E G L I

J

CURRENT PERSPECTIVES
IN
MASS COMMUNICATION RESEARCH

SAGE ANNUAL REVIEWS OF COMMUNICATION RESEARCH

SERIES EDITORS

F. Gerald Kline, *University of Michigan*
Peter Clarke, *University of Michigan*

Volume I

SAGE ANNUAL REVIEWS OF COMMUNICATION RESEARCH

Current Perspectives
in
Mass Communication
Research

F. GERALD KLINE
and
PHILLIP J. TICHENOR
Volume Editors

SAGE PUBLICATIONS

Beverly Hills • *London*

For information address:

SAGE PUBLICATIONS, INC.  SAGE PUBLICATIONS LTD
275 South Beverly Drive St George's House / 44 Hatton Garden
Beverly Hills, California 90212 London E C 1

Printed in the United States of America

International Standard Book Number 0-8039-0171-2

Library of Congress Catalog Card No. 72-84051

FIRST PRINTING

FOREWORD

THE STUDY OF HUMAN COMMUNICATION has emerged as a discipline more quickly than the development of its own channels of communication. New scholarly journals with primary commitment to publish communication research have been slow to appear. Traditional journals often tolerate studies of communication only if they incorporate familiar variables drawn from social psychology (e.g., attitude), political science (e.g., power), sociology (e.g., group structure), or some other recognized discipline. The SAGE Annual Reviews of Communication Research are intended to help overcome these familiar impediments.

For this first volume of the Series the contributors provide a status report on work currently attracting the attention of mass communication research workers affiliated with schools of journalism and mass communication in the United States. This initial choice highlights the vitality of this segment of the communication research community.

Our format, however, is flexible. The Series will seek to identify innovative communication research—whether it is identified with individuals, institutions or schools of thought. As the composition of the advisory board suggests, the Series will cross the coffin-like barriers of academic disciplines. At least three levels of communication will draw our attention—intrapersonal, interpersonal and mass.

Inevitably, organization of volumes in the Series will not represent an exhaustive or mutually exclusive set of categories for viewing the world of communication research. We will publish collections of work that overlap and that leave some vacancies. Neatness will be sacrificed for the goal of moving challenging and competent research into print as quickly as our search process and the realities of book publishing permit.

F.G.K.
P.C.

PREFACE

TWO MAJOR CONSIDERATIONS guided our selection of essays for
this book. First, we wanted to provide an exposition of research
perspectives with emphasis on work being done in the research
centers affiliated with major schools of journalism and mass
communication, and secondly, to provide a context for these
perspectives by applying them to some of the serious problems facing
American society. In neither case do we think it necessary to assume
that these perspectives or problems are unique to the American
situation. Neither do we consider the variety of theoretical viewpoints or the summaries of our knowledge in this area to be the only
ones available. These are some of the current perspectives in mass
communication research.

F.G.K.
P.J.T.

Ann Arbor, Michigan
June, 1972

CONTENTS

ABOUT THE CONTRIBUTORS

STEVEN H. CHAFFEE is Professor of Journalism and Mass Communication and Assistant Chairman of the Mass Communication Research Center at the University of Wisconsin where he has been since receiving his Ph.D. from Stanford University in 1965. A prolific contributor to major communication journals he has served as a special consultant to the Surgeon General's Committee on Television and Social Behavior. He has worked extensively with Jack McLeod in the development of coorientation approaches to communication research.

PETER CLARKE is a professor in the Department of Journalism and the program for Mass Communication Research at the University of Michigan. He was the Director of Communication at the University of Washington. He received his Ph.D. in Communication at the University of Minnesota and has taught there and at Wisconsin. His major research interests include the socialization of children's media behavior, information seeking, and the relationship of communication to social change. He was a co-editor of the *American Behavioral Scientist* issue devoted to "Mass Communications and Youth."

GEORGE A. DONOHUE is a Professor of Sociology at the University of Minnesota. His areas of specialization include social theory, socioeconomic development, and community organization.

BRENDA DERVIN (Ph.D., Michigan State University, 1971) is Assistant Professor of Communications, School of Communication, University of Washington, Seattle. She teaches courses on the communication process, and mass and interpersonal communication research. Co-author with Bradley S. Greenberg of the book, *The Use of the Mass Media by the Urban Poor,* Miss Dervin's research interests focus on poverty, human information processing, and transactional communication. Prior to entering graduate school, she worked for seven years as a public relations specialist for non-profit agencies.

DOUGLAS A. FUCHS is presently a Lecturer in the Department of Journalism at the University of California, Los Angeles. He has served as Consultant and Senior Research Coordinator for the Surgeon General's Scientific Advisory Committee on Television and Social Behavior. Since receiving his Ph.D. from Stanford University, he has taught at the University of California, Berkeley, and Michigan State University. He has published in major communication journals and for a time co-edited *Communication Abstracts* with Jack Lyle.

BRADLEY S. GREENBERG, Professor of Communications at Michigan State University, earned his Ph.D. at the University of Wisconsin. He has published extensively in major communication journals, has co-authored *The Kennedy Assassination and the American Public: Social Communication and Crisis* with Edwin B. Parker, and *Use of the Mass Media by the Urban Poor* with Brenda Dervin.

F. GERALD KLINE is Chairman of the Interdepartmental Doctoral Program of Mass Communication and Research and a member of the faculty of the journalism department. He has served as Director of Research in the School of Journalism and Mass Communication at the University of Minnesota and has co-edited, "Mass Communications and Youth", a special issue of *The American Behavioral Scientist,* with Peter Clarke. His interests center on theory development and methodological advancement as they relate to problems in communication.

JACK LYLE, Professor of Journalism at UCLA has contributed to the Surgeon General's Committee as well as authoring *The News in the Megalopolis* and co-authoring *Television in the Lives of Our Children.*

MAXWELL E. McCOMBS is Associate Professor of Journalism at the University of North Carolina at Chapel Hill and is affiliated with their Institute for Research in Social Science. Recent publications include a chapter in *The Thinking Voter: National and State Electorates in 1968* and numerous journal articles on mass communication and politics. He received his Ph.D. in Mass Communication Research from Stanford University.

JACK M. McLEOD is a Professor of Journalism and Mass Communication, and Chairman of the Mass Communications Research Center at the University of

Wisconsin (Madison). He received his Ph.D. in Social Psychology at the University of Michigan. He has contributed to *Journalism Quarterly,* and *Public Opinion Quarterly.* His research focus over the last decade has been on coorientation and interpersonal communication processes, socialization, and professionalization in the mass media.

GARRETT J. O'KEEFE received his Ph.D. in Mass Communications from the University of Wisconsin and is an Assistant Professor of Mass Communications at the University of Denver.

CLARICE N. OLIEN is an Assistant Professor of Sociology at the University of Minnesota. Her research specialties include community organization, youth development, and mass communication.

JOHN P. ROBINSON is an Assistant Professor of Journalism at the University of Michigan, where he also received his Ph.D. He is also a Study Director in the Survey Research Center. Robinson is a member of the executive committee of the American Association of Public Opinion Research, has served as Research Co-ordinator for the Surgeon General's Advisory Committee on Television and Social Behavior. His publications include "Television and Leisure Time: Yesterday, Today and (Maybe) Tomorrow," and "World Affairs Information and Mass Media Exposure."

KEITH R. STAMM is Assistant Professor of Journalism at Indiana University. His Ph.D. in Mass Communications is from the University of Wisconsin. He also has an M.S. in Agricultural Journalism. Published in several publications including the *Journal of Environmental Education,* Stamm's interest both as a researcher and as a communications practitioner is in communication problems involving the environmental movement.

PHILLIP J. TICHENOR is a Professor of Journalism and Mass Communication at the University of Minnesota. His interests include mass communication theory and methodology, mass media and public opinion, and science journalism.

CURRENT PERSPECTIVES
IN
MASS COMMUNICATION RESEARCH

Chapter 1

THEORY IN MASS COMMUNICATION RESEARCH

F. Gerald Kline

INTRODUCTION

This chapter will try to do two things: first, provide an historical accounting of theoretical developments in the study of mass communication, and, second, attempt an integration or linking of subsequent chapters selected for this volume.

In part one, at the risk of making an overly strict analogy, I would like to view the variety and range of mass communication problems studied as the dependent variable for analysis. By variety and range I refer to studies about certain topics, to those with special substantive interests such as psychology, sociology, political science or marketing research. To complete the analogy, then, we must examine our potential range of independent variables. These could be differences in methods, location of research operation in different institutional settings, or conceptions of man held by the researchers or inherent in the theoretical frame of reference being used. It would be a mistake, however, to take this view as having some direction of causality. The dependent/independent variable distinction has expository purposes rather than a basis in causal sequence. And the list of variables is suggestive rather than exhaustive.

With clearer conception as to the intellectual roots for thinking in this field, we can then evaluate the contributions by other authors to this volume. We have two levels of approach in the eight chapters to follow. We can see the more generalized stance of Donohue et al. toward research on the "gatekeeper" and the system in which the gatekeeper is embedded; Chaffee's overview of the interpersonal influences that mediate mass communication processes; McLeod and O'Keefe's delineation of the socialization processes that are related to, and inherent in, mass media use; and Robinson's position concerning information diffusion in the general population by the various media. All are more general cases of what follows in the last four chapters.

Political activity extends much beyond the two- and four-year campaign periods we are so accustomed to studying. But despite this political fact of life, we are still attracted to what moves the voter to decide in favor of one or another candidate—or does not activate him or her at all. McCombs provides the reader with a summary of our knowledge of politics within the focus of mass media research. In many ways, this has been the most extensively researched area and has attracted some of the seminal thinkers whose works we still draw on. The major questions of power, order, and consensus in the society are all explicitly related to these biennial and quadrennial struggles. It is for these reasons that communication and politics have received sustained social and economic research support.

Dervin and Greenberg have pulled together a vast amount of data, much of which they collected themselves in a systematic program extending over a number of years. Their study of the communication environment of the urban poor contains specific instances of the concerns of the chapters mentioned above. The very specific focus also mirrors the growing concern in the society for the problem of poverty and the need for empirical evidence that will facilitate translating this concern into practical programs for alleviation of the problem.

Fuchs and Lyle deal specifically with the effects media have for transmitting images and messages that are considered taboo. Although not usually emanating from the same philosophical camps, the concern for the violence that seems to pervade our contemporary culture and the anguish expressed over what appears to some to be growing permissiveness and concomitant moral decay, are also forces that have dictated the direction of research interests. Their review also links directly with certain portions of the early chapters in this volume.

Finally, there is the relatively new concern with environmental problems. Stamm, using a predominantly psychological approach, provides the reader with an overview of an area that will undoubtedly expand as practical problems of assessing and shifting public opinion on environmental issues achieve new levels of urgency.

HISTORICAL PERSPECTIVES OF MASS
COMMUNICATION RESEARCH

A number of recent works (White, 1964; DeFleur, 1966; Halloran, 1969; Carter, 1969; Brown, 1970) have made attempts to provide the student with an historical perspective on developments in mass communication research over the last two or three decades. Two of the perspectives dealt with evolution of social theory as used and developed by pioneers in the field. Halloran dealt with various paradigms that, if not being strictly theoretical in the philosophy of science sense of the word, were labeled as models of the communication process.[1] Halloran's major interest in introducing the models was to point to the lack of concern and emphasis on the role of the communicator. DeFleur's efforts were directed toward introducing the student to schools of thought under the set of labels "individual differences, social relationships, and cultural norms." The use of these terms, although not mutually exclusive, covers a set of "classic" research projects.

White chose to provide a perspective on the field by standard disciplinary contributions. Thus the role of the psychologist, sociologist, political scientist, anthropologist, historian and journalist in communication research was described. Carter, in inveighing against this approach, called for the use of "communication" as a field designation in and of itself. His "artistic" account of early workers in the field utilizes a visual accounting scheme. And although Brown pointed to demarcations similar to those of White, he has provided a much more cogent view of where we are and how we got there. His references to the variety of influences on the development of knowledge in the field are similar to those outlined in the dependent/independent variable analogy earlier. Brown's article provides a launching point for a fuller and more extensive examination of the sociology of knowledge in mass communication. Before doing so, we must distinguish the study of how knowledge has accrued from the communication research and the view of mass communication research as an American version of "sociology of knowledge" per se.

Merton's essay on this topic was first published in 1949 and again in 1957 in a revised and expanded edition of *Social Theory and Social Structure.* Merton sees the sociology of knowledge as being basically a European pursuit and belonging "for the most part to the camp of global theorists, in which the breadth and significance of the problem justifies one's dedication to it, sometimes quite apart from the present possibility of materially advancing beyond ingenious speculations and impressionistic conclusions. By and large, the sociologists of knowledge have been among those raising high the banner which reads: *'We don't know that what we say is true, but it is at least significant'* " [italics added] .

Thus, we have the contrast of concerns about how *knowledge* gets to (mostly) elites as opposed to how *information* and *opinion* develop in publics. Merton goes on to say,

"The sociologists and psychologists engaged in the study of public opinion and mass communications are most often found in the opposed camp of the empiricists, with a somewhat different motto emblazoned on their banner: *'We don't know that what we say is particularly significant, but it is at least true'* " [italics added] .

It is obvious that knowledge, information, and opinion are interrelated and they all have an effect on how members of society develop and respond to their impact. It is not entirely clear that mass communication research, to speak only of the American variant, is still to be considered as providing raw truths, with no theoretically significant links to social understanding. We will explore this question in the following pages.

As we pointed out earlier, White, DeFleur, and Halloran tried their hand at delineating major perspectives in mass communication. The approach each took offered different ways to divide up the intellectual activity being discussed. I followed a route similar to White, staying within the slightly shifting boundaries of recent communications, social psychology grouped around reinforcement, macro- and micro-functionalist, symbolic interactionist, and psycho-analytic theories. A close reading of Martindale (1960), Timasheff (1967), Deutsch and Krauss (1965), Hilgard (1956), and Hall and Lindzey (1957) provides further support for these general theoretical views of social life.

Rather than providing *another* outline of each of these schools of thought, it seems more appropriate to start our analysis with clusters of major research figures and groups in the recent past and point out their intellectual debt to the founders and workers in these major schools.

The major investigators have fallen into three main classes—based on their theoretical and disciplinary views. The reinforcement theorists such as Hovland, Lumsdaine and Sheffield (1949), plus the many students and colleagues of Hovland that are considered part of the "Yale" school, were psychological in their orientation, drawing heavily from the work of Hull (1943) and Miller and Dollard (1941) for their inspiration. From a sociological viewpoint, with functionalism and pluralistic behaviorism comingling, there was a great deal of leadership offered by Merton (1949), Lazarsfeld, Berelson, and Gaudet (1948), Berelson, Lazarsfeld, and McPhee (1954), Katz and Lazarsfeld (1955), Klapper (1960), Breed (1955), and Wright (1960). This group from Columbia University Bureau of Applied Social Research had a large impact on subsequent studies. From a micro-functionalist viewpoint, there are the contributions by Heider (1946), Cartwright and Harary (1956), Newcomb (1953), Festinger (1954), and Osgood and Tannenbaum (1955). Interestingly, there were forces at work which helped bring these various schools of thought together. For example, the Research Branch of the Army Information and Education Division during World War II had a mass communication section headed by Hovland and some of his early team members. There was a communication research group at Columbia which did research related to the war, while funded in part by those needing marketing research assistance in the New York area with its dominance in media and media production (Merton, 1957). Kurt Lewin (1943) and his collaborators pursued attitude change in small groups relating to food habits under wartime rationing conditions.

In virtually every instance, we can see that the major impetus to the study of the mass media evolves from a concern with its ubiquitousness, its assumed power (see, for example, Lasswell, 1927; Cantril, Gaudet and Herzog, 1940), and the need for rapid understanding of this phenomenon so that it might be harnessed in the war effort.[2] There is also a need to understand the audiences of the mass media in other than wartime so that the messages that provide economic support for the media can be assured of great exposure and of known effect. Whether the project involves magazine influence (Merton, 1949); fashion leadership through media exposure (Katz and Lazersfeld (1955); drug diffusion in a sociometric sample of doctors (Menzel and Katz, 1955) or whether it links to the raw empiricism of readership studies done for major newspapers by schools of journalism, there has been a bias inherent in "what the media can do to people" (Klapper, 1960).

We need to be aware of how the problem being posed affects the way in which we devise concepts and methods. Thus the experiments of the Yale School were concerned with the manipulable attributes of the communicator and the message. And, of course, the reliance on the experimental method, subjects found in the proximity of the lab (college students), the artificiality of the lab, and the seeking of differential rather than absolute effects, all combined to provide evidence for what the media could do—given the opportunity. The search for these effects in a natural situation using the survey interview approach continued with Lazarsfeld and his colleagues. Despite their movement away from the view of man as an atom isolated from social groupings, there was still reliance on random samples of discrete individuals with only recall data on group affiliations. From a marketing research perspective, the sales of products to people rather than springing from a concern with fundamental questions of social science encourages the persistence of this approach in subsidized research. As Rogers and Shoemaker (1971) point out, the use of unobtrusive measures and the analysis of a sociometric sample of doctors by Menzel and Katz (1955) was a break from this methodological bias. And even though specific sociometric sampling was not carried out by the rural sociologists working in a parallel tradition, their concern for county-level data, demanded by their county extension clients, made them implicitly aware in a practical if not theoretical sense of how important interpersonal influence could be in the diffusion process.

It would be unfair to claim that the developments taking place in the small group laboratories at MIT and later at the University of Michigan under the leadership of first Lewin and then Cartwright had no effect on Hovland and his colleagues. Nevertheless the major impact of the studies such as those done by the Center for Group Dynamics and by Bales (1950) made their debut with Katz and Lazarsfeld (1955) and with Bauer and Bauer (1960). And earlier the notion that the audience for messages was an atomized mass of individuals with messages raining down on them was being attacked by Friedson (1954). We now see emerging the group affiliation of persons in the audience, with an effect on the way in which mass media operate. In the Katz and Lazarsfeld (1955) scheme, which is the most celebrated, the information from the media, within a particular subject-matter scope, flows from an opinion leader to others within the particular group setting. This evidence, despite the overly large impact it had on subsequent research interests, turned the mainstream of media effects thinking away from man as an atom to man as a member of many groups, each providing a context and sometimes a screening mechanism for receiving messages. Katz (1959), in an examination of communication research and the image of society held by different researchers, deals with this and goes on to point to another convergence—that between the newer conception of mass communication research and that of the newly discovered diffusion of innovation tradition central to rural sociology. He notes what might be referred to as the *Gemeinschaft* definition inherent in the rural sociological approach and the *Gesellschaft*[3] quality of mass communication research. Also noted are the psychological concepts that had impinged more on the "urban sociologists" and not on the more traditional sociology of the rural tradition.

One of the major concerns during this period was who controlled the media messages and what effect they would have on the audience. It was not the case, however, that a great deal of effort was expended to examine the professional communicator with organizational support and identification. This is the missing evidence that Halloran (1969) was referring to although he did not point out White's (1950) study, Westley and MacLean's (1957) account, nor Warren Breed's insightful analysis of newsroom socialization in 1958. These are exceptions to the rule, however. The major concern was with the audience and to some extent with the messages that were transmitted to the audience (Smith, Lasswell, and Casey, 1946; Lasswell, Lerner, and Pool, 1952; and Berelson, 1952). Hovland and his collaborators did deal with the communicator in their experimental studies, particularly with the credibility and amount of change advocated by a source. They were not, however, particularly concerned with sources in institutional settings. Their program of research also examined strategies of message presentation to determine the outcomes. As the Yale program in communication research evolved, there was a switch to other variables that encompassed audience characteristics. Personality characteristics such as self-esteem, authoritarianism, other-directedness, as well as physiological attributes such as sex differences were systematically examined. Throughout this program, the learning theory model, often referred to as the "hypodermic model" was used to examine the individual as affected by the communication. This approach, although psychological in character, fitted reasonably well with the conception of man as an "atomistic" entity in contemporary society.

In 1960, Klapper's synthesis and summary of the effects of mass communication provided the field with a reference point for past efforts and new directions. This pulling together of the literature within a "phenomenological" or functional framework has been described by Larsen (1964) as "a significant work in many respects including the fact that it is widely taken as the definitive statement of the effects of mass communication." Larsen, however, notes the emphasis Klapper places on the implication that change ought to be the major intent of the media. Thus the findings of the lack of effect, or conversion from one point of view to another, is implicitly related to his concern for persuasive communication only. Mendelsohn (1964) points to the "definition of the situation" perspective used by Klapper and stemming from work by Thomas and Znanieki (1918-1921). Thus the media are effective, depending on what the individual brings to the situation. It should be noted that the emphasis is still on what the media do to people. Weiss (1969) criticizes Klapper's analysis of the past research by pointing to the reduction of the role of the media to elicit predispositions without noting the distinctive contributions of the media themselves. Larsen (1964), unlike Weiss, is concerned with what the individual brings to the situation. And he points out Klapper's lack of comment on what the homeostatic models in social psychology could provide here in the way of explanation.

The role of personal influence (Katz and Lazarsfeld, 1955) in the flow of mass mediated information, although breaking out of the "hypodermic needle" stance, still relied on an asymmetric perspective rather than one which assumed something like an exchange, either information for time spent with the media or medium, or information for some other exchangeable commodity. Bauer (1964) refers to this as "transactionism" or an exchange of values. Merton (1949) introduced a similar notion of "commodity of exchange." Perhaps this early usage did not have the impact it has had of late because the amount of knowledge we have about the media and how they were used was much less than now. Or perhaps Merton's linking of this notion *only* to influentials, whereas he saw the rank and file using the media as a commodity for personal consumption, had a bearing on its slow diffusion in the research literature. Bauer's transactional point of view was also expressed by him slightly earlier in a comment on Parsons' (1963) exchange model of influence. Although not drawing explicitly on Newcomb (1953), Parsons uses ego and alter (instead of A and B), properties of objects (x's), and a definition of the situation within a normative framework—all with striking similarity. It was not until later, outside of the necessarily narrow view of intrapersonal homeostatic models in general, that the notion of transaction took hold under the rubric of coorientation. I will expand on this point of view at more length later.

Current Status of Communication Research

It has been pointed out by Schramm (1959) that communication is "one of the great crossroads where many pass but few tarry." He referred to this area as a field rather than a discipline. And Tunstall (1969), following Berelson's (1952) lead feels that the field lost its momentum when the major figures from sociology, psychology and political science left, disillusioned that there were no major effects of the media, to find greater variance explanations elsewhere. And he points to the weakness of journalism researchers who moved into the void in the late 1950s (Tunstall, 1969: 4). To correct the record somewhat, it should be noted that the area of journalism he refers to was made up of two parts. The first included those who were more descriptive and historical in scholarly style and often much more concerned with training students for the media. The second, just emerging from pioneer Ph.D. programs in journalism and communication research, were much more concerned with finding out, with social science techniques, what was going on in the media structures and audiences.

Carter (1969), in contrast to Schramm, says, "I think we might quietly cease to define 'communication,' to seek the one subsuming concept, and take 'communication' for what it is, a field designation like 'psychology' or 'sociology.' "

In 1955, a "rump group" of research-oriented journalism teachers met for the first time to discuss theoretical and methodological problems of the day. This group, most of whom are cited and discussed in the pages of this book, provided the basis for a large part of the field of communication research today. Although one can point to the nontheoretical emphasis of early journalism research, it should be kept in mind that much of the research by all disciplinary contributors was a reaction to grand theorizing without data, demands of national ideological stances, availability of funding, and tools available. For bibliographic reviews of this area from 1930 on, see Schramm (1957, 1962), Webb and Salancik (1965), Troldahl (1965), Lyle (1965), Tannenbaum and Greenberg (1968, 1961) and Weiss (1971, 1969). Three of the above citations (Webb and

Salancik, Troldahl, and Lyle) are papers prepared for a symposium on a decade of research in journalism schools.

It may be that stock-taking of this kind is an indication of self-consciousness. Or it may be a rational approach to provide a set of indicators that can illuminate the route one is on. It is the route that will take up the bulk of the next section—the last decade in communication research.

A CURRENT PERSPECTIVE

Brown (1970) asserts on the one hand that the use of functionalism in media studies was mechanical and paradigmatic, yet on the other hand saw the debates as to its usefulness in sociology being ignored. Was it a lack of awareness on the part of those using this approach? He notes the tremendous effect social-psychological developments had, yet he does not see a similar effect from functionalism. In not pointing out that most of the developments in social psychology are micro-functionalist by nature, Brown seems to be confusing theoretical style with disciplinary attachments. It would appear that, in general, the major *leitmotif* of communication research has been functionalist from the beginning. It should be noted we are using functional analysis as described by Merton and cited by Wright (1960):

> "Functional analysis, to a great extent, is concerned with examining those *consequences* of social phenomena which *affect* the normal operation, adaptation, or adjustment of a given system: individuals, subgroups, social and cultural systems."

Or similarly by Stinchcombe (1968): "By a functional explanation we mean one in which the *consequences* of some behavior or social arrangement are essential elements of the *causes* of that behavior." And this analysis may be applied to:

> "standardized (i.e., patterned and repetitive) item[s], such as social roles, institutional patterns, social processes, cultural pattern, culturally patterned emotions, social norms, group organization, social structure, devices for social control, etc." [Wright, 1960].

If we wish to determine whether a functional explanation is called for, Stinchcombe (1968) says,

> "*First,* if many different behaviors or structures are found in different groups, or within the same group, which all have the same consequences,

this suggests that the consequence is causally crucial. . . . *Second,* if the level of activity of a structure varies with the tension which tends to keep a consequence of that structure from happening, this would also be a derivation from a functional theory. *Third,* if we find a consequence remaining steady even though one of its causes is varying . . . we would start looking for the feedback loop from the consequence to a structure tending to maintain it. *Fourth,* if people give erratic and unconvincing reasons for a structure, but the structure keeps functioning when those reasons do not apply, it is likely to be caused by some of its unrecognized consequences. *Fifth,* any structure that occurs in a system we know to be highly selective by certain consequences is likely to have those consequences and to have selected for that reason."

Wright gives examples in contemporary social science that meet one of his requirements. First, he treated mass communication as a social process but held little hope for empirically variable theory. Donohue et al., in the next chapter, are basically taking this approach, although they have supported their claims with a synthesis of many studies. Second, he distinguishes each kind of medium or method of mass communication as an item for analysis. Thus Robinson's look at the diffusion of information via the mass media might be considered as functional capabilities of each of the media. Third, the analysis of newsroom socialization by Breed (1955) is given as an example of institutional functional analysis. Here the units of the mass media are looked at rather than the relation between units that Chapter 2 deals with. Finally, Wright posits a basic communication activity perspective. Drawing from Lasswell's (1949) major paper, and providing the paradigm that Brown (1970) found mechanical, he deals with surveillance, correlation, transmission, and entertainment.

Stinchcombe derives his propositions outlined above from the basic diagram shown in Figure 1. The consequence or end that is maintained he calls H, for "homeostatic" variable. The structure or behavior having the causal impact on H he calls S. Other causal forces or tensions that tend to change H are called T. To link these, he says,

"A causal process, evolution, competition, satisfaction, reward from others, or planning and wanting causes those S's maintaining H to be selected or reinforced. These forces become stronger when the consequence is not maintained, thus increasing the activity of the structure or selecting for it more strongly. Since this force is stronger when H is not naturally maintained (when T is higher) and decreases when H is maintained, it is a causal force with negative direction from H to S."

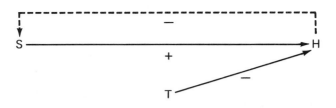

Figure 1.

We can fit Donohue et al. into such a scheme, but first it is necessary to distinguish their different levels of analysis. If we are looking at a total social system in which subsystems are interdependent and the media are seen as conflict management agencies, we can see T as a product of conflict, however arrived at; H as *system maintenance;* $S_1 \ldots S_n$ as the interdependent subsystems; and H → S_i as the *feedback-control* function that allows the subsystems to adjust so that S → H returns the state of equilibrium. It does not appear, nor does it seem necessary, that the state of H at this point is identical to the state of H prior to the conflict beginning. Thus the overall social system has a capability for change. A close examination of S → H will reveal it to be the *distribution-control* function. Where the feedback control function is not a necessary characteristic of system maintenance, it can be seen that with a constant T in the system, the withholding of information S → H would shift to H. A return to H could be brought about by release of requisite information.

In examining a complex social system, the media are seen to be dealing to a large extent with feedback-control. If this control brings about appropriate realignment among the subsystems being reported about in the feedback-control situation, they might then report, or distribute, this realignment. Or the realignment might produce its own information report, either symbolically or in power and status attributes. In a simpler system, such as a small community, the absence of overt tension or a predilection for consensus rather than conflict due to homogeneity and close interpersonal ties, calls for a distributive-control function. Here, the reporting of information might change H slightly and thus shift the state of the whole system. But seldom does the tension erupt in such a way that the media report it to the system participants or individual structures as a feedback-control mechanism. In this system, the information that does parallel feedback-control and distribution-control to realign structures is probably an interpersonal or within-group communication process. Thus, there would be no formal organization for information conveyance such as a local medium. There might, however, be an important person or persons who serve this role in a quasi-formal manner. Opinion leaders, influentials or "liaison persons" would be examples.

In certain situations, where there are blockages of information because of monopoly situations, it is likely the lack of information about the structures or members of those structures that produces a shift in H. One might see it as a steady T with no maintainance linkages from S $\rightarrow$ H by the existing media. Thus a strong feedback loop from H to S should produce a differentiation within the S's to produce a new structure that can fill the S $\rightarrow$ H needs. The growth of radical media or highly differentiated media content would fit into this scheme. As Donohue et al. point out, the differentiation that can be available through the new media technology might be thwarted by centralization. If this is the case and if there is a need for smaller information units to match the differentiated structures, either in larger or smaller communities, then the tension that can arise from lack of distributive-control information should produce a shift in equilibrium that will bring it about. Whether this will be an economic mechanism or a larger system, regulative mechanism is hard to tell.

Kornhauser (1959) makes an argument which has a relation to the above. He talks of the role the media can play as screening agencies between the national leaders, which he calls the elite, and the citizenry at large, the nonelite. The buffering role of the media, recasting messages from elites to nonelites and from nonelites to elites, provides one of the basic needs of a pluralistic society. Removing this buffering capability, he says, will move us rapidly to a mass society with the concomitant danger of mass behavior. Carey (1969), in an essay on the role of the professional communicator, examines aspects of the larger social system and the media that serve it. And, in viewing historical trends in the social sciences, he notes the massification, centralization view of society that is often linked to the mass media, as well as a diametrically opposed perspective (admitting to drawing upon ideal types for his own purposes) of differentiation, dispersal of power, and emphasis on individuality. In examining the media and their relationship to these views, he notes the centripetal force that comes with national media with the potential for centralization of power and authority. He also notes the highly differentiated and more localized media that provide a countering centrifugal force. The general similarity between the above approaches suggests a general need for examining the role of the professional communicators in mediating and integrating the orientations of members of these different subsystems.

In subsequent chapters, there are examples of the above comments. McCombs notes the different viewpoints that emerge in the political arena. The conflict orientation of the political process is not only mirrored in the press via the distribution-control function of the media but there are major feedback-control news flows that force the parties to adjust their issue structure orientation. McCombs' treatment of "agenda setting" is an example. Donohue et al. provide examples of their own in the political realm as well.

Dervin and Greenberg, in discussing the need for a renewed look at communication and development in the American setting, point to the role of the media in modernization. They are "an interactive behavioral system in which improvement must occur simultaneously." Following Rogers and Shoemaker's (1971) basic finding, they note the media's role in creating awareness, which is again a form of agenda-setting. And later they note the differential role played by print and television information as it relates to overall information control. Here interpersonal communication seems to operate in a more homogeneous ghetto environment, as compared to the mass-communicated information that links the ghetto to the outside world. In terms of a larger national system, the media, prior to the riots of 1967, seem to have played a role of the kind Donohue et al. were talking about when the ghetto residents compared their living conditions to those of the people in their immediate surroundings.

Similarly, many of the examples given by Stamm can be seen clearly within the systems conflict model. The local media, concerned with the gains to be made by the Army Corps of Engineers' projects, provided distributive-control information. Not until feedback control information came from "environmentalists" and "rural" objecters did the media finally provide coverage of the conflict that had been latent. In another instance cited by Stamm, the Corps found out, through their own feedback-control capabilities, that their plans had to be modified—a change in the structure of Stinchcombe's paradigm.

The previous discussion has centered on a macro-social perspective of mass communication research in a functionalist framework. Much of the subsequent chapters is of a micro-social nature. This is a concern with linking the individual to the larger social system. The route taken, via coorientation approaches, is through dyadic analysis of the individual, another individual or reified "other," and an object of coorientation. By "other" we mean the individuals who are a continual part of our daily interactions, cliques or reference groups, or larger social system entities.

The roots of this coorientation perspective, according to Chaffee, McLeod, and Guerrero (1969) stem from Wirth's (1948) individual-agreement approach; a symbolic interactionist view as laid out by Mead (1934) but relying on James (1892), Cooley (1902), Burgess (1926), Thomas (1927), and Dewey (1930); the sociometric method of Moreno (1934); the perceptual sociometry of person perception by Tagiuri, Bruner and Blake (1958), and Sullivan's approach to personality and psychotherapy. Although the intellectual roots may be found here, the application and operationization stem more recently from the work of Newcomb (1953) for the writers in the following chapters. And as they point out, Scheff, Morgan, and Laing et al., as well as Chaffee and McLeod (1967), more or less converged from differing perspectives on a coorientational view of social life.

It should be pointed out here that there is a dearth of discussion in the following chapters of homeostatic intrapersonal orientation approaches that were so popular a few years back (Osgood and Tannenbaum, 1955; Festinger, 1954; Rosenberg, 1956; McGuire, 1960). This is due, in part, to the limited usefulness of this approach, alone, to understanding the role of the media in the society, where social interaction and interpersonal contact is so necessary. This is not to say these intrapersonal approaches have not been useful; the point is that there has been a move away from them, as shown in the following pages. The mixed intrapersonal and interpersonal homeo-static approaches of Heider (1958, 1946) and Newcomb (1953) are where much of the current activity is based. Needless to say, the system "balancing," "congruity," "consistency" and "strain for symmetry," all require functionalist explanations of the kind referred to above by Stinchcombe (1968). In fact, the above orientations stem from Gestalt psychology. As Deutsch and Krauss (1965) point out, there are essentially two key notions: (1) psychological phenomena should be conceived "as part of a system of coexisting and mutually interdependent factors having certain properties as a system" and (2) "that psychological processes act to make the state of the [psychological] field as 'good' as prevailing conditions allow."

The A-B-X model that Newcomb adapted from Heider has several basic similarities with approaches in the sociological literature, such as Parsons' (1963) Ego-Alter-X exchange model with some reinterpretation by Bauer (1964) to account for his "transactional" approach.

There are two basic adaptations of the coorientation approach. According to Chaffee and McLeod (1968), each person in a coorientation pair has two sets of cognitions—what each knows and the perception of what others know. Within each person's own field, there can be *congruency* based upon what A thinks of X and what A thinks B thinks of X—a perceived cognitive overlap. This is an intrapersonal construct. There are then two interpersonal constructs that can be generated as well. The first is *agreement,* which is a comparison of what A thinks and of what B thinks—this is seen as the degree of actual cognitive overlap between them (and requires a third party). The second is A's estimate of B's cognitions which may match what B really does think; this is characterized by the term *accuracy.*

A second way in which coorientation has been used and is described in subsequent chapters is a derivation that allows the Newcomb model to be broken into parts (see Figure 1 in the McLeod and O'Keefe chapter). Thus, concentration on the A (child) and X (object) relationship is defined as *concept-orientation,* while emphasis on the A (child) and B (parent) relationship is defined as *socio-orientation.* Full detailing of this approach can be found in the McLeod and O'Keefe chapter. What is of interest here is the usefulness of this mixed intrapersonal and interpersonal approach to communication research, because it bridges not only the individual to larger groups in the society but also allows sophisticated linkages to be elaborated between personal and mass communication.

Although none of the researchers places any great emphasis on the homeostatic character of the coorientation approach being discussed here, it is implicit. Chaffee (1967), in referring specifically to homeostasis, points to Newcomb's belief that communicative acts will produce such an outcome. Carter (1959) and Carter, Pyszka and Guerrero (1969) claim that dissonance should be formulated as a perceived cognitive discrepancy which can be derived from the coorientation paradigm; and Tichenor and Wackman (1971) define consensus as a similarity of orientations toward social objects.

Clarke (1971a), on the other hand, specifically rejects the homeostatic notions of Newcomb and places his emphasis on the intrapersonal "a cognitive state in which person A is aware of another's orientation."

There are some interesting outcomes from the measures generated from the coorientational approach. For example, where the dyad (or group) is more homogeneous one can expect more sharing of information and a greater likelihood of accuracy (Chaffee and McLeod, 1968). Where there is a turning outward for information, there is a likelihood of increased understanding (agreement on what the situation is). These same authors (1967) point out that these cognitive aspects of coorientation, accuracy and understanding seem to be the most reasonable criterion variables for mass communication. And Wackman (1971) relates this approach to information exchange, whereas in the past the intrapersonal homeostatic theories all assumed that the primary function of communication was persuasion. It is not necessarily the case that a successful communication will persuade, even though accuracy is increased. Clarke's (1971a, 1971b) studies of information-seeking by adolescents have relied on the congruency of interest that one child has with some other coorientation partner. Following this point, this author is now working on a project which will attempt to manipulate person A's awareness of what person B's interests are. Where they converge, it can be expected that person A will have a change in congruency (depending on the prior estimate of congruency) and a subsequent seeking of information about the topic of interest, so that it may be used as a social currency for later interactions with B.

Returning to Stinchcombe's outline for functional explanation, it seems plausible to consider the relations between persons, the coorientational system, as the homeostatic dependent variable H; the states of the persons in the system, the characteristics of the structures they are operating in, or their behavior as causal variables (the Ss); and T as the tension that is causing H to move out of homeostasis. By doing so, we can take one example of micro-social communication behavior and examine it from this point of view.

Clarke (1971a) distinguishes between information-*seeking* and information-*sharing*. The former is the purposive search for information rather than incidental exposure. The latter is the exchanging of information between coorientation partners, whether it comes from incidental exposure where both parties have equal probability of being exposed to the material, or whether it is the sharing of information each has independently sought in a purposive way. The sharing of the information might be viewed as the way in which continued coorienting is facilitated. Referring to Figure 1, we can treat continued coorienting as the homeostatic variable, H; the sharing of information, the seeking of information, and the incidental exposure to information as the behaviors or structures that make up the Ss; and the tension, T, as the homogeneity or heterogeneity of the coorientation environment. Clarke (1971a) hypothesized, and supported with data, that, "Persons in a heterogeneous coorientation environment should exhibit greater information seeking in the media than persons in a homogeneous environment." And, second, he said there is no reason to expect pairs in a heterogeneous environment to share information at a greater rate than those in a more homogeneous environment. Apply Figure 1 to this pair of hypotheses and it appears that, as heterogeneity increases, tension increases. As this happens, the homeostasis of the system is diminished, thus providing feedback to the structures, Ss. This in turn produces more activity to return to some more tolerable homeostatic state. In this example, information-seeking would provide more information which, when shared, would reduce the tension by temporarily, or more permanently, reducing heterogeneity.

In both situations, high and low tension, there is still available incidental information that is being provided by equal probability of exposure for the members of the heterogeneous and the homogeneous systems. This may provide enough information for adequate sharing in both situations. However, what is shared in the more heterogeneous system is a mixture of incidental and *sought* information. The lack of tension in the homogeneous system does not require extra effort on the part of the members to return the system to a homeostatic level it did not move from. Of course, there could be other ways to reduce the tension. It is possible that the heterogeneity was brought about in part by the addition to the system of a new person who did not fit in. Adjusting to that person by seeking information that relates to his or her differential character could be one solution. Another is to induce that person to seek information that brings his or her behavior into line. Finally, one could exclude the new person and return to a more homogeneous, less tension-ridden state.

This example, of which many more can be produced by the reader, indicates how the general functionalist approach delineated here subsumes the bulk of the communication research during the last decade or so—whether it be macro- or micro-social in conception.

One point that crops up regularly in discussions of functionalist explanations is the inherent conservative bias that it seems to stem from. That the system being studied must necessarily return to equilibrium, and thus be maintained at the status quo has been the focus for much criticism. As Buckley (1968) points out, it is basically the mechanical-organic approach of Parsons and his students that requires an equilibrium with no change. Stinchcombe (1968) says any notions of it being conservative are due to "sloppy science" and not normatively good or bad theory. Flanigan and Fogelman (1965) and Spencer (1965) also point out that it is not a necessary condition to see a metaphysical ordering or reflection as an ethical preference in functional analysis.

Buckley draws for his modern systems theory approach upon many of the same theorists as do the present-day coorientation researchers. This is basically a structure-elaborating view of social systems wherein homeostasis is distinguished from equilibrium. Buckley examines three basic theoretical approaches in his introduction—mechanical, organic and process models. It is obvious that process as he uses it is closest to a systems theory approach. And although there is some overlap, the process model as one might imagine Schramm and Roberts (1971) using it accepts the society as implicit but not a structure-elaborating entity to study per se. Coorientation stems from symbolic interaction and Newcomb's "communicative acts" approach, as do central aspects of Buckley's view of the world. And it has been pointed out by Buckley that the one-sided emphasis on equilibrium maintenance in the recent past has produced conflict orientations as alternative explanations of social change (Dahrendorf, 1959; Coser, 1956; and Boulding, 1964). Donohue et al. make this conflict approach their major concern and, unlike Buckley, they make overall system maintenance a basic notion in their system.

Martindale (1965) has indicated how the use of functionalism has grown dramatically since World War II. His distinction, holism and elementarism is similar to levels of analysis used by Donohue et al. and by the coorientation researchers. The assumptions of functionalism, for Martindale are that: (1) the social system is the prior causal reality, and (2) all components are best conceived as functionally interrelated.

Functionalism has also been criticized for its weakness for theory construction. Its teleological nature has been its major flaw. Jarvie (1965), however, says it should be used for its heuristic capabilities. Such is the way it seems to be used by the coorientational users in communication research. Chaffee (1971) has specifically warned against using coorientation as a theory, but rather as an approach "separate in our thinking from theories about the relationships between certain coorientational indices and other variables."

A FINAL NOTE

The above review and analysis has obviously neglected certain areas that are currently being explored in mass communication research. This neglect was carefully considered and is not meant to slight those with theoretical approaches not noted here. Given priority were those approaches that have engaged a fairly extensive number of researchers in the field as well as those which were central to the chapters in this volume. Only further explication, testing, and analysis will tell whether the choices made were productive for theoretical developments in the field.

NOTES

1. For a lucid discussion of the relationship of models to theory see May Brodbeck's article in Gross (1959).
2. A compilation of propaganda references in *Public Opinion Quarterly* from 1937-1967 shows the following breakdown: 30 from 1937-1939; 40 from 1940-1949; 23 from 1950-1959; and 3 from 1960-1967.
3. Interestingly, Merton (1949) points to the relationship *Gemeinschaft* and *Gesellschaft* have to the "influential" or "opinion leader" when he coined the best English translation for the words, "local" and "cosmopolite."

REFERENCES

BALES, R. F. (1950) Interaction Process Analysis: A Method for the Study of Small Groups. Cambridge, Mass.: Addison-Wesley.
BAUER, R. A. (1964) "The obstinate audience: the influence process from the point of view of social communication." American Psychologist 19 (May): 319-328.
——— and A. BAUER (1960) "American mass society and mass media," Journal of Social Issues 16: 3-66.

BERELSON, B. R. (1952) Content Analysis in Communication Research. New York: Free Press.

––– P. F. LAZARSFELD, and W. N. McPHEE (1954) Voting: A Study of Opinion Formation in a Presidential Campaign. Chicago: University of Chicago Press.

––– (1969) "The state of communication research," in L. A. Dexter and D. M. White, People, Society, and Mass Communication. New York: Free Press.

BOULDING, K. (1964) The Meaning of the Twentieth Century: The Great Transition. New York: Harper and Row.

BREED, W. (1955) "Social control in the newsroom," Social Forces 33: 323-335.

––– (1958) "Mass communication and social integration," Social Forces 37: 109-116.

BROWN, R. L. (1970) "Approaches to the historical development of mass media studies," in J. Tunstall, Media Sociology: A Reader. Urbana, Ill.: University of Illinois Press.

BUCKLEY, W. (1968) Modern Systems Research for the Behavioral Scientist. Chicago: Aldine.

BURGESS, E. W. (1926) "The family as a unity of interesting personalities," The Family 7: 3-9.

CANTRIL, H., H. GAUDET, and H. HERZOG (1940) The Invasion from Mars. Princeton: Princeton University Press.

CAREY, J. (1969) "The communications revolution and the professional communicator," The Sociological Review Monograph 13: 23-38.

CARTER, R. (1969) The Alchemy of Communication. Paper presented at the Association for Education in Journalism meetings.

––– R. PYSZKA, and J. L. GUERRERO (1969) "Dissonance and exposure to aversive information." Journalism Q. 46: 37-42.

CARTWRIGHT, D. and F. HARARY (1956) "Structural balance: a generalization of Heider's theory," Psychological Rev. 63: 277-293.

CHAFFEE, S. H. and J. M. McLEOD (1967) Communication as Coorientation: Two Studies. Paper presented at the Association for Education in Journalism meetings, August, 1967.

––– (1967) "Salience and homeostasis in communication processes," Journalism Q. 44: 439-444.

––– and J. M. McLEOD (1968) "Sensitization in panel design: a coorientation experiment," Journalism Q. 45: 661-669.

––– J. M. McLEOD, and J. L. GUERRERO (1969) Origins and Implications of the Coorientational Approach in Communication Research. Paper presented at the Association for Education in Journalism meetings, August.

––– (1971) Pseudo-Data in Communication Research. Paper presented to the Association for Education in Journalism, August.

CLARKE, P. (1971a) Co-Orientation and Information Seeking. Paper presented at the Association for Education in Journalism meetings, August.

––– (1971b) "Children's response to entertainment," American Behavioral Scientist 14 (3): 353-370.

COOLEY, C. H. (1902) Human Nature and the Social Order. New York: Scribners.

COSER, L. A. (1956) The Functions of Social Conflict. New York: Free Press.

DAHRENDORF, R. (1959) Class and Class Conflict in Industrial Society. Stanford: Stanford University Press.

DeFLEUR, M. L. (1966) Theories of Mass Communication. New York: McKay.

DEUTSCH, M. and R. M. KRAUSS (1965) Theories in Social Psychology. New York: Basic Books.

DEWEY, J. (1930) Human Nature and Conduct. New York: Modern Library.

FESTINGER, L. (1954) "A theory of cognitive dissonance." Stanford: Stanford University Press.

FLANIGAN, W. and E. FOGELMAN (1965) "Functionalism in political science," in Don Martindale (ed.) Functionalism in the Social Sciences. Lancaster, Pennsylvania: The American Academy of Political and Social Science.

FRIEDSON, E. (1954) "Communications research and the concept of mass," American Sociological Rev. 18: 313-317.

GROSS, L. (1959) Symposium on Sociological Theory. Evanston, Illinois: Row-Peterson.

HALL, C. S. and G. LINDZEY (1957) Theories in Personality. New York: Wiley.

HALLORAN, J. (1969) "The communicator in mass communication research," Sociological Rev. Monograph 13: 5-21.

HEIDER, F. (1958) The Psychology of Interpersonal Relations. New York: Wiley.

――― (1946) "Attitudes and cognitive organization," J. of Psychology 21: 107-112.

HILGARD, E. R. (1956) Theories of Learning. New York: Appleton-Century-Crofts.

HOVLAND, C. I., A. A. LUMSDAINE, and F. D. SHEFFIELD (1949) Experiments on Mass Communication. Princeton, N.J.: Princeton University Press.

HULL, C. L. (1943) Principles of Behavior. New York: Appleton-Century.

JAMES, W. (1892) Psychology. New York: Holt.

JARVIE, I. C. (1965) "Limits of functionalism and alternatives to it in anthropology," in Don Martindale (ed.) Funcationalism in the Social Sciences. Lancaster, Pennsylvania: The American Academy of Political and Social Science.

KATZ, E. (1959) "Communication research and the image of society: convergence of two traditions," American J. of Sociology 65: 435-440.

KATZ, E. and P. F. LAZARSFELD (1955) Personal Influence. New York: Free Press.

KLAPPER, J. (1960) The Effects of Mass Communication. New York: Free Pree.

KORNHAUSER, W. (1959) The Politics of Mass Society. New York: Free Press.

LARSEN, O. (1964) "Social effects of mass communication," in R. Merton, Handbook of Modern Sociology. Chicago: Rand McNally.

LASSWELL, H. D. (1927) Propaganda Technique in the World War. New York: Knopf.

——— (1949) "The structure and function of communication in society," pp. 102-115 in W. Schramm, Mass Communications. Urbana: University of Illinois Press.

——— LERNER, D. and I. POOL (1952) The Comparative Study of Symbols. Stanford, Calif.: Stanford University Press.

LAZARSFELD, P. F., B. BERELSON, and H. GAUDET (1948) The People's Choice. New York: Columbia University Press.

LEWIN, K. (1943) "Forces behind food habits and methods of change." Bulletin of the National Research Council, No. 108.

LYLE, J. (1965) "Attitude measurement in communication research," Journalism Q. 42 (Autumn): 606-613.

MARTINDALE, D. (1960) The Nature and Types of Sociological Theory. Boston: Houghton Mifflin.

——— (1965) Functionalism in the Social Sciences. Lancaster, Pennsylvania: The American Academy of Political and Social Science.

McGUIRE, W. J. (1960) "Cognitive consistency and attitude change." J. of Abnormal and Social Psychology, 60: 345-353.

MEAD, G. H. (1934) Mind, Self, and Society. Chicago: University of Chicago Press.

MENDELSOHN, H. (1964) "Sociological perspectives on the study of mass communication," in L. A. Dexter and D. M. White, People, Society, and Mass Communications. New York: Free Press.

MENZEL, H. and E. KATZ (1955) "Social relations and innovation in the medical profession," Public Opinion Q. 19 (Winter): 337-353.

MERTON, R. K. (1949) "Patterns of influence," in P. F. Lazersfeld and F. N. Stanton (eds.) Communications Research 1948-49. New York: Harper.

——— (1957) Social Theory and Social Structure. New York: Free Press.

MILLER, N. E. and J. DOLLARD (1941) Social Learning and Imitation. New Haven, Conn.: Yale University Press.

MORENO, J. L. (1934) Who Shall Survive? New York: Beacon. (Revised 1953.)

NEWCOMB, T. M. (1953) "An approach to the study of communicative acts," Psychological Rev. 60: 393-404.

OSGOOD, C. E. and P. H. TANNENBAUM (1955) "The principle of congruity in the prediction of attitude change," Psychological Rev. 62: 42-55.

PARSONS, T. (1963) "On the concept of influence," Public Opinion Q. 27 (Spring): 37-62.

ROGERS, E. and F. SHOEMAKER (1971) Communication of Innovations. New York: Free Press.

ROSENBERG, M. J. (1956) "Cognitive structure and attitudinal affect," J. of Abnormal and Social Psychology 53: 367-372.

SCHRAMM, W. (1957) "Twenty years of journalism research," Public Opinion Q. 21 (Spring): 91-107.

——— (1959) "Comments on B. Berelson's 'The state of communication research,'" in L. A. Dexter and D. M. White, People, Society, and Mass Communications. New York: Free Press.

——— (1962) "Mass communication," in Annual Rev. of Psychology 13: 251-284.

SCHRAMM, W. and M. ROBERTS (1971) The Effects of Mass Communication. Urbana: The University of Illinois Press.

SMITH, B., H. D. LASSWELL, and R. CASEY (eds.) (1946) Propaganda, Communication, and Public Opinion. Princeton, N.J.: Princeton University Press.

SPENCER, R. (1965) "The nature and value of functionalism in anthropology," in Don Martindale (ed.) Functionalism in the Social Sciences. Lancaster, Pennsylvania: The American Academy of Political and Social Science.

STINCHCOMBE, A. L. (1968) Constructing Social Theories. New York: Harcourt, Brace, & World.

TAGIURI, R., J. S. BRUNER, and R. R. BLAKE (1958) "On the relation between feelings and perception of feelings among members of small groups," in E. E. Maccoby, T. M. Newcomb and E. L. Hartley (eds.) Readings in Social Psychology, Third Edition. New York: Holt, Rinehart & Winston.

TANNENBAUM, P. and B. GREENBERG (1961) " 'J Q' references: a study of professional change," J. Q. 38: 203-207.

——— (1968) "Mass communication," in Annual Rev. of Psychology 19: 351-385.

THOMAS, W. I. and F. ZNANIECKI (1918-1921) The Polish Peasant in Europe and America. Chicago: University of Chicago Press.

——— (1927) The Behavior Pattern and the Situation. Publications of the American Sociological Association 22: 1-13.

TICHENOR, P. J. and D. WACKMAN (1971) Mass Media and Community Consensus. Paper presented to the Association for Education in Journalism.

TIMASHEFF, N. S., (1967) Sociological Theory: Its Nature and Growth. New York: Random House.

TONNIES, F. (1957) Community and Society. East Lansing: Michigan State Press.

TROLDAHL, V. (1965) "Studies of consumption of mass media content," J. Q. 42: 596-606.

TUNSTALL, J. (1969) Media Sociology: A Reader. Urbana, Illinois: University of Illinois Press.

WACKMAN, D. (1971) Interpersonal Communication and Coorientation. Paper presented to the Association for Education in Journalism.

WEBB, E. and J. SALANCIK (1965) "Notes on the sociology of knowledge," J. Q. 42: 591-596.

WEISS, W. (1969) "Effects of the mass media of communication," in G. Lindzey and E. Aronson (eds.) Handbook of Social Psychology, second edition. Reading, Massachusetts: Addison-Wesley.

——— (1971) "Mass communications." Annual Rev. of Psychology 22: 309-336.

WESTLEY, B. and M. MacLEAN (1957) "A conceptual model for communication research." J. Q. 34: 31-38.

WHITE, D. M. (1950) "The gatekeeper: a case study in the selection of news." J. Q. 27 (Fall): 383-390.

——— (1964) "Mass communications research: a view in perspective," in L. A. Dexter and D. M. White, People, Society, and Mass Communications. New York: Free Press.

WRIGHT, C. (1960) "Functional analysis and mass communication," Public Opinion Q. 24:

Chapter 2

GATEKEEPING: MASS MEDIA SYSTEMS AND INFORMATION CONTROL

George A. Donohue, Phillip J. Tichenor, and Clarice N. Olien

WHEN MAN DEVISED the first rudimentary form of mass communication centuries ago, he immediately developed ways of controlling it. Printer, king, teacher and merchant were almost equally inventive in contriving ways to bring information under control. Their diligence arose from man's historic recognition of a fundamental social principle: knowledge is basic to social power, and immense potential for developing power over other human lives rests with those who man the gates in the communication flow (Bagdikian, 1971; Galbraith, 1967; McDermott, 1969; Park, 1940).

Crises of confrontation between media agencies and government recently and historically should not obscure the fact that both have, as a prime function, the control of information.[1] The main issue is over which organization exerts what control, how, and for what reason (Donohue et al., 1971; Revel, 1971). While knowledge control is as old as mankind, it has become a more prominent feature of modern civilization as more and more human activity becomes directed toward production and accumulation of knowledge (Galbraith, 1967; Harrington, 1967; Boulding, 1964). Mass media today may be seen as part (and only part) of a growing "knowledge industry" which accounts for more than a fourth of the gross national product (Machlup, 1962; Kerr, 1963). Indeed, the very essence of a nation's security and power among nations is dependent upon its structure for generating and utilizing increments of knowledge (Galbraith, 1967).

All large social organizations depend to some extent on information use and control, but now there are vast agencies and firms, in addition to the traditional mass media, whose prime missions center around knowledge development and control. Data processing agencies, quasi-public research agencies, and information retrieval firms represent growing specialization and recognition of the role of knowledge in the total system. Present-day specialists at input and output levels are integrated into a configuration of organized intelligence which is often beyond the comprehension or concern of any one person, but which is vital for the decision-making processes which each person serves in the system (Galbraith, 1967; McDermott, 1969).

Knowledge today is organized to a high degree at all levels of society, and mass media represent one form of this refinement. The way in which mass media knowledge enters into social decision-making may not be the same as the way knowledge is used for executive decisions in industry, but the general principle of knowledge control in the service of other social needs is as applicable to mass communication as to any other level of human discourse. If mass communication is in actuality control of information and knowledge, then, in light of the way decisions are made in a modern, pluralistic society, the study of the gatekeepers who execute control decisions in the knowledge flow is especially urgent.

GATEKEEPING AS INFORMATION CONTROL

Processes of "gatekeeping" in mass communication may be viewed within a framework of a total social system, made up of a series of subsystems whose primary concerns include the control of information in the interest of gaining other social ends (DeFleur, 1966). Questions for mass communication research in this area include *how* such controls are exercised, *where* in the process they occur, and what the *consequences* of these controls are for the overall social system as well as for the interdependent subsystems (Donohue et al., 1971). Mass media make up subsystems that cut across the source and audience subsystems and perform certain functions for both of these other subsystems and for the social system as a whole (Westley and MacLean, 1957; Parsons, 1967; Katz and Kahn, 1966).

"Gatekeeping," then, includes various forms of information or knowledge control. This is a more inclusive definition of the process than may have been intended by others. When White (1950) first applied the term to a wire service editor, he was using it in the specific sense of selecting or rejecting certain messages. That is, the flow of wire messages available to the medium was, for White, roughly analogous to the "flow" of food and other goods potentially available to housewives which Lewin (1951) had been studying when he introduced the "gatekeeper" term into social science literature. But while White was studying one aspect of information control, it is clear that far more than simple rejection or acceptance may be involved in message transmission through channel systems. "Information control," therefore, may be a more inclusive and appropriate term. For this discussion, "gatekeeping" in mass media is viewed as including all forms of information control that may arise in decisions about message encoding, such as selection, shaping, display, timing, withholding, or repetition of entire messages or message components. "Censorship," in this view is a special case of information control.

There is no assumption here that social control is the only function served by mass communication; rather, the assumption is that all communication processes have a control function within them, either manifest or latent.

MASS MEDIA AS SOCIAL SUBSYSTEMS

Growing complexity of modern society has been accompanied by a tendency for communication systems to shift from a consensus approach to more of a conflict model of organization. However, social differentiation is not a uniform process, as Spencer (1898) pointed out when he drew the analogy between biological and social systems. Social differentiation has different effects on different social subsystems and, in the case of mass media, on different parts of a particular subsystem. Along with growth of media systems today, we have sharper differences in the functions which the media serve, and in the segments of the total system for which different media are relevant.

With differing media subsystems and differing functions, considerable conflict and social tension may develop. Social conflict, however, does not necessarily indicate a state of total disorder; conflict and tension, and their management, are fundamental aspects of modern pluralistic social organization (Coser, 1956). In today's pluralistic society, mass media are more likely to accommodate conflict in the interest of controlling it so as to perform certain functions (Olien et al., 1968). To a considerable extent, then, mass media are agencies for conflict management. Conflict control may include the *generation* of conflict situations as well as the direct dissipation of tension. The operations in this conflict management are complex and not always easily accommodated by media actors. Social and organizational strains which media agencies and personnel have in dealing with social conflict have, therefore, provided the focal point for much of the systematic research on "gatekeeper" phenomena which has been done in the past two decades.

In the context of a systems model, mass communication of political, technological, and cultural knowledge is controlled largely in the interest of system maintenance. However, the system (or subsystem) being maintained may vary in different situations. It may be the media subsystem itself. It may be the source subsystem with which the media have systemic relations or it may be the larger social system as a whole. "Maintenance" does not necessarily mean perpetuating the status quo, although that may occur. In the perspective being used here, maintenance refers to sustaining of a system and whatever dynamic processes which it may encompass. Maintenance functions may be fulfilled in at least two different, but overlapping ways.

Two Maintenance Processes

One process serving the maintenance function is *feedback control,* which is defined as the way in which system adjustments are made in response to information about system performance. Feedback takes many forms; a well-known type is feedback within a media system (as through a readership survey). In a more inclusive sense, however, media subsystems themselves may provide a feedback, or regulatory, function for other subsystems or for the total social system. In social philosophy, the feedback-control function is expressed in the conception of the "fourth estate" or "watchdog" role of the press (Hocking, 1947; Hachten, 1963; Rucker, 1968) and this role has been seen as especially crucial in a pluralistic but highly interdependent society. Mass media apply corrective pressures to subsystems that may be out of functional balance in relation to others. In this perspective "muckraking," was not a wayward act of newspapers sensationalizing for sensation's sake. While muckraking *may* have contributed to the sale of newspapers, it also had, quite clearly, a maintenance function for the total social system. Lippmann (1961), for example, viewed the muckrakers as applying certain public standards to the conduct of people in government and other high public office. Both the "surveillance" and "correlational" functions identified by Lasswell (see Schramm, 1960) may be seen as referring to feedback-control processes in system terms. Rachel Carson's *Silent Spring* and the reporting of it in mass media served a feedback function for the total social system. The *Selling of the Pentagon* and the *Pentagon Papers* issues are contemporary examples of the mass media serving a feedback-control function between different social subsystems—in this case, between executive government and one set of interest groups on the one hand and legislative branches and other interest groups on the other. In both cases, both the media and the executive government systems were dealing with information control, and the basic conflict was over whose efforts to control would prevail.

A second process is *distribution control* which may also serve the total system maintenance function without a complete feedback process occurring. Some mass communication is purely distributive, in either a positive or a negative sense.[2] System maintenance may result from either withholding knowledge or selectively distributing it. Media in some communities may serve a maintenance function by avoiding or restructuring certain tension-laden information (Olien et al., 1968). In other communities, maintenance may be served by reporting tension-filled messages on some topics at length. Advertising in all forms may be viewed as contributing to market control or management, so that demand for products can be controlled and predicted (Galbraith, 1967). This principle is most clear in institutional advertising.

Timing of distribution may be a key aspect of control. Holding up release of information until a crucial act has taken place is well known, both in national security cases and in everyday community news management. Some distribution is primarily utilitarian for other subsystems, such as dissemination of certain kinds of information about medicine, household problems, and industry. The vast efforts of public relations and public information offices in public and private agencies reflect the widespread attention given to distributional aspects of information control for system maintenance.

Types of Knowledge

The special concern here is with communication of knowledge, whether it is in the political, scientific, or cultural realm. Knowledge can be thought of as fitting in one of two broad control categories, "knowledge of" and "knowledge about." When a message transmits "knowledge of" a topic, it is creating familiarity and acquaintance with that topic or events associated with it. The recipient gains awareness in a general way, but little more. When a message transmits "knowledge about" a topic or issue, it provides increments of formal and analytic knowledge, or what might approach understanding in depth. These two categories reflect a continuum and relative characteristics rather than discrete types (Park, 1940). In general, most mass-communicated information about public affairs tends to fall toward the "knowledge of" end of the continuum and therefore has special control properties. In the small community, for example, confining public affairs reporting to "knowledge of" (or what some editors refer to as "sticking to the facts") is a standard device for maintaining awareness without delving into the controversial aspects of the issues, which reporting in depth would entail.

Information and Social Stresses

Information control is not the exclusive property of any single social subsystem. Feedback may be functional at one system or subsystem level but dysfunctional for maintenance of another subsystem, leading to some major social stresses. It may be functional for a governmental (or scientific) agency to withhold information and "not rock the boat," whereas such information may be seen by media people as essential for "the public right to know." The latter is an everyday way of saying that if information is widely diffused, it may arouse certain pressures for regulation or change on some social groups or segment. Such observers as Cater (1964) find reporters frequently disagreeing with politicians who think news which is good for their agency is also good for the country as a whole.

Modern media systems exist at least partly for control of conflict, but not necessarily for its elimination; modern society assumes a certain level of conflict as subsystems interact (Coser, 1956). This principle may be recognized widely in the political realm. Yet it also applies to other social sectors, such as science, culture, the arts, and education, even though there may be strong pressures within each sector to maintain a consensus orientation. This pressure for consensus is especially strong in science (Hagstrom, 1965), but it exists to some degree in all subsystems.

NATURE OF MASS MEDIA SYSTEMS

Individuals who make decisions about media messages—reporters, editors, newscasters, writers, publishers—are located in agencies that often reflect a substantial mixing of older and newer forms of social organization. Mass media, rarely mentioned in literature on formal organization, vary widely in structure and function. They range all the way from small-town weeklies and stations where editing, advertising and ownership rest with a single person or two to the large conglomerate where national telecasting, heavy industry and consumer retail firms are tied to one parent firm. Also, it should be kept in mind that family ownership continues to play a major role in media organization. In spite of the present trend toward concentration and the immense aggregations of communication firms that make up some of the conglomerates, the fact is that ownership and management of media have not been divorced as they have in other corporate situations. News and editing operations take place in departments which, apart from size and furniture, from a social organization viewpoint are often nearly indistinguishable from news departments of the nineteenth century. Reporters continue to handle information on the most routine social and political events, confining themselves largely to "knowledge of" issues and rarely delving into "knowledge about." The news room typically is still a patriarchal organization, with each reporter individually responsible to the editor in a direct familistic type of relationship. Thus the reporter is structurally quite removed from the managerial sector of his firm, and accordingly, finds himself ordinarily isolated from much of the decision-making process in his own environment. This social location of the reporter in the structure of the organization is highly relevant to an understanding of the processes by which knowledge transmission through mass media is controlled.

Professionalism and Message Control

While there has been considerable concern about the "professionalism" problem in journalism, this concern has largely ignored or overlooked such aspects of organizational structure as the systemic linkages between persons doing journalistic tasks and persons such as city editors, managing editors and publishers who make ultimate decisions about message flow and media organization. The difference between a newspaper and a hospital may seem obvious on the surface; yet a comparative approach to analysis of the media organization might demonstrate some aspects of "professionalism" in journalism and its bearing on control of message flow. While definitions of professionalism vary (Montagna, 1968), they usually include, as one major ingredient, possession of specialized knowledge which is dispensed in some fashion as inputs for decision processes (Thompson, 1962). Compared with the engineer, cost accountant, medical specialist or lawyer, the journalist is in somewhat of an anomalous situation. With all the knowledge that passes through his hands, he rarely deals directly with a client or user of that information. He is party to a control process but in a different sense than the professional lawyer, medical specialist, or chemistry consultant. The reporter is a specialist in information but hardly ever makes an input into even his *own* firm's decision-making. Nor, for that matter, is he likely to be aware of specific inputs which his information provides for *any* decision-making process—not, at least, in a direct sense. Little wonder, then, that journalists rarely have a sharply defined conception of public audiences, even though they have important systemic relations with the audience.

Low occupational status among reporters has been recognized frequently. Edelstein (1966) in referring to what he terms "false-status" consciousness, says:

> A newspaper man may typically have entry to a bank president, a noted scientist, a cabinet officer, and other high status persons. These contacts actually represent the high points of the newsman's status cycle, extending psychologically, perhaps, through the writing and publishing of the news story. But this status ends with the newsman's assignment to a typically commonplace task.

Reporter's Social Status

If reporting is under close control of editors and other media managers, then it may not be surprising that editors tend to have social status more on a par with doctors and lawyers, whereas the reporter's social status is often more in line with that of other nonmanagerial service-type employees (Centers, 1949; Carter, 1958).

Social status rankings tend to distinguish rather sharply between occupational groups involving decision-making (and inputs into decisions) on the one hand, and persons who perform largely assigned tasks, on the other. To the extent that newsmen and reporters operate largely as servants for editors, their relative status level is almost precisely what one would expect, given their location in the organizational structure of mass media agencies. This may be consistent with Gerald's (1963) view of the negative self-image among journalists, but the fundamental issue may be one of organizational structure as others (Schramm, 1957) have suggested. McLeod and Hawley (1964) found wide variation in the extent to which editorial employees possessed a "more professional" orientation, but did not relate this variation to media structure. In his study of job satisfaction in the news room, Samuelson (1962) found that respondents on larger newspapers (over 50,000 circulation) were less satisfied than respondents on smaller newspapers. Particularly, newsmen in the larger papers were more dissatisfied with the formal arrangements with management and with the routine nature of their duties. Level of salary was independent of other aspects of job satisfaction, although salary *distribution* was a matter for concern, especially among reporters under Guild contracts. Samuelson's study reinforces the interpretation that satisfaction in an occupation may be based on relative rather than absolute conditions (Merton, 1957). The less-well-paid reporter on a newspaper in a small town may be more content and satisfied as long as he has fewer highly paid colleagues for comparison and performs more of a variety of tasks. Furthermore, the small-town reporter is located in an entirely different type of social system and has a different type of role definition than the metropolitan reporter. For the latter type, routinization without highly developed specialization or identity in the total community may be part of the basis for dissatisfaction. Also, status differences between reporters and sources may often intrude into the news-gathering process, as Carter (1958) found in medical reporting and as Tichenor, Donohue, Olien and Harrison (1970) found in science reporting in general. The reporter seeking status with a source community may subject himself to a considerable amount of control by that source system as a result.

Media Ownership and Information Control

A rather common belief is that certain forms of media ownership lead to certain forms of control over message output. Monopoly control, for example, is sometimes expected to lead to certain forms of biased news coverage. Nixon and Ward (1961) challenged that interpretation in their earlier study on newspaper ownership, concluding that one cause of newspaper consolidation was the growth in "objective" reporting in American newspapers. Apparently regarding news dissemination as analogous to a public utility, they saw "little more reason for two competing newspapers than there would be for two competing telephone companies."

Owen (1969), whose criterion of media performance is basically *access* to the media, concludes that form of media ownership may be related to prices which the media charge for advertising. He states, for example, that chain ownership of a daily newspaper results on the average in a 7 percent price increase in newspaper advertising rates, compared with non-chain ownership, and that ownership of a TV station by a newspaper results in an average 10 percent increase in these prices. At least on the business side, then, there is some evidence that ownership structure may be related to price structure.

The question remains, however, whether ownership structure does in fact relate to controls exercised over information which is handled, processed, and disseminated by the media. The general hypothesis is implicit in the notion that mass media have shifted from a "libertarian" to a "social responsibility" mode of operation. Schramm (1957) has argued that the "theory of objective news" reporting followed from the shift to advertising, and away from political subsidy, for support. DeFleur (1966) contends that what he terms "low taste" content serves an economic maintenance function for the media system.

Media Functions and Community Organizations

Media tend to reflect the social systems in which they exist, in size, complexity and function (Riley and Riley, 1965; Porter, 1971). As a social system becomes more differentiated, interdependence among actor roles and among subsystems increases. At the same time, higher levels of autonomy develop among actors and the potential for conflict among actors and subsystems becomes greater. To manage social strains, the more differentiated, pluralistic systems depend more on secondary media than the traditional small communities do (Olien et al., 1968).

In any social system, large or small, complex or noncomplex, system stability is a general need and mass communication systems contribute to the maintenance of that stability. However, maintenance is served in different ways, with a "consensus" approach more common in the less complex system media, and a "conflict" model more common in the more complex one. In less complex systems, then, mass media are more likely to confine themselves to the distributive aspects of system maintenance. The other leg of this proposition holds that the more differentiated and pluralistic the system, the more likely mass media are to perform a feedback control *as well as* a distributive control function.

In the small community, then, the community press frequently reports primarily the positive side of the courthouse, local council room and the political meeting hall. However much of a "watchdog" the community press may have been historically, at least in small communities it largely watches over external forces and it appears to be an infrequent monitor over internal matters. And given its function in its own system, there may be little reason to expect it to do otherwise. For one thing, neither local people nor local leaders ordinarily expect the local press to do other than "put the town's best foot forward" (Janowitz, 1952). Secondly, the "gatekeepers" themselves who edit and own small-town media are more likely to stress the community stability aspect of their functions and are less likely to stress opinion leadership or interest arousal in local issues, as was illustrated in a study (Olien et al., 1968) of Minnesota editors and newspapers. Furthermore, the small-town editors were less likely to report conflict in public affairs, again in line with hypotheses from systems-conflict theory. Weekly newspaper reluctance to deal with conflict appeared to be even greater when the editor was more closely aligned with the local power structure.

Power Status of Editors

Editor location in the community power structure may be a fundamental issue in information control, since there appears to be wide variation in power status of editors and its influence may be different in different kinds of communities. The Minnesota study indicated that power status of editors in larger communities may be associated with *more* conflict reporting, again in line with the functions of the larger system media. Larger communities have more formally organized interest groups and more mechanisms for handling the disputes that do arise. Therefore, the pluralistic social system depends on mass media to communicate different views so that the formal tension management processes can in fact operate. In a less differentiated social system, conflict is more likely to be managed at an informal level. In the large system, it is managed by formalized, open reporting and exchange of views and positions.

Several studies and case analyses, in addition to the Minnesota studies, suggest support for the general propositions offered here. In his study of Chicago-area suburban newspapers, Janowitz (1952) emphasized the differing functions provided by the community newspaper, compared with the metropolitan press. Within the community newspaper field, however, he also noted a tendency for larger ones to deal more with controversy and change and to be more outspoken about their influence in local issues.

GATEKEEPER PERCEPTIONS AND CONTROL BEHAVIOR

Media "gatekeepers" seem to have their own control orientations; their specific performance is related to a wide range of personal and system variables. Although he was not using a systems perspective, White (1950) saw the tendency for knowledge control:

> It is a well-known fact in individual psychology that people tend to perceive as true only those happenings which fit into their own beliefs concerning what is likely to happen. It begins to appear (if Mr. Gates is a fair representative of his class) that in his position as "gatekeeper" the newspaper editor sees to it (even though he may never be consciously aware of it) that the community shall hear as a fact only those events which the newsman, as the representative of his culture, believes to be true.

Gieber (1964) took an even more extreme view than White: that "news is what newspapermen make it." Gieber emphasized, as Breed had earlier, the particular subsystems which the reporter is working to maintain—namely the media system itself and the source system. While one might expect the "gatekeeper" to be mindful of audience values, Gieber among others found evidence that certain kinds of reporters and wire editors had little systematic knowledge of the general reading audience. Not that reporters were unaware of their social environments; what they seemed to respond to most strongly was their immediate bureaucratic surroundings. The "climate of the newsroom" was mentioned frequently. Reporters saw themselves as hired employees of an organization that imposed its news policy upon them. A news policy itself, however, was not necessarily a basis for complaint; reporters were more likely to complain about a *lack* of policy, or an inconsistent one. While Gieber only partially analyzed the functional role of the reporter in the total structure, he saw an organizational basis for information control:

> The fate of the local news story is not determined by the needs of the audience or even by the values of the symbols it contains. The news story is controlled by the frame of reference created by the bureaucratic structure of which the communicator is a member.[2]

This is not to say that a reporter lacks an "audience perception" entirely when he is in the act of encoding. However, the audience perceived is not necessarily representative of the general population of readers or viewers. Working from an individualistic, almost clinical perspective, Pool and Shulman (1959) interviewed 33 newsmen immediately after they had finished writing news articles. Findings were interpreted partly in terms of the "fantasies" which the newsmen experience while writing. One conclusion was that fantasy plays an increased role as the writer has greater freedom. The more unusual the topic the greater the latitude of format, or the "less well organized and professionalized" the newspaper, the more important Pool and Shulman expected fantasy to be. To some extent, the event being reported and the reporter's autonomous tendencies (fantasies) tend to reinforce each other. For example, Pool and Shulman found that newsmen who have supportive images report good news more accurately than bad news, and those with critical images do a more accurate job on bad news. Pool and Shulman did not relate their behaviors to structural conditions or to information control outcomes specifically. Nevertheless, they concluded that "news is a weapon" in the hands of the reporter, and that mental dramas of newswriting fell in two basic categories. One is winning favor from a reader, and the other is verbal aggression to demolish him.

> The communicator is the teacher, instructor, guide, i.e., the authority figure over a passive audience. And since the audience consists of secondary contacts, at best, notions of power and deference replace and symbolize more tangible and intimate rewards. Thus . . . fantasies of our writers as they write are polarized around the power which their pen gives them, power to command affection, or power to destroy.

After repeating their interviews with as many of the newsmen as could be reached two years later, Pool and Shulman concluded, further, that these "imaginary interlocutors" were rather consistent over time and that temperament of the person may be more important than mood in determining who they are. The question of whether media organizational structure and other system variables might bear on this fantisizing process was not raised in this particular investigation.

Who Is the Communicator's Audience?

Studies such as those of Gieber and Pool and Shulman have raised, empirically, the question of the extent to which media gatekeepers have the ultimate audience in mind during the encoding process. In the Pool and Shulman study, 17 percent of the 510 different images identified were of readers, the others apparently including personally known persons, family members, and other specific acquaintances. Tannenbaum (1963) reports data from studies of connotative judgments, suggesting that editors may be badly mistaken in their beliefs about what the public "wants." Specifically, he found more correspondence in judgment about news values between editors and nonreaders than between editors and science readers, leading him to conclude that editors may be the "weak link" in the science communication chain. Martin et al. (1970) found a fairly substantial degree of accuracy among Wisconsin editors in judging their readers' positions regarding student protest demonstrations which had been in the news; editors were less accurate, however, in judging reader opinions of the government's basic position. There was also some correspondence between editor perceptions of readers' beliefs and the direction (favoring versus criticizing) of news articles in their papers about the student protests. Results from some studies suggest that *experimentally* inducing an audience can affect what a person writes and how he remembers information, but there are few studies other than Pool and Shulman's, analyzing audience considerations in mass media encoding as a whole. Implicit in several studies is the view that newsmen may voice a desire to "cultivate the outlook of the average citizen and taxpayer" as Gerbner (1967) found education editors doing. These findings, however, are at best descriptive of behavior at various points within the media and related systems. Again, these studies were designed largely from individualistic, psychological perspectives and do not take system forces or requirements into account.

Attitudes of Communicators and Message Control

From a systems perspective as well as from an individualistic one, attitudes of mass communicators might be hypothesized to be reflected in message control or in the way messages are encoded for mass audiences. One might expect, a politically conservative reporter to write a message which is more supportive of his conservative ideology, compared with a politically liberal reporter working with the same set of data and background details. Gerbner (1964) found support for this general proposition in the handling of a legal case with political overtones in the French press. The "Left" and "Right" papers covered the case from far different positions and perspectives, supporting Gerbner's proposition that under conditions of ideological plurality, there is no fundamentally nonideological, apolitical, nonpartisan news-gathering and reporting system. Dono- hew examined coverage of the Medicare issue by 17 Kentucky newspapers and concluded that publisher attitude was an important force in amount, direction, and display of messages. In fact, Donohew concluded that publisher attitude was a more potent force in this case than either his perception of community opinion or community conditions themselves, such as the percent of persons over 65 or the percentage of the population on old-age assistance. Donohew, however, studied an issue that was still under consid- eration in Congress at the time, rather than programs under way locally. He did not deal with community structure per se; for example, he did not examine linkages between editors and the local health profession.

In some situations, channel communicators seem to compensate for their attitudes in various ways. Carter (1959) matched groups of student newsmen at southern and northern universities and asked them to write crime stories—some of which identified the suspect as Negro and some of which did not. In all cases, writers of the stories with Negro identification were more lenient in their evaluation of guilt of the suspect. Nevertheless, southern students who wrote about the Negro suspect tended to make more use of stereotypic content than classmates who wrote about a white man. In another experiment with student writers, Kerrick et al. (1964) found control forces operating in a special way. Editorial writers who disagreed with newspaper policy were more likely to slant their articles toward that policy than writers who agreed with the policy. If journalism *students* submit to induced "media policy" so readily, it appears that neophyte reporters may be predisposed to accept media system controls with incredible speed. But again, some major system questions have not been studied: what, for example, leads to such control orientations in the first place?

The problem of reporting material that somehow contradicts the writer's feelings has been subjected to study frequently. Greenberg and Tannenbaum (1962) claim that any form of "cognitive stress" may lead to message distortions during encoding. Experimentally, they created situations in which subjects (students, again) wrote from material that in some cases attacked the self-concept. Subjects under such stress took more time, produced at a lower rate, and wrote less readable prose than subjects not experiencing such stress. In a somewhat similar experiment, Bettinghaus and Preston (1964) confirmed the hypothesis that individuals take longer to write statements contrary to their own beliefs, compared with consistent statements. Also, the difference between consistent and inconsistent statements increased among individuals who were more dogmatic.

In none of these studies was information control as such dealt with conceptually. It appears from the Carter and Kerrick studies, however, that certain stress levels may lead to levels and forms of message control deemed functional for the subsystem being served; from the other studies that stress at other levels may be dysfunctional for efficiency and veracity. A key, but open question is whether stress situations may be managed in media organizations at optimal levels, so as to exert control over communicative performance.

MEDIA AND SOURCE SYSTEMS AND INFORMATION CONTROL

While individualistic attitudes and abilities may be related to gatekeeper performance and information control, there is also considerable evidence that the nature of the media *and* the source system—and systemic linkages between the two—may be powerful determinants of information handling. First of all, there is ample evidence that information controls may be exerted by media managers—even by those whose principal task or responsibility is removed a step or more from editorial activities. Bowers (1967) queried managing editors of 613 daily evening newspapers about the extent to which publishers control use or nonuse of content or display of news through direct or indirect means. Bowers found the most publisher activity in the area of local news, where 11 percent were reported by their managing editors as active either "often" or "all the time." At the other extreme was foreign news, with 3 percent at the high activity level. Bowers found publisher interference higher in geographically close topics, in areas related to newspaper revenue, in areas close to the personal concerns of publishers, and on papers lower in circulation. Publisher activity was more pronounced in the way content was reported and displayed, rather than in use or nonuse.

While message shaping may occur frequently, there is nevertheless also evidence that certain kinds of information simply do not get reported in certain kinds of media situations. The general tendency for small community media to avoid controversy and support consensus has been noted above. Breed (1958) in an unusual methodological approach, sought to estimate what would *not* be printed or broadcast. He used a "reverse content analysis" based on statements from 11 community studies that were not used in the mass media. He estimated that about two-thirds of the items presumably "buried by the press" focused around the politicoeconomic area. Religion was second, followed by justice, health, and the family. His interpretation is along functional lines, leading to the conclusion that media withdraw from unnecessarily exposing institutional faults and serve the end of community unity. He does not distinguish functions performed by mass media in more and less differentiated systems. He does, however, view the "quality" and "protest" press as being relatively free to criticize institutions and values. This is consistent with the view that media relating to the total system are more likely to generate conflict among various subsystems, in the interests of bringing about eventual social equilibrium. Such media, in the viewpoint of the model used here, are performing a straightforward feedback-control function for the total system through presentation of various forms of knowledge.

While small community media may practice various forms of distribution control, distributive strategies are also clear in other societal sectors. Scientific organizations, for example, practice "discretionary" communication in the service of social control. In fact, a scientific professional organization is itself a control mechanism. It is true that some things may be communicated *within* the scientific and technological subsystems that would be avoided or denied in, say, political subsystems. Military research journals, for example, were reporting technical details about aircraft performance in certain Indochinese nations at the very time when political spokesmen were denying American presence there (McDermott, 1969). Scientific and technical communication is controlled by a code of conduct and by certain conventions; jargon itself is a control device. The fact that the military journal articles mentioned above were not cited in the mass media for a lengthy period attests to the fact that professional publication itself is a clear case of distributive control.

Subsystem Interdependence and Communication Control

Social status of media personnel was discussed earlier as fundamental to an analysis of information control in mass communication. Where a message encoder is seeking status or feels inadequate, one would quite naturally expect more of the cognitive stresses identified by such investigators as Bettinghaus and Greenberg. Since reporters tend frequently to possess lower levels of status than their sources, then this discrepancy might well be a major factor in determining communication outcomes.

A basic proposition which is suggested in much of the literature, but not tested adequately, is that control over mass media content by a source system is a function of the degree to which media channel members identify with that source system. One would expect, then, that reporters who identify strongly with scientists do submit to a great deal of scientist control over what they write. Political reporters who have strong ties to city hall would be expected to submit to control by political institutions.

Content control by source systems may take several forms. It may be direct; the source may make cooperation contingent upon the right to review copy before publication. This procedure may be more common in science reporting than in less specialized areas, such as politics. Many reporters, if not a majority, may accept a measure of such monitoring when covering science today. Reporters covering space missions regularly subject themselves to extensive controls. Communicators may be coopted by any source subsystem, but cooptation may be especially likely in more highly specialized and high status subsystems, such as medicine and science.

System Controls and Communication Accuracy

In a study of media and science source systems, Tichenor et al. (1970) investigated, as a performance criterion variable, communication accuracy, or the extent to which a message produces agreement between source and receiver. Articles were shown to survey respondents who were asked to read them and state what they said. Scientists quoted in the articles were then interviewed and shown the audience statements, and the proportion of audience statements generally acceptable to the scientist quoted in the articles was a measure of communication accuracy.

A principal conclusion from the study was that communication accuracy, defined in this way, was largely a function of the controls in the process. The most powerful predictors of communication accuracy included specific editor assignment (as contrasted with self-initiative or coverage of a general meeting), administrative responsibilities of scientists, and scientists' awareness of rigid policies for handling public information. Another factor was the press release; articles based on rewritten releases also had higher communication accuracy scores. These are all system-control factors, and were more predictive than reporter attitudes or reporter experience. Personal contact between reporter and scientists was correlated with performance, but in a curvilinear way; up to a point, face-to-face contact increased communication accuracy. But at extreme levels of contact, performance decreased, possibly indicating a breakdown or failure in face-to-face communication processes.

Editor assignment is a control factor with important motivational aspects, since a reporter in the patriarchal structure of a typical newsroom would be expected to perform at a higher level when the editor, his bureaucratic superior, sets out his task for him. Furthermore, editors tended (in this study) to assign reporters, selectively, to articles on scientists who are administrators (presumably well known) with interesting things to say and understandable ways of saying them.

This "editor control" factor stands somewhat in contradiction to Tannenbaum's conclusion that editors may be the "weak link" in the science communication chain. While Tannenbaum (1963) found low correspondence between editors and science readers (and more between editors and nonreaders) he depended heavily on the assumption that such mutuality of perceptions would be strong predictors of communication performance. Actual editorial judgment may be made in terms of source *as well as* content. In any case, the question of systemic linkages among editors, reporters, and sources such as scientists should be reopened for more intensive examination in the context of a systems model.

Control and Channel Member Autonomy

If as the Minnesota study suggested, certain control factors tend to increase levels of observable performance on such criteria as understandability and accuracy, it appears that these control factors may be self-reinforcing. However, extreme levels of such control might raise some questions about the extent to which media can fulfill the feedback, or fourth estate function, in environmental, medical, and other technical areas. The most highly trained substantive specialist in a scientific area might, if he submits to the pressures to cooptation, be reluctant to deal with controversial issues in the areas he reports. There is a need for extensive examination of this tendency in the coverage of environmental crises, which involve highly technical issues and, so far, are rarely covered by veteran, trained science writers. Instead, the environmental issues are covered largely by general reporters, political writers and conservation-environment reporters. A virtually unexamined issue is the extent to which channel members develop *autonomy,* which may be defined as simultaneous achievement of legitimacy and behavioral independence from the source system. Such autonomy could well be a counter-tendency to the predictable effects of channel member identification with the source community. Also, autonomy could arise from channel member prestige in another subsystem. High-status political columnists might elicit far more tension-laden information from a scientist than would an equally high status but specialized science writer. This might follow partly from the fact that when a scientist gets involved in a political issue, his role changes. This involvement puts the scientist into another subsystem and changes his relationship to the larger, total, pluralistic system. Also, compared with the political writer, the science writer tends to assume a consensus model and attributes considerable veto power to his network or sources upon whom he depends for doing his job.

CONFLICT AND INFORMATION CONTROL

The perspective used here in reviewing studies on the gatekeeper area has assumed both the utilization of a conflict model in pluralistic, mass media reporting and the pervasiveness of controls over information in this reporting. The existence of controls seems to be unquestionable; every "gatekeeper" study stands as a study of control processes. Nevertheless, one might question the assumption that a conflict model is being used; more today than, say, a century ago when "yellow journalism" was in vogue.

Form of conflict reporting has changed, and it may be, as Shaw (1967) suggested, that a major change in reporting by daily newspapers accompanied a fundamental innovation in news distribution—the introduction of the wire service. In a historical trend analysis, Shaw depicts the 1880-1884 drop in political news bias in Wisconsin daily newspapers as directly related to an enormous increase in use of relatively unbiased wire news, which had begun there in the early 1880's. Shaw also found evidence suggesting that local reporters may have, to some extent, imitated the less biased style of wire news. Another contemporary study supports the view of wire services as being more or less politically impartial, but supportive of the existing status system in government. Wilhoit and Sherrell (1968) found that "wire service visibility" of U.S. senators was correlated with their seniority and with prestige of committees on which they served. Attitudes and ideology of the wire service managers, the "gatekeepers," and of the senators were not related to senatorial visibility in news reports.

Both the Shaw and Wilhoit and Sherrell findings support the view that wire services have been structured historically so as to prevent, or at least reduce, extreme political bias in the mass media. Perhaps one motivating factor has been the need to serve newspapers holding widely different editorial viewpoints. Nevertheless, the shift to a more balanced reporting of political news is not necessarily a shift away from a conflict model of communication through mass media at the large system, pluralistic level. If anything, "unbiased" reporting may be *more* of a conflict approach; the difference is that compared with the days of "yellow journalism," social conflict in mass media is controlled by a different set of ground rules. The early partisan press was, by definition, speaking for a relatively restricted set of political interest groups and not for the social system at large. When the media became more "mass" in nature and more integrated into a national system, they began to adopt their pluralistic mode of reporting a variety of conflicting viewpoints. Pure "sensationalism" and conflict are not necessarily the same thing. The shift from a "libertarian" model of press behavior to what some observers have described as a "social responsibility" mode of operation (Schramm, 1957) represents a change in forms of information control. Mass media conflict in the United States a century ago was largely *between* media, as it is today in such nations as France. Today, the conflicts are more *within* media, and are managed in a way supportive of the total social system.

INFORMATION CONTROL AND PROFIT MOTIVES

It might be argued that the systems-control approach to understanding gatekeeper behavior overlooks an overriding motivational factor: the motivation to make a profit. This is a widely held assumption and has been stated explicitly by many. Among economists, Owen (1969) represents those who assume that media firms, along with others "seek to maximize profits." DeFleur (1966) while not adhering to the maximization principle directly, sees the function of what he calls "low taste" content (comics, sports, western thrillers, crime, personal advice columns) as maintenance of the financial equilibrium of "a deeply institutionalized social system which is tightly integrated with the whole of the American economic institution."

One can agree completely with DeFleur's point about integration with national economic institutions, and it is reasonable to expect various forms of economic activity by media to be correlated, as Owen found them to be. However, the assumption that the primary motivation of media institutions is to *maximize* profits, and that the profit motive is the only or main one, is open to challenge here as it is for Galbraith (1967) in his discussion of corporate structure in general. It is true, of course, that a primary concern for any social institution is to remain in existence and that growth and differentiation are often necessary for existence; stagnation is often tantamount to absolute destruction for a large-scale organization. To remain in existence, at least a minimal level of profit is essential. A minimum requirement and a drive to maximize, however, are quite different things and much media behavior can better be explained by the motivation to control information and to accomplish professional goals. Such a motivation is basically the same for a columnist as for a professional accountant.

The question of survival is so crucial in many areas of large-scale organization that the profit maximization argument may remain strong. A proponent of this argument might point out (rightfully) that large daily newspapers have remained under single-family ownership longer than most segments of corporate industry. And he might conclude that traditional entrepreneurial motives remain more relevant here than in the public stock corporations of the particular segments of the technostructure that Galbraith is concerned about. Yet, family ownership is itself misleading, since the large newspaper family corporations are themselves highly involved in various forms of regional, multiple, and conglomerate ownership. It would also be misleading to view large-scale broadcast organizations as more like part of the "techno-structure" than newspapers—especially when in some metropolitan centers major television stations themselves are owned largely by newspapers, sometimes ostensibly competing ones.

Economic pressures, of course, comprise part of the field of forces at work in the process of information control through mass media, but the singular-causation argument of economic determinism seems hardly adequate. It will not do to accept Breed's contention that social controversy is often avoided by the media on economic grounds and then try to explain the "playing up" of controversy (such as the "Selling of the Pentagon") as stimulated by the media's desire to make more profits. Fred Friendly seemed to argue that the profit motive often collided with exercise of the news-documentary job at CBS. It would be difficult to accept this rationale and then explain the "Selling of the Pentagon" and the "Pentagon Papers" issue as *purely* profit-motivated.

The issue of who shall control organizations and information has been central to current debates over media content in general, and broadcast media content in particular. In a study of relations between mass media and the legal professions, Gerald (1970) gathered responses from 41 editors and 55 radio-television news editors to this question:

> Would you object to community-wide, all-media postponement to the time of trial, of clearly prejudicial news about persons and evidence in specific criminal cases?

Radio-television editors were more than twice as likely as newspaper editors to answer negatively (58 versus 24 percent). A similar pattern occurred in answers to other, similar questions. An explanation of the difference would be speculative, since it was not the focal point of the Gerald study, but it would be hard to explain on profit maximization grounds. A general broadcast media reluctance to force the issue on such reporting, relative to the newspapers, based on the principle of public licensing of broadcast stations, seems more likely.

INFORMATION CONTROL AND FUTURE DELIVERY SYSTEMS

Although traditional conflict between large-scale media had been declining while pluralistic coverage within media has been increasing, it is nevertheless possible that the future may bring a different type of intermedia conflict. Namely, this may be conflict between the media serving the smaller subsystems and those serving the larger subsystems, or the social system as a whole. It is true that strong tendencies exist to reduce the amount of controversy in the small community mass media. Media in small communities do tend to confine themselves to descriptive, consensual reporting—as long as outside forces do not intervene.

This very intervention of outside forces, however, may be the emerging factor in social problems of today and tomorrow. Confrontations may develop between small subsystems, once independent but now less so, and agencies of the larger overall system. The environment and ecology movement provides an example. In small communities throughout the nation, environmental crises have been generated as a result of pressure group activity on state (or national) level agencies and governments. A state antipollution agency, for example, may issue a report condemning an industrial firm in a suburban or outlying community served by, perhaps, a weekly paper and a radio station. Metropolitan media whose coverage includes that community report the issue immediately, but their coverage is oriented primarily toward their pluralistic feedback function for the larger, total system. Informing various interest groups about a pollution situation has the consequence of bringing "regulative" (in the systems sense) pressures to bear on the subsystems to adjust. Local media can be expected to perform differently. Conflict-systems theory leads to the prediction that local media will structure their reporting so as to emphasize local cohesion and defend local institutions against onslaughts from the outside.

Both kinds of media in such a situation are performing information control operations, but in the service of different functions for different parts of the system. For the *total* system, however, these competing presentations can be seen as functional. If public decisions are to be made in a climate of maximum discussion of varying points of view, local media providing a local perspective would seem to be critical for realization of the democratic ideal. Furthermore, by responding to different subsystem concerns, small and large subsystem media jointly serve to manage conflict and maintain the total system as a whole.

The dynamics of small versus large subsystem media performance, and the behavior of actors within these subsystems, would seem to form an urgent topical area for future investigation and analysis. While future developments in media technology and information delivery are not entirely clear, the question of information control will certainly emerge repeatedly in establishment of community cable television systems. Some have suggested, as Bagdikian has, that community CATV systems might perform a community information and identification service far superior to previous media. Yet, given the integration with national systems required for such operations, it may be questionable whether CATV operations will serve at the local level in a way analogous to community newspapers. Among newspapers, new ownership and merger arrangements need to be studied in terms of potential implications for information delivery. A weekly newspaper joining with a half-dozen others in a central printing operation may continue to operate in a functional way as it has in the past. Multiple chain ownership, however, may be quite different, and the consequences for community identification by the medium may be profound.

NOTES

1. Both the "Selling of the Pentagon" and the "Pentagon Papers" illustrate crises of information control which arose as major public issues in 1971. The first refers to a televised documentary about persuasive techniques allegedly used by the Department of Defense in advancing its public image. The second refers to the issue involving publication by the *New York Times* and, subsequently, other newspapers, of portions of a Defense Department study on the conduct of the Vietnam war. The study had been classified as top secret and the *Times* was enjoined briefly from further publication until the U.S. Supreme Court ruled in the *Times'* favor.

2. Gieber (1964) has argued that the reporter's role is largely "distributive" whereas the position here is that mass communication may be not *only* distributive but also "assimilative" in the sense used by Gieber in reference to political sources. The fact that mass communication serves different functions is basic to the control-systems approach.

REFERENCES

BAGDIKIAN, B. H. (1971) The Information Machines, Their Impact on Man and the Media. New York: Harper & Row.

BAUER, R. A. and C. ZIMMERMAN (1956) "The influences of an audience on what is remembered." Public Opinion Q. 20: 238-248.

BETTINGHAUS, E. P. and I. L. PRESTON (1964) "Dogmatism and performance of the communicator under cognitive stress". Journalism Q. 41 (Summer): 399-402.

BOULDING, K. (1964) The Meaning of the Twentieth Century: The Great Transition. New York: Harper & Row.

BOWERS, D. R. (1967) "A report on activity by publishers in directing newsroom decisions." Journalism Q. 44 (Spring): 43-52.

BREED, W. (1958) "Mass communication and social integration." Social Forces 37: 109-116.

——— (1955) "Social control in the newsroom." Social Forces 33: 323-335.

BURNHAM, J. (1941) The Managerial Revolution. New York: John Day.

CARTER, R. E. (1959) "Racial identification effects upon the news story writers." Journalism Q. 36 (Summer): 284-290.

——— (1958) "Newspaper 'gatekeepers' and their sources of news." Public Opinion Q. 22 (Summer): 133-144.

CATER, D. (1964) The Fourth Branch of Government. New York: Random House.

CENTERS, R. J. (1949) The Psychology of Social Classes. New Jersey: Princeton University Press.

COSER, L. A. (1956) The Functions of Social Conflict. New York: Free Press.

DeFLEUR, M. L. (1966) Theories of Mass Communication. New York: David McKay.

DONOHEW, L. (1967) "Newspaper gatekeeper and forces in the news channel." Public Opinion Q. 31: 61-68.

DONOHUE, G. A., P. J. TICHENOR and C. N. OLIEN (1971) "Mass media functions, knowledge, and social control." Paper presented to the Association for Education in Journalism, Columbia, South Carolina, August.

EDELSTEIN, A. S. (1966) Perspectives in Mass Communications. Copenhagen: Einar Harcks Forlag.

FRIENDLY, F. W. (1967) Due to Circumstances Beyond Our Control . . . New York: Random House.

GALBRAITH, J. K. (1967) The New Industrial State. New York: Houghton Mifflin.

GERALD, J. E. (1963) The Social Responsibility of the Press. Minneapolis: University of Minnesota Press.

GERBNER, G. (1970) "Press-Bar relationships: progress since Sheppard and Reardon." Journalism Q. 47 (Summer): 223-232.

——— (1967) "Newsmen and schoolmen: the state and problems of education reporting." Journalism Q. 44 (Summer): 211-224.

——— (1964) "Ideological perspectives and political tendencies in news reporting". Journalism Quarterly 41 (Autumn): 495-508.

GIEBER, W. (1964) "News is what newspapermen make it," pp. 173-182 in L. A. Dexter and D. M. White, People, Society and Mass Communications. New York: Free Press.

GIEBER, W. and W. JOHNSON (1961) "The city hall 'beat': a study of reporter and source roles." Journalism Q. 38 (Summer): 289-302.

GREENBERG, B. S. and P. H. TANNENBAUM (1962) "Communicator performance under cognitive stress." Journalism Q. 39 (Spring): 169-178.

HACHTEN, W. A. (1963) "The press as reporter and critic of government." Journalism Q. 40: 12-18.

HAGSTROM, W. O. (1965) The Scientific Community. New York: Basic Books.

HARRINGTON, M. (1967) "The social-industrial complex." Harpers Magazine (November): 55-60.

HOCKING, W. (1947) Freedom of the Press. Chicago: University of Chicago Press.

JANOWITZ, M. (1952) The Community Press in an Urban Setting. New York: Free Press.

KATZ, D. and R. L. KAHN (1966) The Social Psychology of Organizations. New York: John Wiley.

KERR, C. (1963) The Uses of the University. Cambridge, Mass.: Harvard University Press.

KERRICK, J. S., T. E. ANDERSON and L. B. SWALES (1964) "Balance and writer's attitude in news stories and editorials." Journalism Q. 41 (Spring): 207-215.

LASSWELL, H. D. (1960) "The structure and function of communication in society," pp. 117-130 in W. Schramm (ed.) Mass Communications. Urbana: University of Illinois Press.

LEWIN, K. (1951) Field Theory in Social Science. New York: Harper.

LIPPMANN, W. (1961) Drift and Mastery. Englewood Cliffs, N.J.: Prentice-Hall.

LYND, R. S. (1939) Knowledge for What? Princeton, N.J.: Princeton University Press.

MACHLUP, F. (1962) The Production and Distribution of Knowledge in the United States. Princeton, N.J.: Princeton University Press.

MARTIN, R. R., G. J. O'KEEFE and O. B. NAYMAN (1970) "Newspaper editors and their readers: a coorientational approach." Paper presented to the Association for Education in Journalism, Washington, D.C., August.

McDERMOTT, J. (1969) "Knowledge is power." Nation (April 14): 458-460.

McLEOD, J. M. and S. E. HAWLEY, Jr. (1964) "Professionalization among newsmen." Journalism Q. 41 (Autumn): 529-538.

McQUAIL, D. (1969) Towards a Sociology of Mass Communication. London: Collier Macmillan.

MERTON, R. K. (1957) Social Theory and Social Structure. New York: Free Press.

MONTAGNA, P. D. (1968) "Professionalization and bureaucratization in large professional organizations." Amer. J. of Sociology 74 (September): 138-145.

NIXON, R. B. and T. HAHN (1971) "Concentration of press owenership: a comparison of 32 countries." Journalism Q. 48 (Spring): 5-16.

NIXON, R. B. and J. WARD (1961) "Trends in newspaper ownership and inter-media competition." Journalism Q. 38 (Winter): 3-14.

NIXON, R. B. and R. L. JONES (1956) "The content of non-competitive vs. competitive newspapers." Journalism Q. 33: 299-314.

OLIEN, C. N., G. A. DONOHUE, and P. J. TICHENOR (1968) "The community editor's power and the reporting of conflict." Journalism Q. 45: 243-252.

OWEN, B. M. (1969) "Empirical results on the price effects of joint ownership in the mass media." Memorandum 93. Stanford, Calif.: Stanford University Research Center in Economic Growth.

PARK, R. E. (1940) "News as a form of knowledge." Amer. J. of Sociology 45 (March): 669-686.

PARSONS, T. (1967) "A paradigm for the analysis of social systems and change," pp. 189-212 in N. S. Demerath and R. A. Peterson (eds.) System, Change and Conflict. New York: Free Press.

——— and N. J. SMELSER (1967) "The primary subsystems of society," pp. 131-140 in N. S. Demerath and R. A. Peterson (eds.) System, Change and Conflict. New York: Free Press.

POOL, I. de SOLA and I. SHULMAN (1959) "Newsmen's fantasies, audiences and newswriting." Public Opinion Q. 23: 145-148.

PORTER, W. E. (1971) "Radicalism and the young journalist." Saturday Rev. (December 11): 65-66.

REVEL, J. F. (1971) Without Marx or Jesus. Reviewed in Saturday Rev. (July 24, 1971): 14-31.

RILEY, J. W., Jr. and M. W. RILEY (1965) "Mass communication and the social system," ch. 24 in R. K. Merton (ed.) Sociology Today. New York: Harper.

RUCKER, B. (1968) The First Freedom. Carbondale, Ill.: Southern Illinois University Press.

SAMUELSON, M. (1962) "A standardized test to measure job satisfaction in the newsroom." Journalism Q. 39 (Summer): 285-291.

SCHRAMM, W. (1957) Responsibility in Mass Communications. New York: Harper.

——— and W. DANIELSON (1958) "Anticipated audiences as determinants of recall." J. of Abnormal and Social Psychology 56: 282-283.

SHAW, D. L. (1967) "News bias and the telegraph: a study of historical change." Journalism Q. 38 (Spring): 3-12.

SPENCER, H. (1898) The Principles of Sociology Vol. I. New York: D. Appleton.

TANNENBAUM, P. H. (1963) "Communication of scientific information." Science 140 (May) 3507: 579-583.

THOMPSON, J. D. (1962) "Organization and output transactions." Amer. J. of Sociology 68 (November): 309-324.

TICHENOR, P. J., C. N. OLIEN, A. HARRISON, and G. A. DONOHUE (1970) "Mass communications systems and communication accuracy in science news reporting." Journalism Q. 47 (Winter): 673-683.

UDELL, J. G. (1970) Economic Trends in the Daily Newspaper Business, 1946-1970. Graduate School of Business Report. Madison, Wis.: University of Wisconsin.

WESTLEY, B. H. and M. S. MacLEAN, Jr. (1957) "A conceptual model for communications research." Journalism Q. 34: 31-38.

WHITE, D. M. (1950) "The gatekeeper: a case study in the selection of news." Journalism Q. 27 (Fall): 383-390.

WILHOIT, G. C. and K. S. SHERRELL (1968) "Wire service visibility of U.S. senators." Journalism Q. 45 (Spring): 42-54.

Chapter 3

MASS COMMUNICATION AND INFORMATION DIFFUSION

John P. Robinson

SOCIAL COMMENTATORS AND OBSERVERS of the changes in modern society are continually amazed by mounting evidence of an incredible increase in the information that flows through society. The rapid diffusion of the electrical devices of radio, television, and more recently the computer, is usually taken as the most impressive evidence on this score, and incipient innovations such as cable television, home video recorders and computer terminals promise to accelerate this "information explosion" even more rapidly in the not-too-distant future. Moreover other indicators point to much the same conclusion: the tremendous proliferation of magazine and book titles over the last 25 years, the increasing audience for education television, and, for the critics of the "vast wasteland" of commercial television, reports from experienced kindergarten and first grade teachers that their students come to school with far greater verbal skills and wider interests than their predecessors.

Against such an impressive array of evidence, elements of which are well wired into the conventional wisdom, the mass communication researcher usually encounters at best a skeptical audience to his proclamation that research fails to corroborate any such utopian effects of the media. To be sure, the researcher does find that people already well informed can become better informed by attention to the media, but for any particular topic these people do constitute a small, and often insignificant, segment of the total mass audience. Such results are consistent with findings from research into the media's effects on audience propensity to engage in violent behavior, to become unduly swayed in their political or electoral decisions, to become less intellectually active as a response to the easier availability of media fare, as summarized in Klapper's (1960) famous summary of the research literature:

> Regardless of the condition in question—be it the voᴛe intentions of audience members, their tendency toward or away from delinquent behavior, or their general orientation toward life and its problems—the media are more likely to reinforce than to change.

But converging evidence of this sort is still likely to be of little consolation to persons conditioned to the argument that modern man's increased exposure to media[1] and other information sources has inevitably resulted in him becoming more informed, occasionally to the point of information overload, than he was in prior eras.

Public opinion researchers have perhaps uncovered the most persuasive evidence of the failure of all segments of the population to share in the information explosion, with their documentation of the shocking ignorance of the American public on matters of basic national concern. In 1964, half of a national sample were unaware of the existence of two Chinas with their opposing political loyalties (Robinson, 1967). In 1969, a CBS survey found only a third of the country had heard of the Kerner Commission Report. In a 1970 national survey, less than a third of the population could provide even rudimentary identification of Ralph Nader, Robert Finch, or Martha Mitchell (Robinson, 1972). Collections of further items on which the public seems ill informed have been provided in Lane and Sears (1964), Erskine (1962, 1963a, 1963b), Schramm and Wade (1967) and Robinson (1967).

Moreover the evidence has been slowly accumulating that more directly links these discouraging information levels to a dearth of information flow from the media to the public, even if one talks only of the actual audience for any given message and excludes the usual majority of the public who are not in the audience at the time of the message. McLeod and Swinehart (1960) found almost no increase in public awareness of the detailed scientific purpose of space satellites six months after extensive media coverage of the implications of the launching of Sputnik I. Robinson and Hirsch (1969) found teenagers unable to describe even the basic themes, much less the subtle meanings, of the lyrics in various popular "message" songs which had received maximum exposure on Top 40 radio stations and which most teenagers indeed claimed to have heard. More disturbing is Stern's (1971) finding that half the audience of a national network news program could not recall even one of the 19 news stories on the program shortly after they were broadcast.

Perhaps the most telling and comprehensive documentation of media ineffectiveness was the "Cincinnati experiment" undertaken shortly after World War II to better acquaint the public with the purposes of the United Nations (Star and Hughes, 1950). Newspapers, radio stations, voluntary associations, schools, and churches were inundated for a six-month period with information slogans, guest speakers, pamphlets, posters and other gimmicks designed to provide knowledge about the functions of the United Nations. Although specifically addressed to those "most in need of enlightenment," that is the less educated and less affluent, it was the educated and affluent who reported being most enlightened by the campaign. The proportion of the Cincinnati residents knowing nothing of the functions of the United Nations was at the same level after the campaign as before.

Now to some extent, the above collection of research is an exaggeration to make a point seldom acknowledged in intellectual debates about the power of the media. Mass communication and public opinion researchers do have evidence of apparently successful transmission of information from the media to the public. Some of these will be examined later in the article. Thus, in the McLeod and Swinehart investigation (1960), the proportion of the population able to describe the less detailed purposes for satellites doubled (although only from 8 to 16 percent) and those larger proportions of the population who saw satellites as the basis of a race with the Russians may have been simply reflecting the framework in which the news media interpreted the importance of Sputnik I. It is unlikely that widespread public awareness of the dangers of cigarette smoking, the signs of cancer, or the causes of forest fires would be possible without the torrent of public service announcements through the media. Public opinion researchers find so few people unable to complete the beginnings of commercial slogans and jingles (Ward, 1972) that they can hardly dismiss the power of media advertising. Public dissatisfaction with the handling of the Vietnam War, growing distrust in the institutions in society, and improving racial attitudes now current in our society may also be seen as directly following from the dominant messages emanating from the media. Nevertheless, these are exceptions rather than the rule, and even though one may dismiss most of the information described in the preceding paragraphs as rather academic, this is the information that the news media feel it is their duty to report, and that policy makers assume the public is concerned about.

How has it been possible for researchers to compile such a dismal scorecard on the effectiveness of the media in conveying news information? One researcher, William McPhee (1956) developed the following line of explanation:

> Imagine trying to transmit complex and sophisticated knowledge to students who walk in and out as they please, when some of the most valuable effects might occur to a passerby who wanders in by chance, when most volunteer students already know what is to be learned, while those who do not already know are not available, when motivation is low, and when neither the subjects nor the teacher have any clear idea about the rewards for learning.

To this, one might add the coping and perceptual mechanisms whereby the public protects itself from the bombardment of media information to which it is exposed. It has been estimated that the average American is exposed to hundreds of messages just about advertising on an average day. Add to this all the "bad news" messages propagated by the news media and it is not difficult to imagine why the audience is highly selective about what news it chooses to attend to or seek out in the media.

More fundamental reasons may be involved. News changes daily and hence cannot be packaged as neatly as a classroom lecture. It is not difficult to imagine that news messages and arguments, designed by news personnel who have undergone considerable exposure to the disciplines of advanced education, could be too difficult to comprehend by a mass audience composed of less than 15 percent college graduates. Moreover, few news stories would seem to provide the fuel for as lively interpersonal conversation among peers in the general public as it would among average members of the news profession, and communications research offers ample evidence of interpersonal conversation being a more powerful transmission mechanism than the media (Weiss, 1970), even among the elites in our society (Bauer et al., 1963).

The research evidence in the following section can be conveniently explained by and subsumed under the above type of arguments. However, while most research results are consistent with this formulation, which builds upon a model of a series of segmented media audiences who tend to become increasingly dissimilar from one another, a significant body of research points to quite different processes of information flow that may operate under certain conditions. These divergent research findings and conditions are then reviewed in the subsequent section, before some final implications and conclusions are drawn.

MEDIA USAGE AND INFORMATION LEVELS

There are, first of all, strong linkages that are found between media usage and information. Briefly stated, heavier users of print media are better informed than light users or nonusers.[2] It is immediately obvious, however, that there are intervening audience factors that need to be taken into account in such a formulation. Of the several factors in the audience itself, research indicates that the extent of the audience member's exposure to formal education is the most powerful factor intervening between media usage and information level.

For example, Figure I breaks the American population down into six groups that were maximally different in terms of their informa-

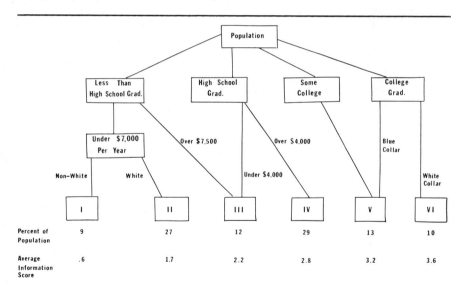

Combinations of background factors for each of the six groups within the United States population showing large differences in information scores about the Far East. Percentage of population estimates are based on the same Survey Research Center data as are the average information scores. Maximum information score = 4.

Figure 1.

TABLE 1
PERCENTAGE WITHIN EACH SOCIAL GROUP IN EIGHT SEPARATE TYPES OF SOPHISTICATED USAGE[a]

Group[b]	Books (Nonfiction)	Analytic Commentary Magazine	News and Business Magazine	Pictoral and Interest Magazine	Read all or most Foreign News in Paper	Read at Least some Foreign News in Paper	Listen to News On Radio	Watch News On TV
I	1	0.0	3	15	7	27	49	10
II	5	0.2	3	21	15	45	58	25
III	8	0.4	9	37	20	63	63	28
IV	8	1.1	13	47	25	69	57	33
V	15	0.5	24	53	36	80	62	34
VI	24	10.0	44	61	40	83	69	42
Total Sample	8	1.1	11	34	21	57	59	28
National Opinion Leaders[c] (Rosenau)	17	30 (est.)	60 (est.)	12 (est.)	NA	94 (est.)	10 (est.)	10 (est.)
National Business Leaders (Bauer et al.)	NA	20 (est.)	88 (est.)	40 (est.)	NA	98 (est.)	NA	NA

a. 1957 Survey Research Center data.
b. See Figure 2 for definition of groups.
c. See Text for explanation of the Rosenau, Bauer et al. data.

tion about the Far East in 1964 (Robinson, 1967). The information index was based on answers to the following four questions:

(1) What kind of government does most of China have?
(2) Have you heard anything about another Chinese government?
(3) Has the U.S. been treating China and Russia the same or differently?
(4) Have you heard anything about the fighting in Vietnam?

The average score in the population on this index, which runs between 0 (no correct answers) and 4 (four correct answers), was 2.2, a score not significantly better than what could be achieved by unembarrassed guesswork on the part of a respondent. Group I (that 9 percent of the sample who were nonwhites with less than a high school education, earning under $7,500 per year) averaged just over half of one of the four questions correct compared to that 10 percent of the sample in Group VI (college graduates in white-collar jobs) who achieved a nearly perfect score of 3.6 items correct. While other factors were important in predicting public knowledge of these items,[3] it is obvious from Figure 1 that education was the dominant factor in distinguishing the six groups in terms of their information levels.

Thus, when one finds significant parallel differences in mass media usage among these six groupings of the population, one strongly suspects that education is the major factor at work here as well. The data are presented in Table 1 and show proportions of a 1958 national sample[4] claiming various usage of the media. While only 1 percent of persons in the Group I category reported reading a nonfiction book in the previous year, almost one in four persons in Group VI did. Even readership of *Look* and *Life,* "magazines for people who can't read," was four times higher in Group VI than in Group I. Similar differences are found for readership of foreign affairs news in the newspaper and claiming news to be among one's usually viewed television programs and, to a much lesser extent, claiming news to be among one's usually heard radio programs.

These two sets of data on information and media usage, unfortunately taken six years apart, still strongly point to a strong relation between the two variables mediated by the factor of education. That is, it is the best educated segments of our population who are both well informed and who keep themselves better informed by more serious usage of the mass media for informational content. Nevertheless these data refer to aggregated groupings in the population and cannot be used to imply that such processes hold for

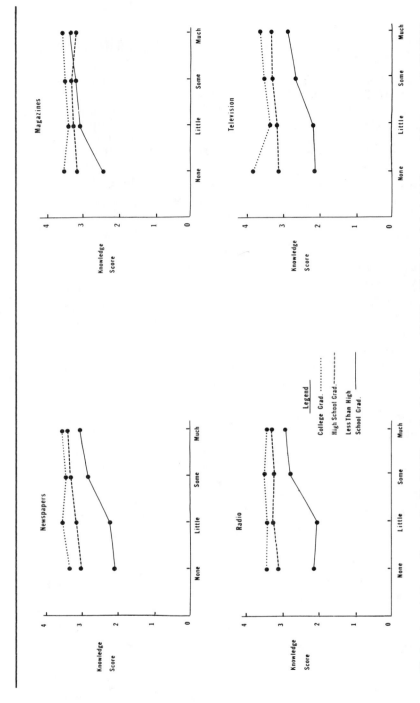

The four knowledge questions dealt with: (1) UN membership of Communist China; (2) Whether Cuba had a Communist government; (3) Which party elected most members to Congress in the last election, and (4) awareness of clash between police and demonstrators at Democratic convention.

Figure 2: RELATION BETWEEN POLITICAL KNOWLEDGE AND MEDIA USAGE FOR VARIOUS EDUCATION GROUPS.

individuals in the society. Indeed, one of the well-known methodo-logical caveats of social science research is that relations that hold for aggregates oftentimes do not hold at the individual level (Robinson, 1950).

However, a study of adults in the Detroit, Michigan area in 1964 did collect simultaneous data on media usage, information level (again about foreign affairs) and education. These data not only corroborate the Figure 1 and Table 1 aggregate findings (Robinson, 1967), but also verify that the above interpretation holds at the individual level as well.[5]

Recent data from more appropriately designed national samples have not only extended these results to information areas beyond foreign affairs, but have allowed analyses by sophisticated multivari-ate methods, more appropriate to verifying the extent to which specific usage of each of the media predicts to information levels once other background factors are taken into account. The data in Figure 2 refer to differences in information level for persons with different educational backgrounds who report varying usage of newspapers, radio, magazines, and television during the 1968 presidential campaign. The data come from the Survey Research Center's 1968 national election study. Since the first two questions which comprise the four-item information index,

(1) Knowledge of whether China had a Communist government and had a seat in the United Nations
(2) Knowledge of whether Cuba had a Communist government
(3) Awareness of disturbances at the 1968 Democratic National Conven-tion
(4) Knowledge of whether Republicans or Democrats elected more men to Congress in the 1968 election

do not ask about campaign information conveyed only in 1968 by the media, our measure of information only can be taken as suggestive of direct media impact.

Nevertheless, the Figure 2 graphs do suggest, importantly, that the various media do not perform the same functions in all segments of the population. Thus, heavy usage of any medium would seem to do little to raise information levels of college graduates, who are well informed whether they use the media or not. The same generally holds true, although not as strongly, and with some exceptions, for high school graduates. Among that majority of the population who did not graduate from high school, however, there are pronounced increases in information level associated with more regular usage of

TABLE 2

AVERAGE NUMBER OF NEWS PERSONALITIES RECOGNIZED
ACCORDING TO MEDIA USAGE (National sample)

		Deviation from Overall Mean	
		Before Correction	*After Correction*[a]
Hours of TV on an average day			
Less than 2 hours (n=64)	1.9	+.4	+.1
Three hours (n=172)	1.8	+.3	+.1
Four-five hours (n=127)	1.3	−.2	−.1
Six or more hours (n=67)	.6	−.9	−.2
Frequency of national news viewing			
At least twice a week (n=270)	1.6	+.1	+.1
About once a week (n=81)	1.8	+.3	+.1
Never (n=82)	.7	−.8	−.3
Reads a news magazine			
Yes (n=60)	3.0	+1.5	+.6
No, but reads other magazines (n=214)	1.5	0	0
Does not read any magazines (n=159)	1.6	−.7	−.2
Reads a newspaper			
Everyday (n=293)	1.8	+.3	+.2
At least once a week (n=99)	1.1	+.4	−.3
Less often (n=41)	.1	−1.4	−.5
Hours of radio on an average day			
Less than 2 hours (n=235)	1.5	0	0
Two-three hours (n=113)	1.6	+.1	0
Four-five hours (n=34)	1.2	−.3	−.3
Six or more hours (n=51)	1.5	0	+.1
Number of movies seen (in previous three months)			
None (n=270)	1.2	−.3	−.1
One-two (n=116)	2.2	+.7	+.1
Three or more (n=47)	1.4	−.1	+.1

a. After correction for usage of other media, sex, race, and education.

the media. While there are still significant differences between persons of different education levels, these become minimal among heavier users of the media. The data strongly suggest, therefore, that more extensive attention to the media can act to level the tremendous differences in information that obtain due to education. Somewhat similar conclusions were reached by Campbell (1966) in his analysis of political information data collected in the 1964 political campaign. Magazines seem especially potent in this regard and in Figure 2, we find that high school dropouts who read several magazines surpassing their counterparts with a high school degree in levels of information. Nevertheless, it is well to remember that, as Table I showed, magazine usage among the less educated is rather uncommon.

A somewhat different tack characterized analysis of the public's ability to identify various people in the news[6] in a small 1970 national survey of television usage (Robinson, 1972). Instead of searching for the complex sort of interactions between variables uncovered in Figure 2, the attempt here was to examine how much of an overall difference usage of each medium made in explaining information levels, once other background factors (such as education, sex, age, race) and alternative media usage had been taken into account. All of these variables were subjected to a Multiple Classification Analysis (MCA), a recent computer program developed by Andrews et al. (1967) to examine the effects of single variables once the effects of all other variables are held constant.

The calculations of Table 2 result from applying MCA to these data. The first column of Table 2 refers to the average number of correct identifications for persons reporting various usage of each of the mass media and the second column refers to the deviation of these scores around the average score of 1.5 (out of a possible 7) correct identifications. Thus persons who report watching television less than two hours per day average 1.9 correct identifications, which is .4 identifications above the 1.5 general average. Entries in the third column refer to the average scores, once all the above-mentioned factors have been taken into account. Here persons who watch less than two hours of television per day now score only .1 identifications above the average, probably reflecting the lighter TV viewers' already-existing higher information levels and better education.

It can be seen that the figures in the third column indicate *print* media usage to be much more crucial in explaining differentials in information levels than does *broadcast* media usage. Readers of news magazines score .6 above average in information levels and nonreaders .2 below average, while regular newspaper readers score .2 above average and nonreaders .5 below average. In contrast frequent TV news viewers score only .1 above average and nonviewers of news programs only .3 below average. These results corroborate Figure 2 in indicating readership of news magazines to be an extremely potent agent for increasing information levels. Unlike Figure 2, Table 2 does not indicate heavy exposure to TV news leading to greater information accrual than occasional exposure.

Our confidence in the Table 2 results is strengthened when we find virtually the same pattern of results among a cross-section of 1,000 teenagers in a single large suburban county (Robinson, 1972) asked the same information and media usage questions. In fact, almost identical results were obtained when the analysis was performed on these teenagers' ability to answer factual questions about foreign countries.

Even further support for the applicability of these results in other areas of knowledge is provided by Schramm and Wade (1967). These authors conducted analyses parallel to those performed here for public awareness of health and science information. In both areas, print media usage was also found to predict to information levels better than broadcast media usage.[7]

Thus a substantial body of survey research data converges on the findings (a) that it is the best-educated segment of society that keeps itself informed about what is happening in the world, and (b) that it is exposure to print media (the favored media mode of the better educated) which is mainly associated with greater likelihood of being informed or becoming better informed. These behaviors have recently been formally described under the hypothesis of an "increasing knowledge gap" by Tichenor et al. (1970), who were able to present several pieces of independent evidence of the phenomena. First of all, they showed larger gaps between information levels of the better educated and the less educated between 1949 and 1969 on three pieces of information—identification of earth satellites, belief that man would reach the moon, and belief that cigarettes cause lung cancer. Thus in 1949, 14 percent of the grade school educated believed men would reach the moon compared to 18 percent of the college educated; by 1965, the comparable figures were 37 percent for the grade school educated and 81 percent for the college educated. In two related experimental studies, the authors showed (1) smaller differences in public affairs knowledge of college educated and non-college-educated persons in a town with a newspaper strike compared to a nonstrike community, and (2) greater gaps in understanding between college graduates and the rest of the population on topics that had been given more publicity in the mass media.

The striking convergence of these three sets of findings strongly suggested to these authors that the mass media largely function to increase those already-existing gaps in information that separate the college graduate from the rest of society and hence may have been responsible for creating even wider divisions of opinion in our society than might have been the case without the media. Certainly the implications of these results need to be taken more seriously by media practitioners.

Tichenor et al. wisely note that their results largely were found with, and hence may only apply to, the print media and to academic "hard" news, i.e., items of public affairs and science rather than audience-specific topics (such as society news or garden care). It is to some similar exceptions to the above pattern of results, some of which do involve the "hard" news items that we have mainly discussed in this section, that we now turn our attention.

EXCEPTIONS TO RESTRICTED INFORMATION FLOW

The above body of literature clearly suffers from a lack of cumulative research enterprises (in which investigators can build upon and extend findings from previous endeavors), but the following exceptions are gleaned from an even more diverse body of research and speculation. These exceptions mainly concern the *type* of information under consideration. That is, it appears that *some types* of information in the media *can be conveyed* to the broader mass audience—i.e., beyond simply those portions of the audience who are already predisposed to absorb the information. Nevertheless, our discussion will touch on other communication variables as well, particularly the type of medium (learning via print as opposed to broadcast media) under consideration.

There is, first of all, the type of information that media observers, following from Lazarsfeld and Merton (1948), have labeled "status conferral." That is, persons, issues, or objects to which the media pay attention have increased status conferred on them merely by being exposed to media attention. Weiss (1970) reviews several examples of this phenomenon, the most well accepted perhaps being the increased importance or salience in the public of issues discussed by candidates during political campaigns (e.g., Eisenhower's raising of the Korean War as a campaign issue in 1952, the issue of bombing the islands of Quemoy and Matsu in the Kennedy-Nixon debates). To this, one might add the apparent correlation between media coverage and public perception of important national problems in noncampaign periods (a recent example being media discussion of ecology and pollution problems). A similar connection is not unlikely for people in news, which perhaps explains why politicians are so anxious for media coverage.[8] Advertising, particularly brand-name advertising, seems predicated on the notion that the public will attach higher status to products that have been brought to their attention by the media. And while there is considerable debate over whether current research has demonstrated a link between televised violence and engagement in aggressive behavior by the audience, it is worth speculation whether all the violence shown in television has conferred status on certain false stereotypes in the public mind concerning the amount of violence existing in our society (less than 5,000 murders are committed in this country per year, which may be less than the number shown in television drama during a year), the nature and motivations for violence (mainly occurring between people who know each other in real-life), the efficacy of law enforcement agencies in solving crimes (in real life crime does pay, which probably accounts for its popularity), and the confidence one ought to have in the correctness of the judgment of law enforcement officials (which may account for public acceptance of the actions taken by Chicago police in 1968 and by national guardsmen at Kent State in 1970).

While this discussion borders on the highly speculative, it is precisely these more subtle and difficultly measured types of information on which appropriate research is in short supply. Despite Herzog's (1944) well-publicized and intriguing finding that soap-opera fans found in these programs solutions to and philosophies about their own everyday problems, researchers have yet to undertake systematic measurement of what people learn from everyday dramatic media fare. Recent television surveys have demonstrated that the public generally perceives television dramatic programs as reflecting real life, and more viewers claim to learn something from their favorite dramatic programs than do not (Robinson, 1972). In terms of what is claimed to be learned, these data suggest that the audience has not changed much in the last 30 years; solutions to life's problems learned from soap operas led the list of things learned, although frequent allusion was also made to accumulating medical knowledge from the "doctor" programs (e.g., Marcus Welby) and to learning about how police solve crimes from detective programs. However complex the task of researching what the audience actually "learns" from viewing each episode of their favorite program may be, it is precisely from such research that we can begin to understand the cumulative effects of this most pervasive medium. Learning from other media should also be considered in such a research endeavor. Some researchers have already produced promising leads about the cumulative effects of television, although not in the context of specific programs. DeFleur and DeFleur (1967) found children more accurate in identifying the job requirements and ranking the socioeconomic status of occupations portrayed in television drama than occupations not portrayed on television. Klapper (1969) speculated that children's moral judgment of the behavior of television dramatic characters might be far more developed than would be predicted from the work of the noted child development theorist, Piaget, suggesting children develop these skills earlier as a result of having viewed so many moral dilemmas on television in their formative years. Schramm et al.'s (1962) finding that first grade children in a community without television showed less verbal skills than first grade children in a matched community with television is also taken as evidence suggestive of commercial television's "teaching" skills, since viewing of regular television programs was presumably the only experiental factor that differentiated children in the two communities. Again the need for more comprehensive research along these directions is obvious.

Turning to other information areas and extending our interest to adults as well as children, Robinson (1972) found heavier television viewers in a national sample to be slightly better informed than less heavy viewers about two principles of weather forecasting (that weather moves from west to east and that low pressure systems signal the arrival of cloudier weather). Presumably, the heavy viewers became aware of these principles because in the process of watching more television of all types they were exposed to more weather forecasts in which these principles are applied night after night (the national weather map showing the directional flow of the weather with pressure systems is a usual prop on these forecasts). Corroboration of this interpretation comes from finding that persons who claimed to watch weather programs every night were significantly more aware of both principles than less steady viewers of weather forecasts, other factors (education, age, usage of other media, etc.) being equal.

The significant factor to keep in mind here is that identical analyses of viewer recognition of news personalities in the same sample (as described in Table 2) indicated the heavy television news viewer to be considerably less able to identify personalities in the news than the less steady viewer. Thus in contrast to their performance on the academic identification items, the heavy television viewer does seem to be reaping some educational benefit from this use of his leisure time. Perhaps these divergent results stem from weather being an area of "life knowledge," with far more day-to-day relevance for the average person than the "school knowledge" required in identifying distant persons in the news. One is reminded of McLeod et al.'s (1968) finding that respondent's performance on "hard" news items was unrelated to their perform-ance on an item requiring problem-solving abilities. The need to examine a broader range of information than has been examined to date again becomes obvious.

Finally, evidence now exists that information camapaigns of the variety studied in Cincinnati need not be doomed to failure. Douglas et al. (1970) have reported a successful six-month media blitz to improve public information about the mentally retarded. Overall information levels on seven of ten information items examined were practically twice as high in the community subjected to the campaign as in a comparable community in which no special campaign was mounted. Moreover, those with least education picked up most campaign information. The authors wisely note the limitations of this study: the topic area was of low salience and little controversy, information items on which change was greatest were straight "awareness" items (e.g., awareness of people or institutions in the community dealing with mental retardation), information gained did not generalize to possibly relevant information not conveyed in the campaign, and the communities were under 5,000 population in which high amounts of interpersonal conversation were observed. But this hardly lessens the intriguing possibility that the negative results from the Cincinnati study have been overgeneralized.

While the major medium used in the Douglas et al. campaign was newspapers, evidence exists of television usage being associated with information accrual. In an earlier footnote, we cited Schramm and

Wade's (1967) finding that heavy users of television for campaign news were better informed on political matters than heavy users of the print media in the 1964 presidential campaign.[9] More dynamic evidence on the accumulation of political knowledge was collected by Chaffee et al. (1970) who, by having identical measures on respondents at two points in time were able to demonstrate significant *gains* in political information during the course of the campaign among a sample of teenagers who were heaviest viewers of public affairs programs on television. Having data on information levels at the beginning of the campaign, Chaffee et al. were able to demonstrate that such gains could not be attributed wholly to public affairs viewers being more informed at the outset of the campaign. Reading newspapers for public affairs was also related to information gain. But, unlike the results in the preceding section, it was no more strongly related to information gain than viewing public affairs on television. What seemed to matter was the manner in which the teenager used each medium, since use of television and newspapers for *entertainment* was not as significantly associated with information gain as their use for *public affairs;* in fact, there was some evidence that greater exposure to TV entertainment was negatively associated with gains in information. Thus the way in which media are used can be more important than the type of media used or the extent of usage.

SUMMARY AND CONCLUSIONS

Like almost every other institution in society, abundant evidence suggests that the mass media tend to reinforce and accentuate existing conditions rather than promote egalitarianism or abrupt change, at least with regard to information diffusion. The evidence is persuasive and pervasive that persons already well informed are more motivated to become better informed through the mass media than persons less well informed. The shocking ignorance of American citizens on issues of vital political and personal concern testifies to the limited fruitfulness of the interaction between the mass media and the public in the governmental process. One suspects that persons who claim to be getting most of their information from television may be euphemistically reporting that they are not receiving much information at all about what is happening.

At the same time, there is precious little evidence that education, the variable which mainly determines the patterns and consequences of media usage examined in this chapter, itself has any effect. One study found college seniors no better informed about public affairs than their freshmen counterparts (Turner and McClintock, 1958). High school students[10] who have had a course in civics are no better informed about government affairs than those who have not (Jennings and Langton, 1968).

How then do we learn anything, if media and education institutions have so little effect? Communication researchers strongly suspect that the key element may lie in the pattern of one's interpersonal social contacts (see Chaffee's chapter on this point). Overwhelming evidence is available to suggest that interpersonal means are more persuasive than mass media appeals (Weiss, 1970); greater credibility and understandability are two of several obvious reasons Robinson (1967) cites for this.

Nevertheless the exact processes whereby information flows through social networks is not well understood. The earlier hypothesis of the two-step flow of information from the media to "opinion leaders" to the rest of the public clearly distorts the nature and complexity of the information diffusion process. To be sure, one could almost define media information which fails to excite interpersonal discussion in the public as having the same impact as the philosophical tree falling in the wilderness. But exactly what information excites discussion, what norms and circumstances allow information transmission in ordinary conversation, how information gets distorted in interpersonal transmissions, or how lengthy or persuasive the claims of information are in these processes have only been vaguely touched in information diffusion research thus far.

The diffusion literature is far more valuable in suggesting an approach whereby media can exploit the powers of interpersonal communication. Rogers and Shoemaker (1971) mention several "media forums" that have worked out well in practice. Relevant individuals in a community are brought together as a group to listen to or watch a salient media presentation. Later, an extension worker leads a group discussion in which arguments in the presentation are debated and discussed in detail, hopefully pointing up irrational or invalid counterarguments. Although life in more modern societies is often too formal for such get-togethers to be practicable in the long run, the more likely the media practitioner successfully approximates interpersonal conditions, the more information will likely be conveyed.

Implicit in both this argument and in our discussion of the exceptions to our main rule-of-thumb is the need for more functional definitions of information so that institutions whose role it is to diffuse information through society should explore more utilitarian methods of reaching people with information they need when they need it. A recent synthesis of what is known about man's selective methods of attending to and processing information to which he is exposed (Sears and Foreman, 1968) concluded by reiterating a point made by researchers on the Cincinnati project, namely that people expose themselves to and absorb information which is useful. Whether one calls it useful or functional, a more rational approach to the business of reaching the public with information vital to a democratic society might begin by taking a thorough inventory of what it is that members of society would like to know more about, what they think they know and do not, and what might be a desirable mixture of the two from utopian conceptions of society.

Prior to such an empirical assessment some thought needs to be given to effective typologies for classifying information. We have tried to distinguish academic knowledge from useful knowledge, or school knowledge from life knowledge, in our earlier discussion. However, this is only one fruitful dimension along which information differs. Rogers and Shoemaker (1971) have distinguished awareness knowledge from "how-to" and "principles" knowledge in their characterization of the innovation diffusion process (which can be conveniently applied to the spread of news information). Awareness knowledge resembles Lazarsfeld and Merton's (1948) notion of status conferral, while how-knowledge refers to specific practical steps involved in applying an innovation and principles knowledge to the hypothetical framework or theory of which the information is only an implication.

A functional approach may be more appropriate. Katz (1960) has clearly performed a service for attitude research by distinguishing the various functional bases of attitudes. One immediate explanation for the failure of informational campaigns to change public attitudes inherent in his typology is that knowledge is but one function of attitudes. Tichenor (personal communication) has speculated about clues to further functions of the media in Katz's three nonknowledge functions of attitudes. Parallel to Katz's adjustive function of attitudes would be an adjustive function of media knowledge, in alerting individuals to more efficient ways of meeting their various role requirements and institutional demands of everyday life. A counterpart to Katz's value-expressive attitudes may be found in media knowledge which functions to provide new modes of expressing existing personality values that the individual holds highly. Finally what social commentators usually refer to as the "escape" function of the media can be subsumed under Katz's ego-defensive function; in addition it is also possible to see many audience information-seeking behaviors that serve to reinforce existing attitudes (like reading columnists or publications that one knows he will agree with) as fulfilling an ego-defensive function.

With such an orientation, we could proceed to explore the functions of an informed public in our society. How much of our national wealth is now being wasted because the public lacks information on the behavioral options open to them in order that they may behave more rationally? Can we begin to devise informational messages that will effect the many dysfunctional attitudes that segments of our society now hold, such as felt needs for more material products than are beneficial for our environment? Answers to these and several other questions of national concern should be alleviated in such an endeavor.

NOTES

1. Evidence from research on how time is spent does suggest that the arrival of a television set results in about twice as much time spent in contact with all mass media as was spent previously (Robinson, 1969).

2. As we shall see below, heavy viewers of television *news* programs are about as well informed as light or nonusers. It is the heavy users of television *generally* who are less well informed.

3. In addition to income, race, and occupation (variables included in Figure 1), sex, age, region of country, and size of place, were consistent predictors of knowledge. Men scored half a point higher than women, persons aged 55-64 scored half a point higher than persons in other age groups, residents of the South half a point less than average, and residents of rural areas half a point lower than average—holding constant all the Figure 1 factors. These same factors were very much associated with amount of print news usage, a leading predictor of information level as noted below.

4. These 1958 data are used in Table 1 because they represent the only such data available from a national sample at approximately the same point in time. No media usage questions were asked of the 1964 sample.

5. One important difference in the Detroit study is that specific questions on the frequency of viewing news programs were asked about radio and television, rather than types of programs to which the set is *usually* tuned. The two types of questions produce somewhat different types of results because the better educated spend much less time in contact with the broadcast media,

especially television (Robinson, 1969). For this reason, the Detroit study finds the better educated attending to radio and television news programs about as often as the rest of the population, rather than the higher frequency implied in Table 1. For more detailed breakdown of the audience for network television news programs, see Robinson (1971).

6. The seven news personalities whom the public was asked to identify were: Robert Finch, Bob Dylan, Calvin Hill, Joseph Tydings, Tom Hayden, Ralph Nader, and Martha Mitchell. Recognition levels for some of the individuals were described in the introductory portions to this chapter.

7. In the area of political information, however, television usage was the stronger predictor. We shall review and discuss this datum in the following section.

8. The phenomenon may also account for participation in certain forms of aberrant behavior. On the one hand, the media confer "status" to some individuals who engage in such deviance and in so doing may create some greater acceptance of the behavior than existed before, and on the other, focus attention on the particular individual who has performed it. Other persons in the audience who feel they are not receiving the attention they deserve may thus engage in some form of the behavior to achieve a similar end. The descriptions of motivations of airplane hijackers, for example, seem consistent with such a formulation as does the rash of imitators who follow the methods of novel crime reported in the media. Certain accounts of James Earl Ray's behavior would be consistent with his murder of Martin Luther King for some status-conferral motivations.

9. There is some inconsistency in the Schramm and Wade data. They report a higher correlation between television and public affairs knowledge than between education and public affairs knowledge (p. 117 and p. 119) but also present a table (p. 118) showing only 16 percent differential in high levels of knowledge between regular and nonusers of TV as compared to 23 percent and 49 percent differentials for education.

10. Few teenagers use the media for informational purposes (Robinson, 1971). Perhaps this is because they seldom learn anything in their high school years about *how* to use the media for such purposes. Educational institutions could profitably incorporate liaisons with mass media (the other educational institution in society) into their curricula so that media could more efficiently continue the education process into and through adulthood. Otherwise we might continue with the competitive model implied in Marshall McLuhan's observation that the child goes to school to interpret his education.

REFERENCES

ANDREWS, F., J. MORGAN, and J. SONQUIST (1967) Multiple Classification Analysis. Ann Arbor, Mich.: Survey Research Center.

BAUER, R. I. POOL, and L. DEXTER (1963) American Business and Public Policy. New York: Atherton Press.

CAMPBELL, A. (1966) "Political information through the mass media." Institute for Social Research.

CBS News (1969) "In Black America." New York: Columbia Broadcasting System.

CHAFFEE, S., L. WARD, and L. TIPTON (1970) "Mass communication and political socialization in the 1968 campaign." Journalism Q. 47: 647-659.

DeFLEUR, M. and L. DeFLEUR (1967) "The relative contribution of television as a learning source for children's occupational knowledge." Amer. Soc. Rev. 32: 777-789.

DOUGLAS, D. B. WESTLEY, and S. CHAFFEE (1970) "An information campaign that changed community attitudes." Journalism Q. 47: 479-487.

ERSKINE, H. (1962) "The polls: the informed public." Public Opinion Q. 26.

——— (1963a) "The polls: textbook knowledge." Public Opinion Q. 27.

——— (1963b) "The polls: exposure to international information." Public Opinion Q. 28.

HERZOG, H. (1944) "What do we really know about daytime serial listeners?" pp. 3-31 in P. Lazarsfeld and F. Stanton (eds.) Radio Research 1942-43, New York: Duell, Sloan, & Pearce.

JENNINGS, M. and K. LANGTON (1968) "Political socialization and the high school civics curriculum in the United States." Amer. Pol. Sci. Rev. 62: 163-204.

KATZ, D. (1960) "The functional approach to the study of attitudes." Public Opinion Q. 24: 163-204.

KLAPPER, H. (1969) "Children's perceptions and moral evaluations of television programs." Paper presented at the 1969 meetings of the American Association of Public Opinion Research, Lake George, N.Y. Abstract in Public Opinion Q. 33: 460-461.

KLAPPER, J. (1960) The Effects of Mass Communication. New York: Free Press.

LANE, R. and D. SEARS (1964) Public Opinion. New York: Prentice-Hall.

LAZARSFELD, P. and R. MERTON (1948) "Mass communication, popular taste, and organized social change," in L. Bryson The Communication of Ideas. New York: Institute for Religious and Social Studies.

McCLINTOCK, C. and H. TURNER (1967) "The impact of college upon political knowledge, participation and values." Human Relations 15: 163-176.

McLEOD, J. and J. SWINEHART (1960) Satellites, Science and the Public. Ann Arbor, Mich: Survey Research Center.

McLEOD, J., R. RUSH, and K. FRIEDERICH (1968) "The mass media and political information in Quito, Ecuador." Public Opinion Q. 32: 575-587.

McPHEE, W. (1956) Unpublished memorandum on Mass Dynamics.

ROBINSON, J. (1972) "Toward defining the functions of television," in E. Rubinstein, G. Comstock and J. Murray (eds.) Television and Social Behavior Vol. 4, Television in Day-to-Day Life: Patterns of Use, Washington: Government Printing Office.

——— (1971) "The audience for national TV news programs." Public Opinion Q. 35: 403-405.

——— (1969) "Television and leisure time: yesterday, today, and (maybe) tomorrow." Public Opinion Q. 33: 210-222.

——— (1967) Public Information About World Affairs. Ann Arbor, Mich: Survey Research Center.

ROBINSON, J. and P. HIRSCH (1969) "It's the sound that does it." Psychology Today: 42-95.

ROBINSON, W. (1950) "Ecological correlations and the behavior of individuals." Amer. Soc. Rev. 25.

SCHRAMM, W. and S. WADE (1967) Knowledge and the Public Mind. Palo Alto/Stanford, Calif.: Institute for Communication Research.

SCHRAMM, W., J. LYLE, and E. PARKER (1962) Television in the Lives of Our Children. Stanford: Stanford University Press.

SEARS, D., and J. FREEDMAN (1967) "Selective exposure to information; a critical review". Public Opinion Q. 31: 194-213.

STAR, S. and H. HUGHES (1950) "Report on an educational campaign: the Cincinnati plan for the United Nations." Amer. J. of Sociology 50: 389-400.

STERN, A. (1971) Article in Time Magazine, October 18.

TICHENOR, P., G. DONOHUE, and C. OLIEN (1970) "Mass media flow and differential growth in knowledge." Public Opinion Q. 34: 159-170.

WEISS, W. (1970) "Effects of the mass media of communication," pp. 77-195 in G. Lindzey and E. Aronson (eds.) Handbook of Social Psychology Vol. 5. Boston: Addison-Wesley.

WARD, S. (1972) "Effects of television advertising on children," in E. Rubinstein, G. Comstock, and J. Murray (eds.) Television and Social Behavior Vol. 4, Television in Day-to-Day Life: Patterns of Use. Washington: Government Printing Office.

Chapter 4

THE INTERPERSONAL CONTEXT OF
MASS COMMUNICATION

Steven H. Chaffee

USE OF THE MASS MEDIA is commonly thought of as a discrete individual behavior, one that can be isolated from the rest of a person's daily living. A moment's self-reflection should be sufficient to convince the reader that this conception is too narrow. We frequently refer to our daily newspapers, to the ubiquitous television set, and to magazines, books, and films for information and insights that we can employ *in our interactions with others.* We do not ordinarily think of these as two separate types of communication. Rather, we are continually—often simultaneously—involved in both mass and interpersonal communication, as we build and cross-validate our interpretations of ourselves and the people and events that surround us.

Mass media content determines, perhaps to a much greater extent than we realize, what things we will argue or agree about with others. In turn—and even less obviously—this interpersonal context plays a major role in shaping the content of the mass media.

Technological innovations in mass communication, which are being introduced into modern society at an ever-increasing rate (DeFleur, 1966), provide much more than an economical means of transmitting messages rapidly. Although Lerner (1958) distinguishes between the "oral systems" of traditional society and the "media systems" of modern society, a more adequate conception of modernity is a complex combination of the two. Interpersonal interaction today takes on a new dimension, growing out of the fact that millions of people can receive the same message at about the

[95]

same time. This enables us to engage a topic as a social system, rather than as atomized individuals, and still deal with it at the level where personal values and meanings can best be defined and expressed—the "micro-social" level of personal interaction.

This paper follows the assumption of Katz (1959) that neither mass communication nor interpersonal processes can be adequately understood without reference to one another. It is by no means a thoroughgoing review of existing research and theory. Rather, it is an attempt to analyze some of the more promising research traditions, in terms of their potential for opening up new avenues of inquiry. The emphasis is on varieties of theory and general research strategies, rather than on the specifics of measurement, operational hypotheses, and particular inference. Individual studies are described primarily for illustrative purposes; data are shown sparingly, and only when otherwise unavailable in published form.

HOW PEOPLE USE THE MASS MEDIA

Like most of the communications media themselves, scientific study of human communication is a product of the twentieth century. Perhaps the earliest attempt at mass communication research was one that took into account the audience's interpersonal character. Like most groundbreaking studies, it was done by a genius. His name was Stanley Laurel; he was not a specialist in behavioral research, but in laughter.

Growing up on the stages of the English music halls, Stan Laurel had early learned the critical importance of timing. He had to learn not to "milk" one gag so long that his audience's laughter died out completely, but still not to begin a new joke so soon that it might get lost in the reaction to the previous one. Onstage, this principle of "laughter theory" was easy enough to follow. But when Laurel arrived in Hollywood he was faced with a very different context. His performance took place in the unsettling privacy of a film studio; there was no audience "feedback" to guide his transition from one gag to the next.

Laurel's solution could well stand as an example for all in communication research. He did not rely on his own well-honed intuitions about humor. Nor did he consult experts, such as his partner Oliver Hardy. Nor did he draw a random sample of moviegoers and administer a survey questionnaire to them. Instead he took unedited versions of each new Laurel and Hardy film to theaters around Los Angeles, and put them on screen in "sneak previews." As each audience laughed, Stan Laurel sat with a stopwatch and timed the laughter. After gathering what a social scientist would call "norms" in several theaters, he went back to the studio and edited his film so that the passage from one gag to the next would be as smooth as if he were back on stage (McCabe, 1961).

The main point here is not simply that Laurel worked a bit of empirical research into his film-making, but that he did so in the film's natural *interpersonal* setting. He obviously realized that laughter is more than the sum of many individual reactions to humor. In a theater it sustains itself in ways that purely personal amusement would not.

Communication in Crisis

Quite a different example of the interplay between mass and face-to-face communication is provided by Coleman's (1957) analysis of the ways in which communities deal with divisive controversial issues. Many of his case studies involve support for public schools, a topic that will be encountered frequently in this chapter.

Coleman concluded that the mass media, which are quite useful in crises such as floods or other disasters when people mainly need to know *what to do,* are much less helpful in community disputes when people need to know *what to think.* As a crisis over an issue such as fluoridation or school bonds grows, personal invective and rumor are generated. The media generally decline to transmit such content, but interpersonal channels thrive on it. As the informal flow of slander and falsehood builds, it tends to create a "market" for itself. At the peak of a controversy, the mass media are frequently inadequate to meet the popular demand for "information" relevant to the conflict (for an example of this phenomenon during a university strike over "black studies," see Nwankwo, 1971).

Eventually, controversies subside and the media reassert their informational role. Coleman notes that the national media may moderate local disputes "by viewing them in a new context, dispassionately, making them appear irrational and sometimes even ridiculous." This too can boomerang, however. Unfavorable national coverage can intensify one-sided local feeling, a principle that has not escaped regional anti-civil rights politicians who attack the "eastern liberal press."

The Interacting Audience

The social nature of the "mass" audience has been stressed in important conceptual papers by Freidson (1954) and Riley and Riley (1951). Many empirical examples support this approach. For example, a nationwide survey showed that television is viewed mostly by household groups, who are also frequently interacting in other ways while a program is on (Steiner, 1963). Similarly, three-fourths of a sample of teenagers in a small midwestern town said they "rarely" watched television alone (McLeod et al., 1971).

Entertainment media can also substitute for social interaction. A California study asked youngsters what they do when they "feel lonely." Among sixth graders the most common answer was to watch TV. Most tenth grade boys said they would listen to music. Only among the tenth grade girls was the most usual response to talk with someone else (Lyle and Hoffman, 1971).

Of the various forms of media use, only reading might be thought of as inherently an individual activity. And it could be argued that books, newspapers and magazines—being so much richer in information than audiovisual media—provide much of the content of our daily interactions. How many conversations begin with the stock query, "Have you read . . .?" (And how many have died aborning when the answer was "no"!)

In a very real way, a principal social function of the mass media may be to facilitate interpersonal discussion. A survey of information seeking during an election campaign showed that voters were much more likely to ask for pamphlets describing the views of the candidates if they expected to talk about the election with friends (Chaffee and McLeod, 1967). The authors suggested that "communicatory utility" may be an important motivating factor in media use (see also Tipton, 1970). They noted that purely personal attributes, such as the individual's voting intentions, made little difference in his information seeking. His personal interest in politics played an interesting role, however. If he "rarely or never" discussed the campaign with anyone, then the greater his interest, the more likely he was to ask for information about the candidates. But among those who "sometimes or often" discussed the election, the greatest information seeking was exhibited by voters who considered themselves about as interested as their friends—not those whose interest exceeded that of their friends. This unexpected finding suggests the important principle that conversations are most likely when two people are about on a par insofar as the topic under discussion is concerned. If one is clearly more "expert" than the other, interpersonal discussion is inhibited because of the social disadvantage this situation poses for the less informed person.

Evidence for this hypothesis of social and informational equivalence can be found in studies of communication regarding public schools. Voters in five cities were surveyed just before local school finance elections; about two of every five respondents reported discussing schools in the previous week. Approximately 70 percent of these conversations were between "peers" in terms of parental role and relationship to schools. That is, parents of public school children talked with one another, as did nonparents; the same was true of parents of preschoolers, parents of private school pupils, and of those whose children had completed their schooling. Highly interested and knowledgeable people similarly tended to talk with one another (Carter et al., 1966).

The hypothesis that "like talks to like" has been demonstrated often enough (e.g., Katz and Lazarsfeld, 1955), and could be expected on the basis of opportunity for interaction alone. People who have similar parental roles are doubtless more likely to find themselves in the same place at the same time than are persons in different parental categories. But the principle of equivalence as a precondition for interpersonal communication holds true even within families, where interaction opportunities are maximal. Carter (1960) reports that husband-wife discussion of local schools is considerably more likely when the spouses are of about the same age and educational attainment.

If interpersonal communication tends to require social and informational equivalence, do the mass media provide an alternate channel for communication between dissimilar persons? There is evidence that they do, under some conditions at least. Again looking at communication regarding local schools, Carter and Chaffee (1966) examined a variety of informational channels. Citizens who had been to college—that is, those who were the social equals of school personnel—tended to use interpersonal channels to find out about school activities. These included direct interaction with teachers and principals, and such formalized channels as parent-teacher organizations and the school board. Many other citizens, however, would find themselves at a clear socioinformational disadvantage in conversations with the highly educated school personnel, or the prestigious school board members. These less educated persons clearly preferred the mass media to direct contact, as a way of learning about their local schools. This tendency was so strong that the newspaper and television ranked first and second, respectively, in "usefulness" as a channel for school information in a nationwide sample—well ahead of the interpersonal institutions that have been established for this specific purpose (see also Chaffee, 1967; Chaffee and Ward, 1968).

The impersonality of mass communication, then, may be socially quite functional in some situations. One can seek information via the media without exposing his ignorance on a subject; thus prepared, he can enter more confidently into interpersonal conversation.

There is also evidence that media sources are evaluated in terms of person attributes (Lemert, 1969), and that these factors influence media believability and effectiveness (Carter and Greenberg, 1965; Stone and Eswara, 1969).

CHOICES BETWEEN SOURCES

There has been a great deal written about the relative importance of the mass media versus interpersonal sources of information. In studies of consumer behavior, the prevailing finding seems to be that interpersonal channels predominate in prepurchase information search (Engel et al., 1968). Similarly, Donohew and Singh (1968) report that social innovations in rural southeastern Kentucky are diffused primarily by word of mouth. Comparative studies of diffusion of agricultural innovations provide a more complex picture. Rogers (1969) found that a slight majority of Iowa farmers first learned of a new weed spray via mass media, but *all* of a sample of Colombian peasants learned of it interpersonally. At the later stage of "persuasion" and adoption of the spray, interpersonal sources were much more important for the Iowa sample, too. The potential usefulness of mass media in Colombia is suggested by the fact that the farmers who adopted the spray early were more likely to consult "cosmopolite" (nonlocalite) sources than were those who adopted this innovation later, or never.

For current news events, the mass media—which are specifically designed to transmit news content—generally predominate, at least in the United States. Greenberg (1964a) asked a California urban sample of persons where they had first learned of a number of news items. He found it quite rare for more than about one-tenth to cite an interpersonal source. The lone exception was that half the sample first heard about the assassination of President Kennedy from someone else. Otherwise there was a slight trend for little known ("minor") news to travel interpersonally more often than "major" news. This general trend, coupled with the unusual instance of the assassination, produced a curvilinear pattern. Whether this is a general curvilinear function that would be replicated with other major events, or simply a freak case growing out of the time of day and overwhelming importance of the assassination, is a question that awaits further research. News media are bound by schedules and delays in processing information; in truly catastrophic situations the need to inform people rapidly can outrun the media's capacity to discharge this function as they ordinarily would. Thus, the situation for major social crises is similar to that discussed above for severe community conflicts (see Coleman, 1957).

Pilot Studies on Topic-Source Relations

To clarify the empirical situation, research should, it seems (a) distinguish between source-use and source-preference, (b) put the media-versus-personal source question explicitly, and (c) work toward some typology of content that is related to differences between sources. Here we shall examine two pilot studies whose sample sizes are too small to merit publication in themselves, but which meet these criteria and thus provide a beginning, at least, for planning broader research. The first (called Sample A here) is part of a larger study of attitudes toward birth control and population growth.[1] The other (Sample B) is from a study of information sources on 22 topics, including birth control and population growth.[2]

In Sample A (n = 66), a four-point scale was used to describe how much attention the person gave to media reports on each topic, and how much he had discussed them with his friends and members of his family. In sample B (n = 43), a seven-point response scale was used, ranging from "none of my information comes from mass media (friends)" to "all of my information comes from mass media (friends)."

Despite differences in wording and measurement, the two samples yielded quite similar patterns of results, as shown in Table 1. The stronger tendency to use mass media than interpersonal sources can be dismissed as an artifact of the topics selected for the studies. What is more important in both cases is that use of mass media is greater

TABLE 1
USE OF SOURCE, BY TOPIC AND SOURCE

Sample and Source	Population Growth	Birth Control	Row Mean
Sample A (n=66)			
Media sources	2.06	1.95	*2.01*
Interpersonal sources	1.64	1.79	*1.72*
Sample B (n=43)			
Media sources	5.00	4.53	*4.79*
Interpersonal sources	2.88	3.51	*3.20*
	Eleven News Topics	*Eleven Consumer Topics*	
Sample B (n=43)			
Media sources	5.38	4.41	*4.90*
Interpersonal sources	2.62	3.63	*3.12*

NOTE: All entries are mean scale scores; higher numbers indicate greater reported use of the listed type of source. Sample A scale scores are not directly comparable to those of Sample B, because different questions and response scales were used.

for information on population, but there is a *relative* tendency to rely on personal sources where birth control is concerned.

This pattern suggests that the media predominate in disseminating information about "news" topics such as population problems, but more personal sources are used when a personal "consumer" topic is involved, such as birth control. This proposition would accord with Katz and Lazarsfeld's (1955) finding that women relied on peers as "opinion leaders" for consumer topics such as fashions, marketing, and movies, but looked to more expert (highly educated) others for ideas on public affairs topics. As a rough test of this hypothesis, the 22 topics of Sample B were divided into two categories. "News" topics included campus demonstrations, the Vietnam War, heart transplants, and Vice President Agnew; among the "consumer" topics were food prices, current movies, effects of marijuana, and clothing fashions.[3] The data at the bottom of Table 1 bear out the general principle that media use is stronger for news than for consumer topics; for interpersonal sources, the opposite is true.

An analogous pattern of data can be found in studies of diffusion of innovations (Rogers, 1962, 1969). As noted above, awareness ("news") of a new agricultural technique often reaches farmers via mass media. But when they progress to the stage of evaluation and adoption ("consumer") decisions, there is heavy reliance on inter-personal sources.

Several reasons probably combine to account for this general pattern. The media are comparatively rich in news content, whereas personal associates are likely to have had relevant "consumer" experience. Further, since consumption is partly a matter of defining one's social "self," other persons would be able to offer normative social guides to appropriate consumption patterns that the media cannot. Finally, some matters may not be dealt with by the media in sufficient depth or detail to satisfy personal information needs. For example, the audience for specific technical details on an agricultural innovation may not be large enough to justify intensive coverage by a general-audience medium. Or the media may shy away from providing adequate information about sensitive topics such as birth control methods, out of fear that they might offend some audience members while informing others.

An alternative hypothesis to this purely information-available approach might be that source use is determined by trust in the media, as opposed to personal sources. Despite frequent complaints about a lack of "media credibility," one might well place even less trust in casual word-of-mouth information if a topic is of real personal importance.

Sample B was also asked how much trust they placed in each type of source. The scores, shown in Table 2, are based on seven-point scales for questions phrased, "How much do you trust the reports

TABLE 2
TRUST IN SOURCE, BY TOPIC AND SOURCE

Sample and Source	Population Growth	Birth Control	Row Mean
Sample B (n=43)			
Media sources	4.88	4.51	*4.70*
Interpersonal sources	4.09	4.60	*4.35*
	Eleven News Topics	*Eleven Consumer Topics*	
Sample B (n=43)			
Media sources	4.25	4.01	*4.13*
Interpersonal sources	3.93	4.41	*4.17*

NOTE: All entries are mean scale scores; higher numbers indicate greater perceived trust in the listed type of source.

you get from . . . ?" on each topic. While Table 2 shows a slight pattern mindful of those in Table 1, the tendency is anything but strong. Regardless of the presumed direction of causality (does use engender trust, or does trust encourage use?), the weak differences in Table 2 are clearly inadequate to account for the strong differential patterns of use in Table 1. Indeed, across the 22 topics the mass media evoke no greater trust than personal sources do. It appears that the media are used more because either (a) they provide more information, or (b) they are more easily available. These pilot studies can barely scratch the surface of such a question, of course. The conclusion that trust in a source ("credibility") is not an important determinant of its use is also supported by a study in Ecuador by McLeod et al. (1968-1969).

Technology and Non-Mass Communication

Development of new communication technologies has generally advanced the art of *mass* communication, and the tendency to rely on mass media may simply reflect the very primitive state of social interaction as it presently exists. Aside from a few widely diffused technological aids (e.g., the telephone), most interpersonal communication today is probably carried on much as it was in ancient times, in terms of form if not content. But it is quite conceivable that technological innovations will begin to expand the range and effectiveness of interpersonal communication. For example, in both cable television and the communication satellite field, there is a good deal of discussion of future possibilities for "narrowcasting" and two-way hookups, which would facilitate small-group discussion and information seeking. Research to date has contributed little to an understanding of interpersonal communication that might pave the way for such innovations.

These and other new technologies could also serve as a vehicle for revival of experimental research on small-group networks. This tradition, which began with conceptual papers by Bavelas (1948) and Leavitt (1951), flourished in the 1950s, but has dwindled since. A summary by Collins and Raven (1969) showed 27 studies as of 1966, yielding a rich set of theoretical relationships. In recent years, the network methodology has been used to manipulate social status (Kimberly and Crosbie, 1967) and communicator-control roles (Hickey, 1968). New forms of "mass" communication that involve two-way (or N-way) audio-video hookups could provide a real-life setting in which to test the many inferences that have been drawn regarding network structure.

DEVELOPMENT OF MEDIA USE PATTERNS

The general topic of socialization of children to the mass media is dealt with in another chapter of this volume, by McLeod and O'Keefe. It should be pointed out here, however, that this is largely a matter of interpersonal influence rather than individual development by a socially independent child.

One interesting hypothesis is that children are socialized to adopt particular patterns of media use, because they follow the example set by their parents (Himmelweit et al., 1958; Schramm et al., 1961). This "modeling" process seems to hold to some extent for television (Chaffee, McLeod and Atkin, 1970), but not for reading (Clarke, 1969a, 1969b). This difference underscores the assertion made earlier here, that reading is a more individual form of media use. Close examination of data on TV indicates, however, that parents are at least as likely to follow their children's example as vice versa (Bottorff, 1970; Chaffee et al., 1971). That is, there seems to be a general "social contagion" of viewing patterns, within families at least. It should be noted that this cannot be ascribed simply to the increased "availability" for all family members of a program that one person in the home is watching; the parent-child viewing similarity is as strong in households with two TV sets as it is in one-set homes (Chaffee, McLeod and Atkin, 1970).

A more pervasive—if less obvious—form of parental influence on a child's media use grows out of the habitual structure of parent-child communication over the many years of child development (McLeod and Chaffee, 1971; Chaffee et al., 1971). In homes where the parents enforce a strong orientation toward maintaining social harmony, the youngsters and their parents both tend to spend a great deal of time watching entertainment programs on television. By contrast, where there is a strong "concept-orientation" in family discussions, with each person encouraged to develop and express his own ideas on current topics, all family members display heavy attention to media news reports—via both TV and newspapers. There is evidence that these influences of family communication patterns persist beyond childhood and the home environment, becoming part of the "personality" that the individual carries to new social situations (McLeod et al., 1967).

A person's choice of a newspaper has been shown to be related to his personal social contacts within a community, in studies of both urban (Bogart and Orenstein, 1965) and rural samples (Blexrud, 1971).

HOW THE MEDIA AFFECT PEOPLE

The most researched type of mass communication effect is attitude or opinion change. Pioneer studies early showed that audience interaction is a key factor in persuasion. For example, Knower (1935) found that an argumentative speech had more influence on persons who listened to it alone, than on those who heard it as members of an audience. Hovland et al. (1949) discovered a "sleeper effect," in that conversion to the modal opinion within a social subgroup continued for some months after exposure to a persuasive film. It is widely assumed that mass communication has little direct persuasive power, because interpersonal influence mediates and counteracts inputs from the media (consult Klapper, 1960, for an extended statement of this view).

This "media impotence" hypothesis is, of course, hard to accept at face value. The advertising and public relations industries are apparently built on the assumption that the media have strong persuasive capabilities, and there is a vast research literature to support their faith (as well as an undoubted mass of unpublished studies in secret files of advertising agencies). But as a comparative statement, most writers seem to agree with Rogers (1969) that "mass media are able to create a generally favorable mental set toward change but are seldom able to change specific attitudes toward new ideas, a task better accomplished by interpersonal communication channels." Rogers probably puts the case too strongly when he goes on to describe the "possible effects" of the media as limited to increasing knowledge, while the function of attitude change is reserved for interpersonal channels.

The Two-Step Flow

The proposition that there is a "two-step flow" from mass media to opinion leaders and thence to the general audience (Berelson et al., 1954; Katz and Lazarsfeld, 1955) has come in for considerable criticism and revision in recent years (e.g., Troldahl, 1966-1967;

Arndt, 1968; Bostian, 1970; Lin, 1971; Rosario, 1971), as well as some empirical defense (Allen, 1969). The two-step concept is probably more useful to bear in mind as a factor that should not be overlooked, than to posit as a powerful hypothesis for test. The weight of evidence indicates that direct flow from the media is the rule for most people, more often than not. Even in the famous Decatur study that was designed to demonstrate personal influence, a majority (58 percent) of the reported opinion changes "were apparently made without involving any remembered personal contact, and were, very often, dependent upon the mass media" (Katz and Lazarsfeld, 1955).

The proposition that opinion givers use the media more than do other people has been supported in studies ranging from the early voting surveys (Berelson et al., 1954) to an analysis of cliques in a Colombian pueblo (Rogers, 1969). It should be noted, though, that the term "flow" can be seriously misleading, because it implies a unidirectional communicatory impulse from media to opinion giver to general audience. A good bit of the causal impetus can be characterized as "information seeking" on the part of receivers, which is a thriving research field beyond the scope of this paper.

The companion hypothesis that interpersonal influence is stronger than direct persuasive effects of the mass media is much more robust than the two-step flow model. It is, however, no more than a statement about the present stage of development of media persuasion techniques. And not all research evidence would support it. For example, a sample of adolescents attributed more influence on their opinions about current state and national news topics to the mass media than to parents, teachers, or friends (Chaffee, Ward and Tipton, 1970). And it is by no means necessarily the case that interpersonal influences will counteract media sources; we might expect the two to persuade in the same direction at least half the time (by chance), thus providing an especially powerful total communication influence on the individual (Douglas et al., 1970). In contemplating possible avenues to societal modernization, Rogers (1969) comments that a combination of media and interpersonal channels, "used in complementary roles," could be "an unbeatable force."

Nonpersuasive Effects

Communication influences are not, of course, limited to opinion change or other forms of direct persuasion. Interpersonal relaying of information from the mass media has been demonstrated in a number of instances where no direct persuasive implications are involved (e.g., Deutschmann and Danielson, 1960; Greenberg, 1964b). News of the assassination of President Kennedy first reached a majority of a California sample by word of mouth; their immediate reaction was typically to turn on radio or television for confirmation and details (Greenberg, 1964a).

As has been suggested above, the notion that mass media are somehow pitted against interpersonal sources is a synthetic one, which may make sense to an armchair commentator more than to an information user. We should expect a constant interplay between these kinds of sources, which could have mutually reinforcing functions. To try to allocate variance to one source or the other in such a situation is bootless. As an example, consider some additional data from the pilot study of attitudes toward birth control, referred to above as Sample A.

One of the questions asked in this survey was, "What do you feel is the number of children you would eventually like to have in your own family?" There was a strong tendency toward the norm of wanting *two* children, no more and no less. Of the respondents in the 16-21 age range, nearly half gave this number; of those over 21, more than three-fourths said they wanted to have exactly two children. (Some added that they would like to adopt more.)

This magical number of two children per couple had been suggested by some campus advocates of "zero population growth" in the months preceding the survey (even though statistical projections suggest that it would produce a birthrate that would guarantee continued population explosion). Whatever the merits of the two-child norm, one might be tempted to ask whether it was propagated primarily by the media, or by word of mouth. The answer, as shown in Table 3, seems to be approximately a dead heat. Higher use of *both* interpersonal *and* media sources for information on population growth and birth control is associated with the two-child norm. Those desiring either fewer or more offspring use both types of source less, although probably for somewhat different reasons.

It should be noted that the apocalyptic tone of much of the information (from all sources) available on population would argue against having *any* children, as a general proposition. But the practical effect is instead to shift people toward a realistic "com-

TABLE 3
NUMBER OF CHILDREN WANTED, BY AMOUNT OF SOURCE-USE
ABOUT POPULATION PROBLEMS

	Number of Children Wanted		
	Less Than Two	*Two*	*More Than Two*
Reported mass media use on population growth and birth control	1.62	2.20	2.00
Reported interpersonal communication about population growth and birth control	1.37	1.88	1.55
(n)	(8)	(39)	(18)

NOTE: Data are from Sample A (see note 1). Cell entries are combined mean source-use scores for the two topics.

promise" norm of two, rather than away from a desire to have children as a general pattern of persuasion. The interested person apparently uses any information he can get on the subject, then comes up with a personal solution that is within the bounds of social acceptability. The precise functions of each type of source in this sort of process deserve much closer study.

Possible Dysfunctions of Communication

One normally thinks of communication and information-gain as "a good thing." But from the point of view of social functioning, this is not necessarily the case. For example, one result of having vast quantities of information available via the mass media is apparently to widen the "knowledge gap" between the well educated and the rest of society (Tichenor et al., 1970; Chaffee, Ward and Tipton, 1970). However satisfying this might be for the highly informed individual, it does not seem particularly healthy from the viewpoint of the social system as a whole.

The hypothesis that forms of behavior that are socially undesirable (from some perspectives, at least) can be learned from the mass media—and then later carried out in personal interaction—is a burgeoning research proposition. It has been demonstrated most often in experimental studies of aggression as a consequence of exposure to film or TV violence (e.g., Berkowitz et al., 1963; Bandura et al., 1963; Liebert, 1971), with recent corroboration from field surveys (Lefkowitz et al., 1971; McLeod et al., 1971). There is also evidence of learning of "pro-social" forms of behavior via television (Stein and Friedrich, 1971). However, research to date has not dug deeply into the more general possibility that people might learn prototypic patterns of interpersonal communication from media. The many family situation comedies on television, for example, may be shaping parent-child interaction patterns in the homes in which these programs are regularly seen. (If the reader finds this hypothesis disquieting, he can take comfort in the fact that it has yet to be demonstrated empirically.)

McLuhan (1964) has proposed that it is the structure of perception inherent in a mass medium that accounts for its principal effect. Thus the use of print forces one to learn to think "linearly," whereas television permits a "simultaneity" of cognitive organization. The Whorfian hypothesis of the influence of language structure (Whorf, 1956) is of a similar nature, positing that the "world view" of a society is determined by the lexicon and grammar it uses. In both cases, the authors see these asserted effects as *limiting* the capacity of people to structure reality appropriately. An analogous view of the influence of interpersonal communication is the parent-child interaction research of McLeod and Chaffee (1971). They propose that family communication structures partly determine the way in which a developing child learns to structure new situations, and to relate information to them. In a somewhat similar vein, Bernstein (1964) suggests that social stratification is reinforced by forms of address and interaction learned as "restricted codes" that are appropriate only for the person's particular subculture. To date, these various formulations have not been synthesized in a fashion that would demonstrate a close relationship between structures of mass and interpersonal communication. And unfortunately some of the key propositions (notably McLuhan's) could not be readily subjected to empirical investigation.

In an influential early paper, Lazarsfeld and Merton (1948) discussed several latent functions of mass communication. One is that media reports about a person tend to enhance his social prestige, perhaps beyond the level that would be intrinsically merited. This "status conferral" hypothesis has some empirical support (Lemert, 1966), and deserves further study. Lazarsfeld and Merton also suggest a possible dysfunction, which they call "narcotizing." The gist of this notion is that close attention to media accounts of public affairs substitutes for social action for many people; from the perspective of the social system, this tends to leave a large (and presumably informed) sector of the population "politically apathetic and inert." (Although the authors consider such a situation dysfunctional, from some political viewpoints it would be all to the good; value judgments are inherent in functional analyses of this type.) In the decades since they wrote that the extent to which the narcotizing dysfunction operates "has yet to be determined," there has been little or no research that would alter that conclusion.

A COORIENTATIONAL METHODOLOGY

One probable reason for the lack of systematic research on the effects of mass communication on interpersonal interaction is the absence of a general methodology for analyzing small social systems. A recent development that might prove quite important, then, is the emergence of several varieties of a model of "coorientation." This strategy finds its conceptual origins in Newcomb's (1953) A-to-B-re-X model of communication, and research on "person perception" (Tagiuri et al., 1958). Rather similar models, using different terminology and applying it to different types of communication problems, have been published by Laing et al. (1966), Scheff (1967), and Chaffee and McLeod (1967, 1968).

The general procedure in all these methods is to analyze a *pair* of persons as if they were a dyadic or "microsocial" system, rather than as isolated individuals. For each person, two separate measures are taken on each topic under study: first, the person's own view of the matter is assessed; second, his perception of the other person's view is estimated. Cross-comparisons provide dyadic measures of the similarity or overlap between the two persons, and of the accuracy of each's perception of the other's orientation. A third derivative measure can be calculated within individuals, by comparing each person's orientation with his estimate of the other person's; this has been called congruency.

The measures of similarity, accuracy and congruency are quite versatile, in that the model can be applied to any kind of content on which two persons might coorient. For example, in person-perception research, measures are made of the degree of personal attraction each person has toward the other, and the degree to which he thinks the other is attracted toward him. Similarity of attraction is called mutuality. In opinion research, similarity of opinions is called agreement. In studies of communication about "what the situation is," similarity of definitions of the situation is called understanding. (It might be well to reserve an assumption-laden term such as consensus to apply to a situation that includes a high degree of agreement, accuracy, and understanding.)

Needless to say, such situations are rare. The point here is that communication can help to facilitate them. In particular, communication is a likely road toward accuracy and perhaps understanding. It is probable that conditions of high agreement and mutuality, which involve affective feelings that are normally deep-set, demand more than is usually implied in the simple concept of communication. But some social situations may require these difficult goals. The coorientational model provides a set of terms by which to measure the effectiveness of attempts to achieve them.

For example, a study of husband-wife pairs by Pasdirtz (1969) shows interesting differences between family communication types (see above). Coorientational measures on several current news topics were taken for both husband and wife before and after a 15-minute session in which they discussed these topics. In the "pluralistic" families, where concept-orientations are stressed, there was a marked before-to-after improvement in the accuracy of cross-perceptions of opinions. In the "protective" homes, where the emphasis is on socio-orientations, congruency (perceived similarity of opinions) increased although true agreement did not. The main increase in opinion agreement was found in "consensual" families, where both concept- and socio-orientations are important. These findings accord well with expectations from other results of family communication pattern research. It should be mentioned, though, that coherent outcomes from coorientational studies appear to be limited to experiments or quasi-experiments of this type, where interactive communication on the topic is "forced" on the coorienting persons. Survey studies in unperturbed field situations have tended to disappoint the investigators, probably because the persons under study have not really cooriented on the topic (Chaffee, 1971).

The coorientational measures appear to be fairly reliable, and therefore useful as dependent variables. Even with as few as 11 cases (pairs) per cell, Chaffee and McLeod (1968) were able to find statistically significant results in line with their hypotheses.

Aside from its methodological applications, the coorientational model can help to clear up some conceptual confusions. An example is the use of the vague terms "homophily" and "empathy" in writings on societal development (e.g., Lerner, 1958; Rogers, 1969). Although it is usually operationalized as a sort of fantasized role-taking, the core concept of *empathy* is rather close to coorientational *accuracy*. Wackman (1969) considers the terms interchangeable, and proposes an elaborate technique for measuring accuracy (empathy) that would be independent of agreement. This is fortunate, since homophily is a concept very much like agreement, and Rogers (1969) suggests that homophily is a necessary condition for empathy. To test such a remarkable proposition, it would be essential that the two measures be independent of one another. (In other places, Rogers uses homophily to refer to mutuality, and in others it simply means similarity in terms of some noncommunicable attribute such as socioeconomic status. A careful explication would reveal half a dozen or more distinct coorientational concepts covered by the two terms empathy and homophily.)

A 1971 symposium explored a variety of applications of coorientational concepts. These included studies of both interpersonal communication (Wackman, 1971; O'Keefe, 1971; Pearce and Stamm, 1971) and mass media use (Clarke, 1971a; Tichenor and Wackman, 1971). Each research area yields its special emphases and conceptualizations. Stamm and Pearce (1971), for instance, have extended the concept of congruency to an ingenious process model that successfully predicts communication behavior as a dependent variable. Tichenor and Wackman have examined "community consensus" as an indicator of the role of local media in developing common value orientations within a subsociety. This is an example of an application of the coorientational model, which grows out of interpersonal communication studies, to mass communication research.

INTERPERSONAL INFLUENCES ON THE MASS MEDIA

There is a tendency to conceive of the mass media as relatively fixed and monolithic institutions, generating communicatory inputs to society on a predetermined schedule. But of course the structure and content of the media change constantly. It would be strange if some of this change were not attributable to influences generated at the interpersonal level. But surprisingly little research has been organized in a way that would demonstrate this type of influence.

There have been many attempts to modify the impersonal

procedures of the mass media, to render them more like interpersonal communication. Letters to editors and "Talk of the Town" columns are time-honored examples from the newspaper and magazine industry. Radio programs that feature live telephone conversations with listeners are becoming fairly widespread. Television news shows have begun to include a casual "chat" session among the newscasters. But research to assess these efforts is lacking; the critical test would seem to be whether they do, in fact, create a situation that is more like interpersonal communication. One reason for the absence of such research may well be that we have no clear idea of the kind of atmosphere that is created by either interpersonal or mass communication. Hence it would be difficult to determine whether the one is becoming more like the other.

A more subtle hypothesis about the influence of interpersonal interaction on mass communication might be proposed as an explanation for the tendency of some media to rely heavily on "lowest common denominator" content. When audiences consist of groups of heterogeneous persons, the media must provide material that will have some appeal to everyone in the group. When audience members are isolated, the media are free to present specialized content without fear of losing the interested individual.

This proposition is quite different from the usual elitist complaints about the "mass" audience (e.g., Ortega y Gasset, 1932; MacDonald, 1953). Media audiences are not masses in any serious sense, and do not behave as if they were. But television, for example, is watched by small family groups, as mentioned above. For a program to be acceptable to an entire family (which it must be if all want to watch something at the same time) it cannot be very specialized. The young, the old, and the in-between must all be attracted to it in some degree (see Wand 1968, for evidence on this point). The result is frothy light comedies and action-dramas throughout the early evening hours. What is more, the family audience members are likely to talk, interrupt one another's viewing, and engage in other activities while a program is on. So plots need to be predictable, dialogue redundant, and programs broken up intermittently; this last function is served by commercial breaks on network TV, but even educational channels have found their audiences require some pauses in programs.

All this is conjectural, although it coincides with what little is known about programing decisions. To blame TV's "vast wasteland" on malevolent executives seems misdirected. We can assume that programing directors will happily broadcast any material that will attract enough audience to hold its sponsors. But, faced with a multi-personally used medium, they must seek a common denominator in their audience; whether it is "lowest" is a matter of private taste, but few would argue that optimally attractive fare for anyone is common on TV. Some viewers complain of too few news shows, others of too many. The same is true of situation comedy, or almost any other type of program.

By contrast, print is "consumed" individually, so such media as books and magazines are relatively free to specialize in content. Indeed, the "general interest" magazine typified by *Collier's, Look,* and the *Saturday Evening Post* has all but vanished. A similar change can be seen in motion pictures. Until the 1950s, the movie theater was a gathering place for all sorts of people, and the content was of the "common denominator" variety. Since TV, film audiences have become predominantly young adult in makeup, and the industry has been able to specialize in a decidedly superior type of product for that homogeneous audience—at least compared to the banal "teen" films of the 1940s.

As the absence of research citations suggests, this general area has not been treated as a field of study to date. It may, however, become one in the near future. As Hirsch (1971) points out, technological innovations often bring unanticipated changes in the media. The advent of new communication technologies such as cable and satellite broadcasting, and the increasing number of multi-receiver homes, could render "narrowcasting" feasible for television, and free the industry from the constraints of a heterogeneous family audience. Whether this will constitute an important "natural experiment" for research depends largely on the kind of conceptualization that is brought to bear on the problem. It seems that the influence of the audience on the medium will be at least as important in this case as will the more conventional question of the medium's influence on the audience.

CONCLUDING NOTE

In his introduction to a special issue of *American Behavioral Scientist* on mass media and youth, Clarke (1971b) noted that the contributors shared "a loose intellectual bias . . . that mass communication behavior has social origins and social consequences." This paper has been devoted to a subset that might be called microsocial origins and consequences of mass communication. The field of macrosocial or societal-level communication processes is often referred to in discussing mass media. Indeed, even the term "mass" implies this sort of conceptual orientation. But it may well be that processes that appear on their surface to consist of mass behavior are nothing more than the sum of many interpersonal events, which comprise the real stuff of human communication.

NOTES

1. Data were gathered as a class project in the author's discussion section of Journalism 201 (Introduction to Mass Communication) at the University of Wisconsin, fall 1970-1971. Each student was assigned to interview one person of his (her) own sex in each of five age groups: 16-17, 18-19, 20-21, 22-23 and 24-25. Given these nonrandom procedures, the students tended to interview other students, plus some relatives and neighbors (since the interviews were mostly done during Christmas vacation). The fact that the sample cannot be generalized to any definable population is unfortunate, but not crucial here since each respondent provides data for each cell in the table—thus acting in effect as his own "control" for analysis.

2. This study was an undergraduate independent study project by Timothy Cowling, under the direction of the author. All respondents were University of Wisconsin students, interviewed in living units. As with Sample A, this sample is nonrandom but each person provides an entry in each cell in the tables.

3. The full lists: *Consumer topics* were food prices, lake pollution, interest rates, marijuana effects, birth control, medical costs, draft laws, current movies, popular music, new car models and clothing fashions. *News topics* were campus demonstrations, heart transplants, Vietnam War, federal budget, supersonic transport, local schools, unemployment rate, hard drugs traffic, population growth, Vice-President Agnew, and the Arab-Israeli war.

REFERENCES

ALLEN, I. L. (1969) "Social relations and the two-step flow: a defense of the tradition." Journalism Q. 46 (Autumn): 492-498.

ARNDT, J. (1968) "A test of the two-step flow in diffusion of a new product." Journalism Q. 45 (Autumn): 457-465.

BANDURA, A., D. ROSS, and S. A. ROSS (1963) "Imitation of film-mediated aggressive models." J. of Abnormal and Social Psychology 66: 311-318.

BAVELAS, A. (1948) "A mathematical model for group structures." Applied Anthropology 7: 16-30.

BERELSON, B. R., P. F. LAZARSFELD, and W. N. McPHEE (1954) Voting: A

Study of Opinion Formation in a Presidential Campaign. Chicago: Univ. of Chicago Press.

BERKOWITZ, L., R. CORWIN, and M. HEIRONIMUS (1963) "Film violence and subsequent aggressive tendencies." Public Opinion Q. 27: 217-229.

BERNSTEIN, B. (1964) "Elaborated and restricted codes: their social origins and some consequences." American Anthropologist 66 (2): 55-69.

BLEXRUD, J. (1971) "Rural community identification and the press." Master's thesis, University of Wisconsin.

BOGART, L. and F. E. ORENSTEIN (1965) "Mass media and community identity in an interurban setting." Journalism Q. 42 (Spring): 179-188.

BOSTIAN, L. R. (1970) "The two-step flow theory: cross-cultural implications." Journalism Q. 47 (Spring): 109-117.

BOTTORFF, A. (1970) "Television, respect, and the older adolescent." Master's thesis, University of Wisconsin.

CARTER, R. F. (1960) Voters and Their Schools. Stanford, Calif.: Institute for Communication Research, Stanford University.

――― and S. H. CHAFFEE (1966) Between Citizens and Schools. Stanford, Calif.: Institute for Communication Research, Stanford University.

CARTER, R. F. and B. S. GREENBERG (1965) "Newsapers or television: which do you believe?" Journalism Q. 42 (Winter): 29-34.

――― and A. HAIMSON (1966) Informal Communication About Schools. Stanford, Calif.: Institute for Communication Research, Stanford University.

CHAFFEE, S. H. (1971) "Pseudo-data in communication research." Presented to Assn. for Education in Journalism, Columbia, S.C.

――― (1967) "The public view of the media as carriers of information between school and community." Journalism Q. 45 (Winter): 730-734.

――― and J. M. McLEOD (1968) "Sensitization in panel design: a coorientational experiment." Journalism Q. 45 (Winter): 661-669.

――― (1967) "Communication as coorientation: two studies." Presented to Assn. for Education in Journalism, Boulder, Colo.

――― and C. K. ATKIN (1971) "Parental influences on adolescent media use." American Behavioral Scientist 14 (3): 323-340.

――― (1970) "Parent-child similarities in television use." Presented to Assn. for Education in Journalism, Washington, D.C.

CHAFFEE, S. H. and L. S. WARD (1968) "Channels of communication in school-community relations." Journalism Monographs, No. 8.

――― and L. P. TIPTON (1970) "Mass communication and political socialization." Journalism Q. 47 (Winter): 647-659.

CLARKE, P. (1971a) "Co-orientation and information-seeking." Presented to Assn. for Education in Journalism, Columbia, S.C.

――― (1971b) "Some proposals for continuing research on youth and the mass media." American Behavioral Scientist 14 (3): 313-322.

――― (1969a) "Parental print use, social contact about reading and use of the print media by teenage boys." Presented to Pacific chapter, American Assn. for Public Opinion Research, Napa, Calif.

――― (1969b) "Identification with father and father-son similarities in reading behavior." Presented to Assn. for Education in Journalism, Berkeley, Calif.

――― and L. RUGGELS (1970) "Preferences among news media for coverage of public affairs." Journalism Q. 47 (Autumn): 464-471.

COLEMAN, J. S. (1957) Community Conflict. New York: Free Press.

COLLINS, B. E. and B. H. RAVEN (1969) "Group structure: attraction, coalitions, communication, and power," pp. 102-204 in G. Lindzey and E. Aronson (eds.) Handbook of Social Psychology. Reading, Mass.: Addison-Wesley.

DeFLEUR, M. L. (1966) Theories of Mass Communication. New York: McKay.

DEUTSCHMANN, P. J. and W. A. DANIELSON (1960) "Diffusion of knowledge of the major news story." Journalism Q. 37 (Summer): 345-355.

DONOHEW, L. and B. K. SINGH (1968) Community Action in Appalachia. Lexington, Ky.: School of Communications, University of Kentucky.

DOUGLAS, D. F., B. H. WESTLEY, and S. H. CHAFFEE (1970) "An information campaign that changed community attitudes." Journalism Q. 47 (Autumn): 479-487.

ENGEL, J. F., D. T. KOLLAT, and R. D. BLACKWELL (1968) Consumer Behavior. New York: Holt, Rinehart and Winston.

FREIDSON, E. (1954) "Communications research and the concept of the mass." Amer. Soc. Rev. 18: 313-317.

GREENBERG, B. S. (1964a) "Diffusion of news of the Kennedy assassination." Public Opinion Q. 28 (Summer): 225-232.

――― (1964b) "Person-to-person communication in the diffusion of news events." Journalism Q. 41 (Autumn): 489-494.

HICKEY, J. R. (1968) "The effects of information control on perceptions of centrality." Journalism Q. 45 (Spring): 49-54.

HIMMELWEIT, H. T., A. N. OPPENHEIM, and P. VINCE (1958) Television and the Child. London: Oxford Univ. Press.

HIRSCH, P. M. (1971) "Sociological approaches to the pop music phenomenon." Amer. Behavioral Scientist 14 (3): 371-388.

HOVLAND, C. I., A. A. LUMSDAINE, and F. D. SHEFFIELD (1949) Experiments on Mass Communication. Princeton, N.J.: Princeton Univ. Press.

KATZ, E. (1959) "Communication research and the image of society: convergence of two traditions." Amer. J. Sociology 65: 435-440.

――― and P. F. LAZARSFELD (1955) Personal Influence. New York: Free Press.

KIMBERLY, J. C. and P. V. CROSBIE (1967) "An experimental test of a reward-cost formulation of status inconsistency." J. of Experimental Social Psychology 3 (October): 399-415.

KLAPPER, J. T. (1960) The Effects of Mass Communication. New York: Free Press.

KNOWER, F. H. (1935) "Experimental studies of changes in attitudes: I. a study of the effect of oral argument on changes of attitude." J. of Social Psychology 6: 315-347.

LAING, R., H. PHILLIPSON, and A. R. LEE (1966) Interpersonal Perception: A Theory and a Method of Research. New York: Springer.

LAZARSFELD, P. F. and R. K. MERTON (1948) "Mass communication, popular taste and organized social action," in L. Bryson (ed.) The

Communication of Ideas. New York: Institute for Religious and Social Studies.

LEAVITT, H. J. (1951) "Some effects of certain communication patterns on group performance." J. of Abnormal and Social Psychology 46: 38-50.

LEFKOWITZ, M. M., L. D. ERON and L. C. WALDER (1971) Television Violence and Child Aggression: A Follow-up Study. In G. Comstock and E. Rubinstein (eds.), Television and Social Behavior, Vol. 3. U.S. Government Printing Office.

LEMERT, J. B. (1969) "Components of source 'image': Hong Kong, Brazil, North America." Journalism Q. 46 (Summer): 306-313.

――― (1966) "Two studies of status conferral." Journalism Q. 43 (Spring): 25-33.

LERNER, D. (1958) The Passing of Traditional Society. New York. Free Press.

LIEBERT, R. M. (1971) "Television and social learning." Overview of J. Murray et al. (eds.), Television and Social Behavior, Vol. 2. U.S. Government Printing Office.

LIN, N. (1971) "Information flow, influence flow and the decision-making process." Journalism Q. 48 (Spring): 33-40.

LYLE, J. and H. R. HOFFMAN (1971) "Children's use of television and other media." In E. Rubinstein et al. (eds.) Television and Social Behavior, Vol. 4. U.S. Government Printing Office.

MacDONALD, D. (1953) "A theory of mass culture." Diogenes, No. 3 (Summer): 1-17.

McCABE, J. (1961) Mr. Laurel and Mr. Hardy. New York: Doubleday.

McLEOD, J. M., and S. H. CHAFFEE (1971) "The construction of social reality," in J. Tedeschi (ed.) The Social Influence Processes. Chicago: Aldine-Atherton.

――― and D. B. WACKMAN (1967) "Family communication: an updated report." Presented to Assn. for Education in Journalism, Boulder, Colo.

McLEOD, J. M., C. K. ATKIN, and S. H. CHAFFEE (1971) "Adolescents, parents, and television use." In G. Comstock and E. Rubinstein (eds.), Television and Social Behavior, Vol. 3. U.S. Government Printing Office.

McLEOD, J. M., R. R. RUSH, and K. H. FRIEDERICH (1968-1969) "The mass media and political knowledge in Quito, Ecuador." Public Opinion Q. 32 (Winter): 575-587.

McLUHAN, M. (1964) Understanding Media: The Extensions of Man. New York: McGraw-Hill.

NEWCOMB, T. M. (1953) "An approach to the study of communicative acts." Psych. Rev. 60: 393-404.

NWANKWO, R.L.N. (1971) "Communication in campus crisis: a study of symbolic interaction." Journalism Q. 48 (Autumn): 438-446.

O'KEEFE, G. J. (1971) "Agreement, accuracy and congruency as dependent variables in field interaction studies." Presented to Assn. for Education in Journalism, Columbia, S.C.

ORTEGA y GASSET, J. (1932) The Revolt of the Masses. New York: W. W. Norton.

PASDIRTZ, G. (1969) "An approach to the study of communication processes." Presented to Assn. for Education in Journalism, Berkeley, Calif.

PEARCE, W. B. and K. R. STAMM (1971) "Coorientational states as antecedents to communication behavior." Presented to Assn. for Education in Journalism, Columbia, S.C.

RILEY, M. W. and J. W. RILEY (1951) "A sociological approach to communication research." Public Opinion Q. 15: 445-460.

ROGERS, E. M. (1969) Modernization Among Peasants: The Impact of Communication. New York: Holt, Rinehart & Winston.

――― (1962) Diffusion of Innovations. New York: Free Press.

ROSARIO, F. Z. (1971) "The leader in family planning and the two-step flow model." Journalism Q. 48 (Summer): 288-297.

SCHEFF, T. J. (1967) "Toward a sociological model of consensus." Amer. Soc. Rev. 32: 32-46.

SCHRAMM, W., J. LYLE, and E. B. PARKER (1961) Television in the Lives of Our Children. Stanford, Calif.: Stanford Univ. Press.

STAMM, K. R. and W. B. PEARCE (1971) "Communication behavior and coorientational relations." J. of Communication 21 (September): 208-220.

STEIN, A. H. and L. K. FRIEDRICH (1971) "Television contact and young children's behavior." In J. Murray et al. (eds.), Television and Social Behavior, Vol. 2. U.S. Government Printing Office.

STEINER, G. A. (1963) The People Look at Television. New York: Knopf.

STONE, V. A. and H. S. ESWARA (1969) "The likability and self-interest of the source in attitude change." Journalism Q. 46 (Spring): 61-68.

TAGIURI, R., J. S. BRUNER, and R. R. BLAKE (1958) "On the relation between feelings and perception of feelings among members of small groups," in E. E. Maccoby, T. M. Newcomb, and E. L. Hartley (eds.), Readings in Social Psychology. New York: Henry Holt.

TICHENOR, P. J. and D. B. WACKMAN (1971) "Mass media and community consensus." Presented to Assn. for Education in Journalism, Columbia, S.C.

TICHENOR, P. J., G. A. DONOHUE, and C. N. OLIEN (1970) "Mass media flow and differential growth in knowledge." Public Opinion Q. 34 (Summer): 159-170.

TIPTON, L. P. (1970) "Effects of writing tasks on utility on information and order of seeking." Journalism Q. 47 (Summer): 309-317.

TROLDAHL, V. C. (1966-1967) "A field test of a modified 'two-step flow of communication' model." Public Opinion Q. 30 (Winter): 609-623.

WACKMAN, D. B. (1971) "Interpersonal communication and coorientation." Presented to Assn. for Education in Journalism, Columbia, S.C.

――― (1969) "A proposal for a new measure of coorientational accuracy or empathy." Presented to Assn. for Education in Journalism, Berkeley, Calif.

WAND, B. (1968) "Television viewing and family choice differences." Public Opinion Q. 32 (Spring): 84-94.

WHORF, B. L. (1956) Language, Thought, and Reality. New York: John Wiley.

Chapter 5

THE SOCIALIZATION PERSPECTIVE AND
COMMUNICATION BEHAVIOR

Jack M. McLeod and Garrett J. O'Keefe Jr.

STUDIES OF THE EFFECTS of messages have dominated the past quarter-century of mass communication research. This dominance is reflected in the theoretical research literature of the field as well as in the kinds of public policy questions examined. Characteristics of message content and source are sought that will cause changes in the attitudes or behavior of the audience. Thus, communication is almost always either the causal independent variable or the intervening process through which influence flows. Much less often is some attribute of communication behavior studied as the dependent variable, a factor affected by other variables.

As a result of this research imbalance, it is easy to overestimate the potential of communication messages for producing change in a mass

AUTHORS' NOTE: The research reported here in tables has been supported by a grant to the first author and Steven H. Chaffee by the National Science Foundation (GS-1874) and by contracts with the National Institute of Mental Health (HSM 42-70-30, HSM 42-70-77). Other sources of support for portions of the research include the University of Wisconsin Graduate School and the National Science Foundation through a grant to the University of Wisconsin Madison Academic Computing Center. The studies have been conducted in the Mass Communications Research Center of the School of Journalism and Mass Communication. We are also indebted to Charles K. Atkin who served as Study Director on the Television Use project, to Lee B. Becker for his thoughtful reading of the manuscript, and to William R. Elliott for assisting in the analysis of data.

audience and to underestimate the role of the audience in determining media use and effects. The mainstream of experimental communication research makes this even more likely in that it has been built on an implicit assumption of "perfect transmission" of messages (Chaffee and McLeod, 1970; McLeod and Chaffee, 1972). Attitude change studies, for example, have adopted the strategy of holding "all other factors" constant while measuring the effects of messages. While this strategy makes good sense in experimental design, among these "other factors" communication variables are typically held at a *high level* of constancy by isolating the subjects, by making sure they read the message, and by other means that should maximize attention. These ideal conditions are seldom met in the real communication world where "noisy" conditions and varied motives of reception dull the impact of the message. This is not to say that the poorly designed nonexperimental research cited by writers who are wed to a "no direct effects" of mass media position are any less misleading (cf. Klapper, 1960). A more balanced view should give additional weight to constraints or impediments to communication and to the conditions that produce them.

Mass media audience members have considerably more latitude in communication behavior than is implied in the experimental effects literature (cf. Hovland, 1959). Not only may the person ignore or misinterpret the messages that impinge on him, but he can more actively cope with media by controlling and seeking messages appropriate to his needs. Bauer (1964) warns against adopting a one-way effects model that sees the communicator as *doing something to* a relatively passive audience and urges its replacement with a model that describes what people *do with* mass communication. The more active role of the audience suggests that *communication behavior* rather than the more restricted *media use* should be our focal concept.

COMMUNICATION BEHAVIOR AS A DEPENDENT VARIABLE

The above arguments provide a strong rationale for studying communication behavior as a *dependent* variable. Empirical research results rather than force of argument should be the test of the utility of this strategy, however. The requirements for productive research of this kind unfortunately are rather stringent: (1) identify meaningful patterns of communication behavior; (2) tie these patterns to their functional antecedents; and (3) show that the antecedent-communication behavior sequences have functional consequences in the form of communication effects. While these requirements are seldom met in existing research, they can serve as ideal standards for the design of future studies.

In this chapter, we review various attempts to treat communication behavior as a dependent variable and analyze some types of explanations that have been given as to why people use media in different ways. We offer a detailed look at one such explanation—the socialization perspective that potentially ties together some of the loose ends found in this research area. We then review the meager body of communication research relevant to the socialization paradigm and look ahead to the kind of research data needed to more adequately satisfy the requirements of that perspective. We begin with a review of the conceptual and operational alternatives in the measurement of communication behavior.

How Communication Behavior is Measured

At least four major types of communication behavior categories have been used as research concepts: media exposure, communication processes, motivational gratifications, and media credibility and preferences.

Media Exposure

The most frequently used category among the four is probably media exposure as indexed by time spent with a medium and frequency of use of various media content categories. Although the "time spent" measures are quite easy for sample survey respondents to answer, they have a serious disadvantage in that the responses to such questions are comprised of a number of confounded factors such as interest, availability of the medium, and the amount of recreation time open to the person. Unless careful controls are used (e.g., Samuelson et al., 1963; Robinson, 1971a), time spent with a medium is psychologically uninterpretable and unlikely to produce clear results when related to other variables.

Considerable precision is added by looking at "frequency of use" of specific content categories within a medium. For example, considerably higher correlations with political knowledge are shown for the "reading of hard news" than for "time spent reading newspapers" (McLeod et al., 1968-1969). There is some danger, however, in using content category systems that represent solely the ideas of the "experts" of the field. What may be a media use pattern for the researcher may not represent the actual content groupings as used by the audience. A recent study shows that the usual television program categories (e.g., westerns, situation comedies) have lower intracategory viewing correlations than did a two-dimensional system of auditory and visual variation based upon production measures (Watt and Krull, 1972). It is also true, of course, that knowing how often a person reads or watches a given content item tells us very little about what function that particular behavior has for the person.

Communication Processes

Process classifications of communication behavior seem to describe more closely what people do with communication. Classifications include activities like "opinion giving," "information seeking," "selective exposure," and the like. Most researchers using these process variables have not attempted to specify an exhaustive set of categories, although more elaborate systems are available in the work of Bales (1950) and others. Unfortunately, the more elaborate the process category system, the less likely it is to have been used to identify various factors producing systematic variations in communication pattern. One, or at most two process categories at a time have been studied as dependent variables.

The lack of agreement among researchers about the conceptualization of process categories limits convergence of research findings in this area. Some investigators even treat process as an implied constant and ignore it in their research concepts. For example, Katz and Lazarsfeld (1955) seem to treat opinion leadership as an *intrapersonal* property of the person, although by implication it is better seen as an *interpersonal* relationship indexed by a sequence of two acts—opinion- or information-seeking by one person followed by opinion- or information-giving by the "opinion leader." Other researchers view information seeking and other process concepts as *situational* variables rather than as relatively stable reflections of personality (e.g., Lanzetta and Driscoll, 1968; Chaffee et al., 1969b). In any case, process categories have an advantage over media exposure concepts in that they are applicable to both interpersonal and mass communication.

Motivational Gratifications

Media exposure and communication process variables are both

restricted to relatively observable overt behavior of audience members. The function or "why" of watching "I Love Lucy" or reading the news must be inferred backward from the behavior, e.g. "If he reads the news, he must need information." A more direct approach is to try to measure the person's motives for (or gratifications from) using the media in a particular way. The "classic" study in this tradition is Berelson's (1949) study of what people said they missed during a newspaper strike. He inferred the following list of newspaper functions: information about and interpretation of public affairs; a tool for daily living; respite from personal cares; social prestige; and social contact. While strikes and other abrupt changes bring gratifications into sharper focus, it is also possible to study motives for using various media under more usual circumstances (Waples et al., 1940; Herzog, 1944; Wolfe and Fiske, 1949; McLeod et al., 1965-1966; Mendelsohn, 1968; Lyle and Hoffman, 1971a).

The advantage of the motivational approach is that it is conceptually closer to the "why" of media usage; its obvious weakness is that its measurement depends upon the ability of respondents to have insights into their own motives and upon their willingness to give more than socially acceptable responses. While we should not blindly accept the statements of people giving various reasons at face value, there is probably sufficient validity to warrant using these measures to supplement other measures.

Media Credibility and Preferences

The question of credibility or believability of the various news media has been investigated with almost monotonous regularity for many years. To a great extent this reflects the crossfire between the public relations offices of the television and newspaper industries. While television regularly appears as the most credible medium, Carter and Greenberg (1965) and Clarke and Ruggels (1970) present evidence to show it very much depends upon the way you ask the question, and who is asking it.

Our research interest in credibility, of course, rests on the assumption that it has some impact on the effect of media messages. While source credibility studies following Hovland and Weiss (1951) have generally shown positive if complex effects (direct changes from "expertise"; interactive changes from "trust") on attitude change, it should be kept in mind these studies generally use sources much more divergent in credibility than are found in everyday mass media. Whatever impact credibility may have on attitude change in field situations, it does not appear to alter the transmission of information. For example, McLeod et al. (1968-1969) found that in Ecuador, at least, the relationship between reading of hard news in the newspaper and political knowledge was not at all affected by controlling for newspaper credibility. People apparently learned just as much when they distrusted their papers as when they did not. Credibility was unrelated to use of a medium and only slightly and inconsistently associated with knowledge.

There is some doubt that the medium per se has credibility; perhaps people simply have varying evaluations of content that typically appears in a given medium. This suggests an alternative approach measuring preferred sources for news would be highly correlated with the use of that medium; however, this is not the case for television and radio (Clarke and Ruggels, 1970). Similarly, the correlation between television program preferences and frequency of viewing of these programs is only moderate (Chaffee, 1971b; Chaffee and McLeod, 1971a). It appears that the areas of media attitudes and overt behavior represent rather different domains and should be studied as such.

Alternative Explanations of Communication Behavior

The great variety of potential explanations of communication behavior vary according to the location of the causal force as being *in* the social organization, in the relationships *between* people, or *within* the person. Demographic variables like sex, age and social status indicators are most commonly used in social organizational explanations. In most cases they fail to indicate functional explanations of communication behavior and merely locate behavior patterns within the social structure. DeFleur (1970) has suggested assumptions underlying demographic differences in media behavior, calling the result *social categories* theory. People occupying a given position in the social structure are said to face a similar set of social stimuli and produce rather uniform behavior as a result. While the homogeneity of behavior within a social grouping is a straightforward prediction, there is no reason to expect any *particular form* of communication behavior from such an assumption.

The informal social relations between people serve as a second focus for the explanation of communication behavior. The concern with communication process helps to overcome some of the weaknesses of demographic analyses; however, the fact that social relations are often *defined* as communication processes presents the danger of tautologically mistaking description for actual explanation. The well-known approach of Katz and Lazarfeld (1957), unfortunately for our purposes, implies that the "two step" flow is equivalent throughout the community. Since opinion leaders are distributed throughout the social structure, their behavior and methods of influencing others might be expected to be the same. This is simply not very useful for understanding the diverse patterns of communication behavior. The sampling of interpersonal networks used by Katz and Lazarsfeld has gained increasing support in recent years (see Coleman, 1958; Blau, 1962; Arndt, 1968; Rogers and Bhowmik, 1970-71). If we define communication as a process of exchange *between* persons, it seems logical to extend the sample strategy to the interpersonal conceptual definition and measurement of variables (see Newcomb, 1953; Westley and MacLean, 1957; Laing et al., 1966; Scheff, 1967; and Chaffee et al., 1969a).

Intrapersonal personality variables have not been very successful predictors of communication behaviors (Weiss, 1971), perhaps because of their definition as stable trans-situational properties of the individual. While they are most likely to be useful in predicting interactive effects with other variables (McGuire, 1968), they might be better reconceptualized as interpersonal concepts (e.g., communication style in a given situation). Personal values have been used with some success particularly in studies of mass media communicators (Breed, 1955; Stark, 1962; Donohew, 1967; Coldwell, 1970; Flegel and Chaffee, 1971; Graf, 1971; McLeod, 1971a; Martin et al., 1972). Attitudes and values may also affect audience members in their selection of newspapers (McLeod et al., 1965) and attention to content (Atkin, 1970), although the principle of selective exposure is by no means universally accepted (Sears and Freedman, 1967; Katz, 1968).

THE SOCIALIZATION PERSPECTIVE

Socialization explanations of communication behavior are quite different from those already discussed in being more elaborate and in demanding more of the data required to validate them. These requirements are clarified in a key assumption of the socialization perspective: *to understand human behavior, we must specify its social origins and the processes by which it is learned and maintained.* This implies we must specify the learning conditions as well as the location of the behavior in the social structure. We will discuss later the implications of these requirements for data.

The socialization perspective has been adapted for communication research from the larger field of social psychology. Its historic roots go back to Freud and psychoanalytic theory and later to the child development interests beginning in the 1920s. For anthropologists, it became the central concept linking culture and personality (Benedict, 1934; Linton, 1945), and has been regarded as one of the key functional prerequisities of a society (Aberle et al., 1950). G. H. Mead (1934), by emphasizing the development of the self through social interaction, tied socialization to the emerging discipline of social psychology. More recently it has played a crucial role in the meta-theory of Parsons (1955) as the mechanism connecting social systems and personality systems.

The adaptation of the socialization perspective to communication research in the past decade is logical in that communication would seem to be the major vehicle through which learning takes place and shared cognitive systems are made possible. We have purposely used the term *perspective* rather than *theory* because there is no agreed-upon set of socialization concepts, assumptions and hypotheses to guide us; rather, there is only a rough blueprint for what data should be included and what a socialization theory of communication behavior might look like.

Most alternative explanations of communication behavior involve two, or at most three, variables. The socialization perspective is more demanding in including five types of variables: (1) age or life cycle position of the influencee; (2) social structural constraints operating to affect learning; (3) agent or source of the influence; (4) learning processes involved in socialization; and (5) content or criterion behavior being explained as the dependent variable. While any given research is unlikely to handle all five types as measured or manipulated variables, a complete socialization theory must deal with all of them. We will discuss the importance of each of the five types of variables to the socialization perspective before turning to the rather fragmented research literature relevant to this approach.

Age or Life Cycle Position

The emphasis on describing the original conditions of individual learning in socialization explanations of behavior requires that careful attention be paid to the age at which behavior patterns change. The specification of the age of learning can be accomplished in three ways: through recollection backward in time, for example in asking adults to remember certain experiences or influences from their childhood; by sampling various age categories to ascertain the contemporary situation in phases of childhood, adolescence and adulthood; and with panel designs following the same respondents across various stages of their life. Among these, recollective studies are the least satisfactory because of memory limitations that become more severe with the passage of time. Sampling age levels is better, although maturational and generational differences may be confounded because different subjects are used in the various age groups. Panel designs overcome this problem, but are seldom used because of the considerable cost and time requirements involved in carrying them out. We will return to the topic of ideal research designs for the socialization perspective later in the paper.

As a result of its origin in psychoanalytic theory, the study of socialization was once synonymous with the study of early childhood. In recent years, however, socialization research has been extended to learning throughout the person's lifetime (Brim and Wheeler, 1966). While there is undoubtedly a reasonable degree of consistency across age categories for some behavior patterns, it is clear that new behavior patterns emerge at all stages of development.

The growing emphasis on adult socialization has brought with it a change from consideration of age per se as the critical variable to a more differentiated focus on *life cycle* position. In the post-adolescent period, persons enter the occupational world, get married and so forth, at rather different ages. It is, therefore, the life style associated with a particular part of the cycle rather than age that becomes the critical concern of the adult period. The points at which persons move from one part of the life cycle to another are likely to be periods of considerable reorganization of communication and other behavior. This increased potential for change at critical junctures in the life cycle is a point not lost on insurance salesman and others who profit by following wedding and birth announcements and other signals of changing informational and consumer needs.

Social Structural Constraints

Social structural explanations involve *direct* influence on communication behavior. The socialization perspective retains an emphasis on the social structural variables, but makes the influences *indirect* through their effect on the practices of various socialization agents, the practices in turn altering communication behavior. Socialization explanations thereby do much more than social structural ones to specify the process by which social structural influence is carried out, although the question of the relative importance of direct vs. indirect effects is answerable only through empirical research.

The most frequently used social structural variable is social class, measured either by subjective self-report or through objective indices like education, occupation, and income. Despite its frequent use, the relationship of social class to socialization practices remains equivocal and often contradictory (cf. Zigler and Child, 1969). Of course, this may be as much a problem of using faulty measurement of socialization practices or learning mechanisms as it is the weaknesses of social class as a variable. Social class is likely to remain an important control variable, but it should not deter the researcher from searching for within social class variations in socialization practices. Religious affiliation, race, ethnic background, and organizational membership are a few of the other possibilities for investigation.

These social groupings are more likely to be useful if they are treated as indicants of underlying variables rather than as simple categorical distinctions. For example, Elliott (1972) treated religious affiliation by arraying the various denominations along two separate dimensions (degree of hierarchical constraint in church structure and strength of conviction in dogma) rather than using the more customary nominal categories (Catholic vs. Protestant). Although the nominal categories showed little relation to child-rearing practices, the dimensional analyses provided rather clear and theoretically interesting results. Similarly, Miller and Swanson (1958) found within social class differences in socialization practices that were ordered by whether the head of the family worked in entrepreneurial or bureaucratic occupational settings. That which was held desirable in the work setting was presumably mirrored in the values emphasized in the raising of children.

It should also be mentioned that the effects of social structural constraints may be dependent upon such characteristics as the sex of the person being socialized. It is possible that the working class, for example, emphasizes the differences in the sex role more than does the middle class (Bronfenbrenner, 1961). For that reason, it is important that socialization studies conduct separate analyses by sex wherever possible.

AGENT OR SOURCE OF INFLUENCE

Socialization explanations of communication behavior see influence as coming from the behavior of a specific agent or source. The early socialization approaches to areas other than communication were rather closely confined to parents because of their focus on early childhood. More recently, increasing attention has been paid to siblings and to peers whose influence becomes greater during the adolescent years. Teachers are also potentially studied as socialization agents for adolescents. Spouses, children, work associates and friends may be influential in studies of adult socialization.

The key implication of including specific influence agents in the socialization model is that the unit of analysis becomes the source-receiver combination rather than the individual person being influenced. In terms of theory, this suggests selecting interpersonal rather than intrapersonal variables for describing the socialization process. For research design, this means that a multi-person sampling unit is more appropriate than the usual procedure of sampling individuals. We would sample agencies like families, peer groups, classrooms, and work sites and gather data from the agent and others in the group as well as from the person being socialized.

It is not assumed that the socializing agent has a particular goal in mind nor even that he is aware that he is exerting influence. If the agent serves as a role model or positive reference person, his behavior may be modeled regardless of his intent. Indeed, the socialization process may be viewed as a reciprocal process between persons, particularly among adults.

Learning Processes

We have chosen to avoid using the term "child-rearing practice" or the more general "socialization practice" in the socialization perspective model because these terms seem to imply too much of a conscious attempt to influence by the socialization agent. Our term "learning process" is more general in that less conscious teaching can be included under it. It also places what seems to us to be the more appropriate focus on learning rather than on teaching. The specification of the learning process is a key element in socialization explanations in that without it no functional relationship can be established between social structural variables and the person's behavior.

Learning processes used in socialization explanations can be grouped into three general types: *modeling, reinforcement,* and *social interaction.* Modeling processes involve imitation as the key mechanism, either through the conscious attempts to emulate the socialization agent or simply because the agent's behavior is the most salient alternative open to the person. The early studies of children's use of television, for instance, used the correlation between the parent and the child as the basis for concluding that "parental example" has a direct influence on the child (Himmelweit et al., 1958; Schramm et al., 1961). In an effort to be like his parent, the child presumably watches programs that his parent watches and avoids those he does not watch. While the simplicity of this explanation makes it attractive, it is logically inadvisable to consider parent-child behavior correlations sufficient to establish causality of the modeling process. We will discuss this point along with relevant data later in the chapter.

Reinforcement explanations of learning processes focus either on reward mechanisms (positive reinforcement) or on punishment (negative reinforcement). The person learns to duplicate his past behaviors that have been rewarded by the socializing agent and/or to avoid repeating those for which he has been punished. This statement of the learning paradigms is quite broad and obscures many nuances among the many varieties of reinforcement theories (cf. Berger and Lambert, 1968). In nonexperimental field research on parent-child relations, the frequency of parental affection is the most common operational definition of positive reinforcement while negative reinforcement is most often indexed by the frequency of physical punishment. Various types of psychological punishment (e.g., denial of privileges, restriction to own room) have also been studied.

The application of reinforcement learning variables to communication research can take a number of forms. The most direct approach is to study hypotheses that predict greater agreement between the agent's intent (i.e., what he is trying to teach) and the communication behavior of the person under conditions where the agent uses positive rewards frequently. Greater avoidance should be found for communication behaviors that have been punished in the past. A second type of analysis looks for interactive effects of positive reinforcement in producing greater similarity (modeling) between the agent and the person. The prediction for punishment is less clear. A third type of prediction is that the control styles of parents and other agents serve as frames of reference for the person being socialized, such that high levels of affection will develop in him a warm supportive world view and, conversely, excessive physical punishment will lead him to see his environment as hostile and violent. In each case, he would be predicted to seek out media content that agrees with his world view.

The social interaction view of the learning process is less specific as to the exact mechanism involved—combinations of modeling and reinforcement may be involved. This explanation holds that the characteristic social norms involved in the person's interactions with relevant others shape his behavior, including his communication style and preferences. What is learned is a series of complex interpersonal relationships (Brim and Wheeler, 1966). A specific example of trying to treat social interaction processes as variables has come from studies of family communication patterns by various researchers at the University of Wisconsin's Mass Communication Research Center (Chaffee and McLeod, 1971b; Chaffee et al., 1966, 1971, 1972; McLeod et al., 1966, 1967, 1968-1969, 1969; McLeod and Chaffee, 1972; Stone and Chaffee, 1970). These studies, conducted in many different populations and cultures have shown consistently that there are two general dimensions of communication structure in the family. The first, *socio-orientation,* is an environment in which the child is taught to be deferent to elders, to maintain harmonious personal relationships and to withhold his feelings. The second dimension, *concept-orientation,* is virtually uncorrelated with the first. It involves encouraging the child to express his ideas and exposing him to controversy. The child learns to cope with the world in terms of these family structural constraints and serves as a cognitive map to guide him in situations outside the home. The specific communication behavior relevant to these two dimensions will be discussed in a later section of this chapter.

Content or Criterion Behavior

The socialization perspective requires a choice between two major forms of dependent variables that are unfortunately confused in much of the research literature. The first is the *similarity* of the person's behavior to that of the socializing agent. The second type of criterion is the *absolute level* of the person's behavior. These two forms of criteria are obviously quite different and it is possible they are not influenced by the same set of socialization factors.

The absolute criteria further subdivide into those defined by their theoretical relevance to the functioning of a given social system and those focused around the constellation of individual behaviors regardless of their function for any larger system. This distinction may be clarified by citing a typical example of the former approach implied in the following definition of political socialization: "the learning process by which political norms and behaviors acceptable to an ongoing political system are transmitted from generation to general" (Sigel, 1965). The difficulty in this definition is that it is hard to determine which norms and behaviors are functional for the system and which are not. A similar problem exists in communication research. In the national development literature, for example, the communication behavior functional to modernization is assumed to be greater use of mass media relative to use of interpersonal channels (cf. Lerner, 1958). This "more the better" media assumption is questionable as is the "less the better" assumption about interpersonal communication.

While we cannot entirely avoid gratuitous assumptions about communication behavior (e.g., the world would be better off if people paid more attention to public affairs media content), it seems advisable to use relatively homogeneous patterns of individual communication behavior as the criterion variable. That is, we would like to group those behavior which perform some function for the person (Robinson, 1971a). We should be particularly on guard against a natural tendency of journalistic researchers to overemphasize the informational functions of the media; the evidence points to various types of entertainment functions as being predominant in media use patterns of most persons (Steiner, 1963; Stephenson, 1967).

Summary of Socialization Perspective

We have attempted to clarify the socialization perspective that takes as its main assumption the necessity to specify both the social origins and the learning conditions of communication behavior. The emphasis is on changes in the person's behavior as he moves through the life cycle. Since a different set of variables may be dominant at each stage of the person's development, all generalizations are conditional to a particular phase of the life cycle. A given factor may vary in influence depending on the age of the person. Socialization takes places through the interaction of the person and various agents in specific social settings; therefore, the person-agent is the unit of sampling and analysis. Within each life cycle stage and person-agent unit, three types of variables are selected for analysis: social structural constraints, learning processes, and functional patterns of communication behavior.

RELEVANT RESEARCH LITERATURE

In the previous section we have developed a model that implies the ideal pattern of research design and data to satisfy the socialization perspective. Unfortunately, the reality is that available research findings are far from this ideal. We have adopted a minimal definition for relevant literature as being any study that describes communication behavior specific to the person's age or life cycle stage. The bulk of the literature, therefore, is simply a description of single communication variables. Maturation rather than socialization is thereby the dominant focus. Other studies relate demographic characteristics to communication variables, but analyses of third variable interactions (e.g., social class by frequency of parent-child communication by child's use of public affairs media) are rare indeed.

The available research is also limited by dealing almost exclusively with media exposure, and with the less interpretable "time spent" measures at that. Attention is usually confined to a single medium rather than to a group of media to identify functional patterns of communication behavior.

Our literature review is divided into three sections: children (up to age 12); adolescents (roughly ages 12 to 18), and adults. Within each section, we consider first the single variable studies describing normative or average communication behavior during that stage of the life cycle, and, following that, we examine studies relating other variables to various communications behaviors.

Childhood

The most striking feature of children's use of media in the era of television is that it begins at such an early age. Long before the child is able to read, he is already watching television at regular times and has chosen favorite programs (e.g., "Flintstones," "Sesame Street"). Differences between boys and girls in program preferences are already evident (Lyle and Hoffman, 1971b). By the time the child gets to first grade, he is apt to expand his viewing to include many programs ordinarily categorized as "adult" or "violent" (Lyle and Hoffman, 1971a; Murray, 1971).

While the preschool child is exposed to television over 30 hours per week, or one-third of his waking hours (Stein and Friedrich, 1971), the school child's viewing actually is likely to increase even more. Situation comedies are added to cartoons as the favorite program in the early grades; cartoons gradually decline while crime and adventure shows are becoming more popular (Lyle and Hoffman, 1971a). While his television tastes are becoming more diversified, his attention to radio, records and the entertainment portions of the print media grows steadily.

The early school years also find the child changing in the way he reacts to media. In the first grade the child understands little of the motivation and consequences of television program content; by the start of adolescence he is apt to understand more than half (Leifer and Roberts, 1971). By second grade the child is aware that commercials are trying to sell him something and by the fourth grade he is likely to have developed critical and skeptical attitudes towards advertising (Ward, 1971; Ward et al., 1971). The increasing diversification in media use does not mean that there is any great increase in interest in public affairs content. Throughout childhood there is little attention to educational programing (except for an interest in "Sesame Street" among the younger children). Research on political socialization shows that, although the child is becoming more knowledgeable about politics, his view of government is personalized and concrete and not concerned with abstract processes (Adelson and O'Neil, 1966; Easton and Dennis, 1965). The Government *is* The President and God and Country are often synonymous. More abstract concern with principles and procedures has rarely begun by the fifth grade.

It is apparent from the available research that at no age is television viewing the passive activity that it is often assumed to be. Instead, the child's viewing is best thought of as a series of short periods of attention interrupted by other activities such as eating, looking at other objects in the room, and talking and playing with siblings and friends. For the most part, childhood viewing is opportunistic and unplanned. The Lyle and Hoffman data indicate a considerable amount of channel switching. It is likely that this relatively unselective pattern of choice and attention extends to use of other media as well.

Structural Constraints

It is clear even from the sparse amount of research on children's communication behavior that social class differences are already evident in the earliest years of media use. Stein and Friedrich found that nursery school children from lower-socioeconomic-status homes were more interested in the violent non-cartoon shows than were the higher-status children. By the middle of grade school, the working-class children are spending more time with television (Greenberg and Dominick, 1969a; McIntyre and Teevan, 1971). There is some evidence, however, that the social class differences in time spent with television may be lessening. Although comparisons are somewhat tenuous because of different samples, Lyle and Hoffman (1971a) found weaker social class differences than were found using similar measures a decade earlier (Schramm et al., 1961). It appears that much of the lessening of differences stems from the increased use of television among the younger middle-class boys in the recent study.

Other class differences are noted in the way children use television. Working-class children are more likely than others to say that they use television to learn and to see program content as true to life (Greenberg and Dominick, 1969a). The same research found middle-class children were the more likely to say they watch television to be excited and Lyle and Hoffman report that these children are more critical and skeptical about the medium. With respect to violent content specifically, lower-income youngsters consider media violence more acceptable, liked it more, and saw it as more realistic (Greenberg and Gordon, 1971a).

Greenberg and his associates also have studied racial differences in communication behavior, controlling for socioeconomic status. Greenberg and Dominick found that Black children spent more time watching television, were more likely to evaluate program content as being realistic, and more often said they watch television to learn than did other children. The Black fifth-grade boys studied by Greenberg and Gordon perceived less violence than did white boys shown the same set of videotapes. They also found the violence more acceptable, although we should be cautious in accepting the racial differences in that the controls were based on simple dichotomous control for socioeconomic status. An alternative hypothesis is that the racial differences are spurious in that large status differences between races remain *within* status levels even after SES is dichotomized and used in an analysis of variance. This suggests using instead the analysis of covariance treating status as a continuous variable. The findings of Greenberg and associates are nevertheless challenging and represent a healthy step in bringing communication research closer to economic reality.

Learning Processes

Research on the modeling of communication behavior by young children unfortunately is lacking. Lyle (1971) does speculate that modeling should be greater for children than for adolescents presumably because of the dependence and closer affectional ties at the younger ages. On the other hand, the actual overlap of viewing behavior by children and adults is low and the chances for modeling are less. Without data we cannot know, but it does seem that siblings and peers may be more important socializing agents for children's communication behavior.

Whatever the effect of parental attempts to influence children's communication behavior, a considerable amount of research evidence points out that relatively few parents make such influence attempts very often. Lyle and Hoffman (1971a), for example, found that a majority of mothers did nothing to set hours or to restrict total viewing time although most did prohibit the viewing of certain types of programs. Positive encouragement to watch specific types of programs appears to be even less frequent. Such control over children's viewing as does exist is largely confined to middle-class parents (Greenberg and Dominick, 1969a). Evidence is lacking regarding the effect of the more general parental behaviors, affection and punishment, on young children's communication behavior.

There is some indirect evidence that the child's social interaction with others affects his use of media. Lyle and Hoffman found that among their sample of first graders those who infrequently played with other children often turned on television to find companionship. Of course, this raises the question of direction of causation.

Does the isolation cause the excessive television viewing or does the reverse causal sequence account for the correlation? Murray (1971) cites longitudinal data from a sample of 27 five- and six-year-old Black males in support of the inference that the lack of satisfactory interpersonal relationships lead the child to become "addicted" to television (up to 42 hours per week) as a means of maintaining a "solitary environment." Additional research is needed on this point.

Adolescence

Adolescence, the period of youth covering the ages between 12 and 18, is a fruitful area for illustrating the socialization perspective. Not only is there more communication research specific to ages in that range than for children or adults, but there are also a host of theoretical questions that are particularly relevant to the adolescent period. In the short space of a half-dozen years, the relatively dependent child is transformed into the relatively autonomous young adult. The result is seldom the informed citizen who uses the mass media to make rational decisions, but a fledgling adult he is, nevertheless.

Adolescence is a period of rapid change in communication behavior. The time spent with television is at its peak at the start of adolescence; it declines by ten percent or more by the end of that phase of the life cycle (Lyle and Hoffman, 1971a). Most of the drop in television time comes in afternoon and prime time evening viewing. The later bedtime of the older youths does allow them to watch more late evening TV. Lyle and Hoffman also report a decline from the sixth to tenth grades in the use of books and comic books while radio listening and record playing show sharp gains. The reading of a daily newspaper is also more common among the older adolescents while no consistent trend is shown for movie attendance.

The changing patterns of attention to various television program categories during adolescence were examined in two studies conducted at the Mass Communications Research Center of the University of Wisconsin. The first, which we call here the "Political Socialization" study, was carried out in five Wisconsin cities in 1968. The data consist of an interview with a randomly selected parent in each of 1,292 families along with two questionnaires completed six months apart by one of the children in the family. Roughly half the children were in the seventh grade on the first administration of the questionnaire and the other half were tenth graders. Further details of the study design are available elsewhere (Chaffee et al., 1970). Here we will be concerned only with the measures of communication behavior of the child and his parent and certain variables of parent-child relations potentially related to the socialization of the adolescent.

The second study, called here the "Television Use" study, presents data from two reports included in the Television and Social Behavior program series (McLeod et al., 1971a, 1971b). Respondents in two samples from different parts of the country filled out questionnaires: 230 seventh graders and 243 tenth graders in eight public schools in Prince Georges County, Maryland; and 68 and 83 adolescents respectively from those two grades in Middleton, Wisconsin. In the latter sample, we also conducted personal interviews with the mothers of the adolescents. The two samples are combined for this paper.

The changes from junior to senior high in the use of television are shown in Table 1. Both studies show substantial decreases in viewing time from junior to senior high parallel to those shown by Lyle and Hoffman. The drop is somewhat larger for girls than for boys. Table 1 also shows changes for specific types of programs. (Data are not shown for two categories for the Political Socialization study because they were not included in the questionnaire.) While a loss in viewing from junior to senior high is shown for almost all comparisons, the greatest decline is shown for situation comedies and variety comedy shows. The only category to show even a trace of an increase is news and public affairs, and then only for girls. The contrast to other types of programs is marked, however. Other comparisons not presented here show a clear if unspectacular increase in use of print news media among the senior high students.

Of some methodological interest is the similarity of standard score patterns between the two studies across the various program types. This is the more surprising when we consider that very different questions were used on each study to index the viewing of specific program types. In the Political Socialization study, the adolescents were given the program type (e.g., westerns) and asked to indicate on a five-point scale how frequently they watched this kind of program. In the Television Use study, the respondents were presented with a list of 65 prime time evening shows and asked how often they watched each on a four-point scale. Despite the different measures, there is remarkable comparability between the two sets of data. Perhaps the exact wording of media use questions is less of a problem than we ordinarily assume it is.

While the amount and kind of media used changes markedly during adolescence, apparently the reasons for using the various

TABLE 1
ADOLESCENT'S USE OF TELEVISION (standard scores)
BY SEX AND GRADE

Television Use Index		Political Socialization Study			Television Use Study		
		Junior High	Senior High	Diff.	Junior High	Senior High	Diff.
Adolescent's TV Time	Boys	+40	−27	−67	+13	−05	−18
	Girls	+36	−46	−82	+19	−27	−46
Adventure- Drama	Boys	+29	−01	−30	+26	−09	−35
	Girls	+08	−28	−36	+07	−24	−31
Westerns	Boys	+21	−01	−22	+30	−14	−44
	Girls	+05	−24	−29	+08	−24	−32
Crime- Detective	Boys	−	−	−	+36	+07	−29
	Girls	−	−	−	−01	−40	−39
Situation Comedies	Boys	+18	−19	−37	+15	−62	−77
	Girls	+28	−24	−52	+64	−16	−80
Variety- Comedy	Boys	−	−	−	+21	−11	−32
	Girls	−	−	−	+22	−29	−51
News-Public Affairs	Boys	+14	+09	−05	+28	+14	−14
	Girls	−17	−05	+12	−30	−11	+19
(Number of cases)	Boys	(343)	(287)		(160)	(138)	
	Girls	(298)	(364)		(150)	(176)	

NOTE: Standard score entries are weighted cell means, setting the overall mean at zero and the standard deviation at unity, for all four cells in each sample. Scores are calculated to two decimal places; decimals are omitted for simplicity. Statistical significance (.05 level) for differences between grades is: Political Socialization study, ± 16 or greater; Television Use study, ± 23 or greater.

media remain relatively constant. The Lyle and Hoffman (1971a) data show that both sixth and tenth graders turn to television for entertainment, relaxation and relief from loneliness; much less often is television sought when the person is angry or when his feelings are hurt. Listening to music is more evenly divided according to reasons for use and turning to it under conditions of anger or hurt feelings is considerably more common than for television. Clearly, television serves no special function to vent anger and frustration as is sometimes thought. As was true with younger children, the adolescent's involvement in the television he watches is fragmented and partial. Foulkes et al. (1971) found that eye contact with the television set drops when books, games and other objects of interest are around to distract the viewer.

There are a few other changes in television use worth mentioning. The use of programs logs becomes somewhat more frequent in the tenth grade in contrast to the dial twisting that reaches its peak with the sixth graders. The same Lyle and Hoffman data show a decline in perceiving television as real among the older adolescents. Compared to the sixth graders, the tenth graders were also more likely to agree that television should be for fun, not for education and to have less objection to the amount of sex and violence presented on television.

It is likely that adolescent communication behavior cannot be properly understood without reference to changes in other areas of behavior that take place during these years. It is useful to think of two independent and contrasting trends of adolescence: a strong tendency toward independence from parental dominance among most teenagers, and a somewhat weaker movement among some youngsters toward an active and informed role in the political and economic life of their community and society.

The former trend toward independence is best understood as parent-child conflict over specific behaviors and life styles rather than rebellion with respect to central political and economic values. Conflict over staying out late, hair style and school performance are very common. In terms of communication behavior, the parent-child conflict is manifested in attention to peer-defined tastes in such activities as record playing and radio listening. Attention to the adult-defined television programs and book reading shows a contrasting decline in importance. More of the time devoted to television and other media is spent with peers or alone; viewing with the family becomes less common in later adolescence (Lyle and Hoffman, 1969a). The emphasis on peer tastes and peer interaction helps to account for the sustained disinterest in public affairs content among most adolescents. There is no evidence that interest in one medium or type of content generalizes to any other. Clarke (1968) found that attention to teen columns in the newspaper did not generalize to other types of items. Whatever medium is used, it is apparently tied to its potential for discussion with friends (Troldahl and Costello, 1966).

The second adolescent trend toward greater public affairs participation is more complicated than the emerging pattern of parent-child conflict. The trend affects only some of the adolescents and its magnitude varies depending upon the criterion used to index participation. If we use the values like political trust, efficacy and support or the identification with a political party as the criterion, then we find very little indication of "growth" among the senior high students as compared with their junior high counterparts (Political Socialization study). If we treat attention to public affairs media content as an index of activity, then we find a moderate yet discernible increase from the junior to senior high groups. At neither age level does anything like a majority participate actively in public affairs media. McIntyre and Teevan (1971) found no more than 20 percent of their adolescent sample to be viewers of television news. Our own data in Table 1 show an actual decline in television news and public affairs viewing.

It appears that the adolescent period is one of considerable public affairs "tracking" in which a substantial minority of youngsters "turn on" to public affairs in anticipation of active citizen roles in adult life, while another sizeable minority become discouraged in school and elsewhere and "tune out" of active citizenship roles. For them, the teenage subculture is more rewarding and less frustrating. A third group, perhaps a majority, become interested in public affairs occasionally (e.g., during elections) but follow the dominant adolescent trend for the most part. The testing of this tracking formulation requires a design that studies changes in individuals over time.

Other criteria for public affairs participation show much larger and more consistent increases from junior to senior high. Political knowledge, in our Political Socialization study for example, shows a junior to senior high gain much greater than that shown for any public affairs media variable. Adelson and O'Neil (1966) found another type of criteria that showed considerable development through adolescence. They showed that, while the pre-adolescent tends to think of government in highly personal terms, the thirteen-year-old begins to demonstrate causal thinking. By fifteen, he is likely to be able to handle abstractions fairly easily but lacks sufficient information to make balanced judgments. As Lane and Sears (1964) point out, the child becomes opinionated long before he becomes informed (if indeed he ever becomes informed). Adelson and O'Neil found the eighteen-year-old apt to be able to elaborate his ideas with relative fluency and to think ideologically. This trend, so important to the democratic political process, was also evident in our Political Socialization study. The senior high adolescents were much more likely than those in junior high to have impersonal views of government, to see wholes rather than parts, to have positive rather than negative approaches, to emphasize the future rather than the present, and to place stress on community and principle rather than individual gain in their answers to various open-ended questions. Such criteria may begin to play a more important role in the application of the socialization perspective in the political area.

Structural Constraints

In keeping with the section on childhood, we will confine our literature review of structural constraints to those studies that link the constraints to communication behavior. Our model implies, however, an *indirect* path of influence from the constraints through learning process variables to communication behavior. This makes the very large body of literature of social class differences in child rearing practices relevant to our model; however, we have chosen not to include that literature here partly because of the large amount of space such a review would take and partly because the relevant learning processes are not well specified at this point. For an excellent review of the social class and child rearing literature, see Zigler and Child (1969).

There is a considerable amount of evidence regarding the direct connection between social class and communication behavior among adolescents. The Lyle and Hoffman (1969a) data show that youngsters from blue-collar families watched considerably more television and used newspapers less than did those from white-collar households. Differences in the use of radio, records and comics were small and inconsistent. The authors assert the social class differences in media behavior were generally smaller than those in their research of a decade ago, although the samples are not directly comparable. Greenberg and Dominick (1969a), as well as our Political Socialization and Television Use studies, provide further evidence of greater television time for lower-income and working-class adolescents. It is also interesting to note that in the Lyle and Hoffman data, the social class differences in television use are greater for the tenth grade than for the sixth grade, especially among girls. This contradicts the Kline et al. (1970b) proposition that the predictive power of socioeconomic status would lessen as the child becomes older. Clarke (1969a) also found social class had widely varying predictive power among different age groups. While the education of each parent predicted strongly to book reading of that parent, it had no influence at all on their adolescent child's reading or purchase of books. Future research should make similar comparison of the predictive power of social class and other structural constraints at various age levels.

The social class differences also appear for content within the media. Lyle and Hoffman show a decided blue-collar preference for "hip adventure" programs, particularly at the tenth grade; the white-collar adolescents have a contrasting preference for comedy and family shows. Regarding the frequency of viewing various types of television shows, data from both our Political Socialization and Television Usage studies indicate more frequent viewing of westerns among the lower-socioeconomic-status adolescents. Other entertainment categories show less strong correlations in the same direction. News and public affairs programs have an opposite pattern being watched more often by the higher-status youngsters; however, the correlations while consistent are not large. Similarly, low positive correlations are shown between socioeconomic status and use of public affairs materials in the print media. Apparently, social class makes some difference in the child's use of public affairs media content, but it is hardly the complete explanation of the public affairs tracking during adolescence discussed earlier.

Adolescent attitudes and perceptions regarding media may also be related to social class. The trend toward greater agreement with the statement "television should be for fun and not for education" that Lyle and Hoffman found among the older adolescents was especially noticeable for those from blue-collar families. Greenberg and Gordon (1971b) found that among eighth graders, those from low-status families expressed more liking for violent content and found it more humorous and more realistic.

Learning Processes

While it is commonly held that "example is the best persuader" (cf. Schramm et al., 1961), there is insufficient evidence to defend such a sweeping generalization. Clarke (1969b) found that the similarity of father and son in reading behavior was contingent upon the identification of the son with the father regarding achievement. There is no evidence of modeling of book buying or book reading, and parent-child similarity in magazine reading is strong only for newsmagazines (Clarke, 1969a). Low positive parent-child correlations are shown for adolescent news reading (Chaffee et al., 1971).

Parent-child correlations for television use are shown in Table 2. The number of cases for the Television Use study is considerably smaller than shown for Table 1 because mothers were interviewed in the Wisconsin sample but not in Maryland. In neither state did we contact fathers. It is apparent that, except for the television time measures, the correlations are stronger for the Television Use sample than for the Political Socialization study. Quite possibly the differences are accounted for by the fact that the more reliable specific program lists were used in the Television Use study, while single categories of programs were the basis for use measures in the latter study. The television time measures were more comparable and very similar results are shown.

The results presented in Table 2 also suggest that mothers are somewhat more important sources of influence than fathers and that same-sex correlations are higher than those shown for opposite-sex parent-child combinations. However, neither of these differences is strong nor totally consistent across the various measures.

It is important to note that the presence of parent-child correlations of whatever magnitude represent necessary but certainly not sufficient evidence of modeling—the imitation of the parent's

TABLE 2
PARENT-CHILD TELEVISION USE CORRELATIONS
BY SEX OF PARENT AND CHILD

Television Use Index		Political Socialization Study		Television Use Study
		Fathers	Mothers	Mothers
Adolescent's TV Time	Sons	.14	.15	.12
	Daughters	.09	.18	.13
Adventure-Drama	Sons	.11	.13	.23
	Daughters	.02	.13	.27
Westerns	Sons	.19	.29	.19
	Daughters	.19	.25	.42
Crime-Detective	Sons	—	—	.26
	Daughters	—	—	.24
Situation Comedies	Sons	.07	.13	.25
	Daughters	.01	.09	.24
Variety-Comedy	Sons	—	—	.30
	Daughters	—	—	.33
News-Public Affairs	Sons	.11	.07	.18
	Daughters	.14	.17	.28
(Number of cases)	Sons	(297)	(333)	(119)
	Daughters	(301)	(361)	(106)

NOTE: Cell entries are Pearson r's, and differ from zero at the following significance levels: Political Socialization study, $r \geq .12$, $p < .05$; $r \geq .15$, $p < .01$; Television Use study, $r \geq .19$, $p < .05$; $r \geq .25$, $p < .01$.

behavior by the child in order to be like the parent. This argument is made more extensively elsewhere (Chaffee et al., 1971), and we can only summarize the central points here. One alternative explanation of the data is *reverse modeling,* the child's media use influences the parent rather than vice versa. Indirect evidence of various kinds indicates that child to parent influence may be at least as strong as the influence emanating from the parent (Clarke, 1963; Bottorff, 1970; Chaffee et al., 1971). Another possibility is that the *opportunity* to watch, which increases if another person is already viewing, accounts for the parent-child correlation. While the Chaffee et al. research found no support in the analysis of one-set versus two-set home (the opportunity explanation suggests higher parent-child correlations in one-set homes), it is possible that the higher correlations we found in the Television Use study reflects opportunity. A control for specific programs watched did reduce the correlations by about one-third, but apparently opportunity cannot account for the entire correlation.

A final explanation of the parent-child correlation is that both the parent and the child are located similarly in the social structure, therefore some combination of *third variables* common to both may account for the media use associations. Control for socioeconomic status, for example, does reduce the parent-child correlations shown in Table 2, but they do not disappear altogether. Given the fact that the correlations are only low to moderate to begin with and the potential of several other alternative explanations, modeling (or parental example) does not seem to be a very strong explanation of adolescent communication behavior.

Reinforcement learning, the parent's use of rewards and punishment, is an alternative to the modeling learning formulation. In terms of direct attempts to influence the child's media behavior, reinforcement appears to be an unlikely explanation in that the number of parents who attempt to control their child's television viewing declines markedly through adolescence (Greenberg and Dominick, 1969a; Lyle and Hoffman, 1971a; McLeod et al., 1971a). There is some evidence consonant with a reinforcement explanation, however. Jeffres (1968) found that explicit parental rewards in the form of book giving and taking the son to the library did have a presumed effect on the child's newspaper reading behavior. Maccoby (1954) suggests that in middle-class families, oversevere reaction (and to some extent, underreaction) to the child's aggressive behavior leads to increased television viewing.

Our Political Socialization and Television Use studies included one reward measure (frequency of parental affection) and three punishment indices (physical, verbal, and restrictive—taking away privileges, grounding, etc.). In neither study did we find the expected relationship between affection and low levels of viewing violent television content; in fact, there were tendencies in the opposite direction. Physical and verbal punishment tended to show low positive correlations with violence viewing, but the relationships were inconsistent across comparisons. Restrictive punishment showed somewhat stronger and more consistent positive correlations with violence viewing. It also showed low positive associations with other types of entertainment viewing and low negative ones with exposure to news and public affairs media content.

In contrast to the rather meager amount of evidence regarding modeling and reinforcement learning in the development of adolescent communication patterns, studies of social interaction are more numerous and persuasive. One indication of the importance of social interaction in shaping media patterns is the relative salience of the media as topics of conversation. Lyle and Hoffman (1969a) found that movies and the entertainment aspects of television were particularly important discussion topics with friends and parents. While school events was the most frequently discussed topic among the thirteen categories presented, television was considerably more salient than student protest, pollution, politics and Vietnam. This provides at least indirect evidence of a positive social facilitation function of the mass media.

More direct evidence is found in the above-mentioned Jeffres (1968) study where the frequency of parent-child interaction regarding books was positively related to the child's exposure to newspapers. Clarke (1969a), however, found no correlation between parental contact and the child's book buying. It is likely that the content of the interaction determines the effect and that communication in a given area does not necessarily generalize to behavior change in another area. Our Political Socialization study data show that the adolescent's use of public affairs media is strongly related to parent-child interaction about politics but bears only a slight relation to the overall frequency of communication.

It is also possible that the lack of communication with significant others can affect communication behavior. Riley and Riley (1951) found that youngsters lacking in integration into a peer group showed a preference for action and violence in the media. Similar results were reported by Himmelweit et al. (1958) and Schramm et al. (1961). Our own Television Use study, however, did not replicate this finding and instead found a slight positive correlation between peer group integration and viewing of violent television content (McLeod et al., 1971b).

An interesting variant of the interaction learning formulation is found in the Clarke (1971) study of coorientation and information-seeking regarding symphonic music. The key predictor of information-seeking was the presence of a favorable coorientation partner, either parent or peer. The perception that such a partner existed was a better predictor than actual interaction on the topic, thus diverging from a straightforward frequency of communication explanation. The presence of an unfavorable partner (someone opposed to symphonic music) did not seem to matter and the fact that who the partner was is unimportant also argues against a simple reference group interpretation. In another study, Clarke (1971) found that the *congruency* of interest (similarity of own interest and perception of other's interest) predicted information-seeking about popular music, especially when the adolescent's judgments about other persons depended on what music they liked or disliked. The key coorientational variable may not always be the intrapersonally measured *congruency*, however. In our Television Use study, neither the congruency of the child, nor the mother regarding goals of education bore a strong inverse relationship to the child's violence viewing (both correlations −.07). On the other hand, interpersonal *agreement* (the similarity between the actual positions of the mother and child on educational goals) showed a much higher negative correlation (−.21) with violence viewing (McLeod et al., 1971b). *Accuracy* (the similarity of the perception of other's position and actual position of the other) had negative correlations with violence viewing intermediate in size between agreement and congruency.

Our research on family communication processes has been described earlier in "The Socialization Perspective: Learning Processes" section of this paper. We have found it useful to think of the two dimensions of parent-child interaction, *socio-orientation* and *concept-orientation* in terms of Newcomb's (1953) A-B-X paradigm making A the child, B the parent, and X the topic or focus of communication. We have adopted an assumption alternative to Newcomb that each relation varies in strength. A socio-oriented communication pattern involves stress on A-B relations, whereas a concept-oriented pattern emphasizes A-X relations. Although both

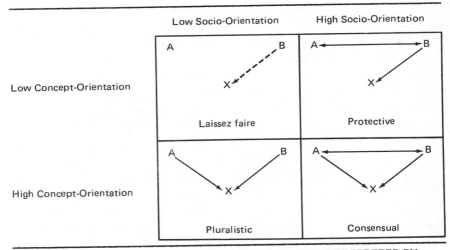

Figure 1. FAMILY COMMUNICATION PATTERN TYPOLOGY INTERPRETED BY RELATIONS FROM NEWCOMB'S ABX PARADIGM. Key: A = the child; B = the parent; X = the topic; arrows indicate relations stressed in particular family type.

dimensions are continuous variables, it is easier for analysis to cut each at the median forming the four-fold typology shown in Figure 1:

Laissez faire families lack emphasis on either type of relation. The adolescent is not prohibited from arguing with his elders, but neither is he exposed to conflicting sets of ideas.

Protective families stress the obedience and social harmony of sociorelations (A-B) only and there is little concern with conceptual matters. The child is not only prohibited from speaking up, but he is not likely to encounter controversial ideas that would make him speak out.

Pluralistic families emphasize the development of strong and varied concept-relations (A-X) without insisting on obedience to authority. The child is encouraged to explore new ideas and to express them without fear of retaliation.

Consensual families place stress on agreement through both types of orientations (A-B and A-X). The child is faced with a seemingly incompatible situation in that he is encouraged to explore controversy, but he is also constrained to develop and maintain ideas consonant with those of his parent.

Media use comparisons for the Political Socialization study adolescents are shown in Table 3. It is apparent that adolescents from *protective* homes spend the most time with television of any group; however, their interest in entertainment programs clearly does not generalize to attention to news and public affairs. One interpretation of the heavy television use among protective adolescents is that their behavior represents an attempt to escape from the strictures of the strong A-B relation emphasis, but it should be pointed out that their parents also watch far more television than the average parent.

Adolescents from *pluralistic* homes present a striking contrast to the protective media use pattern. While they spend far less time with television than the average child their attention to news and public affairs programs is quite high. While it might be expected that the pluralistic adolescent would also be very high on use of the newspaper, he apparently is only slightly above average in his attention to print news. The reasons for this are not entirely clear, but it is certain from other analyses that the pluralistic adolescent is a very busy youngster engaging in outside activities in school and elsewhere. It is likely that these competing activities limit the time he spends with the print media.

Apparently the strategy in *laissez faire* homes of letting the child develop his own interests does not lead to a lively interest in public affairs. The laissez faire adolescent resembles his protective counterpart in being uninterested in public affairs content on television or in newspapers. Adolescents from *consensual* homes present somewhat of a paradox. The public affairs interest, particularly with respect to newspapers, tends to be well above average. In other analyses not shown here, however, the consensual youngster has been found to be clearly below average in his knowledge of politics. Apparently, his gain in knowledge is not commensurate with the time he spends with the public affairs media.

Table 4 presents data from the Television Use study (McLeod et al., 1971b). Because of the small number of cases, grade and sex have been combined. The adolescents from protective homes are again extremely high television users, in terms of time and viewing of violent programs and Saturday morning cartoon viewing. They are also the most likely group to say that television presents a chance for them to learn behaviors that the adult world considers antisocial. Again, the pluralistic adolescent has an opposite pattern in being below average in television viewing time. He is unlikely to see television as a source of antisocial learning, in keeping with a general pluralistic tendency to be low on antisocial aggressive behavior.

TABLE 3
ADOLESCENT'S MEDIA USE (standard scores) BY FAMILY
COMMUNICATION PATTERNS (Political Socialization study)

Media Use Index			Family Communication Pattern			
			Laissez faire	Protec- tive	Plural- istic	Consen- sual
Adolescent's	Jr. Hi	Boys	00	29	−38	02
TV Time	Jr. Hi	Girls	−09	27	−30	12
	Sr. Hi	Boys	11	28	−32	−03
	Sr. Hi	Girls	01	24	−13	−05
TV Adventure-	Jr. Hi	Boys	−24	07	17	−06
Drama	Jr. Hi	Girls	−16	09	−01	09
	Sr. Hi	Boys	−02	31	−23	00
	Sr. Hi	Girls	−14	02	03	12
TV Westerns	Jr. Hi	Boys	04	10	−33	10
	Jr. Hi	Girls	−10	28	−13	−02
	Sr. Hi	Boys	−14	13	−09	13
	Sr. Hi	Girls	−14	09	04	−10
TV News-Public	Jr. Hi	Boys	−08	−26	12	17
Affairs	Jr. Hi	Girls	−17	−06	22	04
	Sr. Hi	Boys	−21	08	22	−07
	Sr. Hi	Girls	−23	−08	15	16
Newspaper	Jr. Hi	Boys	−13	−11	03	14
News	Jr. Hi	Girls	−00	−20	03	14
	Sr. Hi	Boys	−14	12	08	−03
	Sr. Hi	Girls	−13	01	03	11
Newspaper	Jr. Hi	Boys	−01	−19	09	08
News	Jr. Hi	Girls	−04	−33	−02	31
	Sr. Hi	Boys	−09	01	03	06
	Sr. Hi	Girls	−17	02	07	12
Newspaper	Jr. Hi	Boys	14	−11	−01	−01
Entertainment	Jr. Hi	Girls	09	−05	−06	00
	Sr. Hi	Boys	04	−07	10	−11
	Sr. Hi	Girls	−09	05	01	06
Total Public	Jr. Hi	Boys	−22	−33	29	04
Affairs Media	Jr. Hi	Girls	−15	−32	24	22
	Sr. Hi	Boys	−15	−03	18	00
	Sr. Hi	Girls	−31	−11	17	25
(Number of	Jr. Hi	Boys	(78)	(81)	(70)	(114)
Cases)	Jr. Hi	Girls	(82)	(65)	(68)	(83)
	Sr. Hi	Boys	(81)	(61)	(77)	(68)
	Sr. Hi	Girls	(104)	(70)	(102)	(88)

NOTE: Standard score entries are weighted cell means, setting the overall mean at zero and the standard deviation at unity, for all four cells in each row. Scores are calculated to two decimal places; decimals are omitted for simplicity. Statistical significance (.05 level) for differences between a given cell and the total of all other cells in that row ranges between 17 and 22 depending on the size of the cell and the other cells in the row.

TABLE 4

ADOLESCENT'S TELEVISION USE AND REACTIONS (standard scores)
BY FAMILY COMMUNICATION PATTERNS (Television Use study)

Television Use/ Reaction Index	Family Communication Pattern			
	Laissez faire	Protec- tive	Plural- istic	Consen- sual
Adolescent's TV time	−23	+40	−22	+08
TV violence viewing	−14	+25	−41	+32
TV Saturday morning viewing	−31	+21	−31	+42
Agrees that TV presents chance to learn antisocial behavior	−04	+19	−29	+14
Sees close similarity between TV violence and real life	−27	−02	−06	+33
Becomes involved with characters and stories of action TV shows	+24	−11	−02	−07
(Number of cases)	(34)	(40)	(34)	(39)

NOTE: Standard score entries are weighted cell means, setting the overall mean at zero and the standard deviation at unity, for all four cells in each row. Scores are calculated to two decimal places; decimals are omitted for simplicity. Statistical significance (.05 level) for difference between a given cell and the total of all other cells in that row is 29 for Laissez faire and Pluralistic groups and 27 for Protective and Consensual groups.

Adolescents raised in laissez faire homes from this sample appear to be light television viewers. They also show a somewhat surprising pattern in seeing little similarity between television and real life, but conversely, reporting greater involvement with the characters and stories on action shows. The consensual youngsters, perhaps reflecting the cross-pressures they face in their family situation, watch heavy dosages of violent content and are the most likely group to see similarity between what they watch and the real world.

Kline et al. (1970b) used the family communication typology and obtained results for adolescent media use generally consistent with the data presented here and with earlier research (Chaffee et al., 1966; McLeod et al., 1967). Children in protective families watch television most among the four types and are low on newspaper use. Pluralists are low on electronic media use relative to their use of newspapers. The laissez faire youngsters are lowest on newspaper use while the consensuals are highest in their use of both newspapers and radio. The same data were used to test a theoretical model of socialization through the use of path and dummy variable cohort analyses (Kline et al., 1970a). In the model, the family communication dimensions, autonomy from family, and autonomy from peers were the independent variables. While the results were less satisfactory in their prediction of media time budgeting than for other dependent variables (political behavior and mass institution evaluation), the study represents an important first step in the application of multivariate analysis to socialization models of communication behavior.

Adulthood

The completion of high school, roughly corresponding to the end of adolescence, is a key point of discontinuity in the socialization process. Some of this discontinuity appears in the form of communication behavior patterns of early adulthood that are rather different from those of adolescence. As individuals leave parental homes, begin independently exploring their physical and social environment, acquire new educational and occupational skills and responsibilities, begin planning families of their own, form new peer and friendship groups, and generally move about in society, their communication behavior is affected and often radically changes.

The immediate post-high school years produce the most divergent system of economic, political and social tracking to be found throughout the life cycle, although as we have argued earlier this tracking really begins to be apparent somewhere between junior and senior high school. The tracking becomes more obvious after high school when slightly less than half the age group go on to college and the remainder enter the occupational world. The two emerging life styles are dramatically different.

In the first year of college, the student's media behavior changes markedly from that of high school years. While his reading of books connected with classes occupies a considerable portion of his time, his viewing of television is only about one-sixth of its frequency of a year or two earlier and he is likely to be either a non-reader or a light reader of newspapers (O'Keefe and Spetnagel, 1972; McLeod et al., 1972). In part, this reflects the lessened availability of these media in dormitory situations and in part his lack of interest in world and community affairs. Radio, which has a high level of use early in college life, declines while television and newspaper use increase steadily into the senior year. This follows an apparent broadening of interest of some students as well as the increased availability of television and newspapers in apartment living situations. McLeod et al. found that political position and major in school were rather strongly related to media preferences for news, with the more liberal students and Liberal Arts majors looking more toward the print media while the more conservative and vocationally oriented stayed with the electronic media.

In contrast to the large amount of research on college students, very little is known about the majority of young adults who go to work after high school. In terms of political activity, it is apparent that they are less likely to vote and participate than older adults. Presumably, their attention to public affairs media is also below that of older adults.

Generally, adult newspaper readership seems to increase with age (Kline, 1971; Samuelson et al., 1963). Greenberg and Kumata (1968), however, using data from a national survey of adults, found no association between number of newspapers read and age. This finding does not necessarily contradict the other studies in that multiple readership of papers is dependent upon the presence of multiple newspapers in the area where the person lives. Older people tend to live in less populated areas and, hence have less chance for exposure. Time spent with newspapers also presents a problem in that older people may read more slowly. In studies of age by reading behavior, it would be more important to measure the content rather than time or number of newspapers.

No relationship between age and the number of magazines read or time spent reading magazines was found in the Kline, Greenberg and Kumata, or Samuelson et al. studies. Greenberg and Kumata do report that women spend slightly more time with magazines than men do and our Political Socialization study data showed that the mothers in the sample used newsmagazines more than did the fathers. Radio listening apparently declines somewhat with age (Greenberg and Kumata, 1968; Mendelsohn, 1968), although other researchers have found no relationship (Kline). There is general agreement that women spend considerably more time listening to the radio than do men at all ages (O'Keefe and Spetnagel; Greenberg and Kumata; Mendelsohn).

As was the case with the literature for children and adolescents, there is considerably more recent research done on television than other media. The Kline and Samuelson et al. studies both report a strong association between age and television viewing time. Both the Greenberg and Kumata and Mendelsohn studies, on the other hand, show a curvilinear relationship with respondents in the middle age categories showing the lowest amount of time spent. In total, most adults spend more than two hours a day in front of television screens, but about twenty percent do not watch at all on a given day (LoSciuto, 1971). Most researchers report higher viewing levels for women than for men; however, this appears to be largely a function of available time rather than preference for television per se.

Regarding television program preferences, it appears that entertainment programs take precedence over heavier fare at all age levels. Violent programs are popular, but not necessarily the most popular type of show. LoSciuto reports higher attention levels for dramatic and family comedy programs while Bechtel et al. (1971) show the highest viewing levels for movies (many of which are violent, of course). Israel and Robinson (1971 report only about twelve percent of the adult population can be categorized as television violence "fans"; however, this fairly small group makes up one-third of the audience for these shows. Attention to violence shows peaks after the age of fifty, partly as a function of greater time spent viewing during these years. Not surprisingly, men are more consistent viewers of violence than are women.

The viewing of news programs also becomes more frequent with advancing age, according to the Israel and Robinson data. Their results also show considerable overlap in the news viewing audience with the twenty percent who are regular viewers constituting the bulk of the audience on any given day. Available time may account for some of the difference in news viewing and some of the non-viewing may be attributed to avoidance of the disturbing aspects of news. LoSciuto found that, although relatively few adults were emotionally upset by any kind of television content, the negative comments centered around news programs. Their specific complaints about general programing, however, dealt more with commercials and to a lesser degree with violence and sex.

Structural Constraints

There is considerable ambiguity as to the relationship between education and time spent with the various media. Samuelson et al. (1963) found a positive correlation between education and newspaper reading time that was strengthened by controlling for age. Greenberg and Kumata (1968) also found a high correlation between number of newspapers read and education. Kline (1971), however, using path analysis found a slight negative relationship between education and time spent reading newspapers.

McLeod et al. (1965-1966) found a $-.42$ correlation of education and time spent with television. Samuelson et al. report a much lower negative correlation that disappeared when job-connected hours, hobby hours, organizational membership and number of children were controlled for. Greenberg and Kumata found a curvilinear relationship between television viewing time and education with the peak occurring among adults with a high school education. Finally, Kline found a −.33 correlation for these same two variables, but this was reduced to zero when income and anomia were controlled for. None of these studies found any marked association between education and radio listening; however strong positive correlations have been shown for education and magazine reading (Greenberg and Kumata; Kline).

Other indicators of social class, income and occupational status, show diverse findings. Taken as a whole, the results indicate the need for careful control of a host of extraneous factors. In fact, they cast doubt on the wisdom of using media time spent measures because they are so confounded and difficult to interpret. Most of the research also assumes a direct path between social class and media use that may not be justified. The McLeod et al. (1972) findings indicate that for the college population at least there is no direct path, but rather an indirect one from education to orientation toward education (scholarly versus vocational) and college major and from these to media use.

With respect to watching violent programs on television, Israel and Robinson (1971) found considerably higher viewing levels for the lower-status groups in terms of their education, occupation and income. This relationship held for both men and women. Interestingly, the greatest educational differences in violence viewing were shown for the 18- to 24-year-old males where tracking may have its greatest effect. In this same connection, the high school dropout group showed particularly high levels of violence watching.

The Israel and Robinson data show surprisingly little connection between the various socioeconomic status measures and television news viewing. There is somewhat of a curvilinear relationship with the "some college" group being lowest and college graduates the highest on news viewing. Stronger relationships are found between various social class measures and use of news in the print media and public affairs use generally (McLeod et al., 1965-1966; Donohew and Thorp, 1966; Greenberg and Kumata, 1968; Bogart, 1968-1969). Our Political Socialization study data also support this inference.

One of the weaknesses of most studies of adult media use is that they tend to treat socioeconomic status as a simple locator and do not try to deal with the process by which these social constraints affect the communication behavior of the adult. Wilensky (1964) in his study of working conditions, career orderliness, and unemployment record of the adult's occupational history and Elliott (1972) in translating religious affiliation into organizational dimensions are notable exceptions to this pattern.

SOME CONCLUSIONS

We have argued that the preponderance of research devoted to the effects of communication has resulted in a distorted picture of the process and effects of mass communication. To correct this imbalance, more attention should be paid to the causes or antecedents of communication behavior. We have reviewed the problems of measuring communication behavior in terms of four types of variables: media exposure; communication processes; motivational gratifications; and media credibility and preferences. As used in research treating communication behavior as a dependent variable, the measures tend to be narrow, nonfunctional and confounded.

A socialization perspective was presented, containing five elements: age or life cycle position; social structural constraints; agent of influence; learning processes, and content or criterion of the communication behavior. Each of the five elements must be specified in order to have a complete socialization explanation.

Relevant research literature was reviewed within each of three life-cycle stages: childhood, adolescence, and adulthood. Existing research falls far short of specifying all five elements necessary for the socialization perspective. Most studies simply describe a single type of communication behavior for a particular age group, and almost all of the studies cited have been conducted in the United States. Systematic cross-national studies using comparable measures are badly needed.

The generalizations from the literature are also contingent to this particular point in time. We have avoided using media studies done prior to the era of television assuming that use of that medium affects all other aspects of communication behavior. Almost all the research on adolescents, then, involves sampling of the first generation in history to grow up entirely with television. The content of television may have become the dominant source for the validation of social reality for this generation. It would be interesting to ascertain the effect of television as a socializing agent by examining the communication behavior of today's adolescents when they become adults. Comparisons with the behavior of today's adults could be obtained by careful long-term cohort analyses using comparable measures.

Within the next decade, communication technology will introduce changes in communication behavior that are likely to make obsolete the research findings cited here. The advent of cable television, for example, will allow for a growing segmentation of the television audience with special programing for specialized tastes. The violence "fan" potentially will be able to watch a steady diet of gore unbroken by news at his supper hour. The minority attentive to public affairs programing will be able to seek a richer diet of information. The consequences for the society may be a greater disparity in information levels and tastes. As media patterns become more distinctive, it will be all the more useful and necessary to study communication behavior as a dependent variable and to investigate influences operating to develop these patterns. In the future, as mass communication control changes, the independent variables may be less "independent" and more under the control of specialized audiences.

While the present state of research evidence is inadequate, we believe that the socialization perspective can serve as a useful guideline to future research if appropriate procedures of measurement and design are followed. In terms of measurement, we have argued that the social structural constraints should be treated as theoretical variables rather than as static categorical locators. Their influence is best understood if they are tied to specific learning processes. The best available evidence indicate that the most fruitful conceptualization of these learning processes involves the interaction patterns between people rather than the more usual modeling and reinforcement formulations.

The most perplexing measurement problem involves the need to establish *functional patterns* of communication behavior that cut across various discrete media use and interpersonal behaviors. Focus on narrow time spent with a given medium measures is not likely to produce meaningful results. Receiver-oriented categorizations of media functions combined with specific use patterns of content categories would seem to be the optimum strategy for measuring communication behavior.

The socialization perspective requires the sampling of social units rather than individuals. While most of the research has dealt with the family as the agency of socialization, it is obvious that this by no means exhausts the sampling possibilities. For the older adolescent, the peer group and the classroom may be more influential than the family and are thereby suitable sampling units. Most of the analyses of adult media use have focused on the person's location in the social structure in terms of education, income and social class. The socialization perspective implies that the organizational structure and social relations of the work place, voluntary association and neighborhood may be as important as the more general societal location in determining communication behavior.

It is quite possible that communication behavior even if functionally defined represents too narrow a scope for an adequate research program. That is, that communication behavior is best understood in its relationship with other kinds of behaviors as dependent variables. Our own inclination is to study communication behavior as part of a broader investigation of political socialization. Chaffee et al. (1970), for example, found evidence that indicated adolescent public affairs media use leads to an increase in political knowledge during a political campaign. This would add a sixth element to our socialization model. While political socialization represents a natural affinity for researchers interested in the news media, such areas as the socialization of youth into the economic system remain relatively unexplored.

Our division of the life cycle into the three broad stages (childhood, adolescence, and adulthood) is obviously much too gross a breakdown for meaningful analysis. Research designs should use much finer age gradations, breaking childhood and adolescence down into five or six periods and adulthood into perhaps six or eight stages categorized by occupational and family obligations. Particular attention should be paid to the relative importance of various structural constraints, agents, and learning processes at each stage of the life cycle.

The development of research designs appropriate to the socialization perspective must meet two basic requirements: they must be capable of handling the large number of variables contained in the socialization model; and, in view of the emphasis on change, they must deal with change over time and sequences of cause and effect. Path analysis, a procedure that examines the adequacy of complex causal models using nonexperimental data gathered at a single point in time, is one promising approach (Blalock, 1964, 1969; Duncan, 1966).

The ideal research design, however, is the panel design that has often been suggested but seldom followed in communication research. More specifically for research on children and adolescents, we would obtain data from samples of youngsters at three year age intervals from age five through seventeen. Data also would be obtained from potential agents of socialization in the family or peer group. Three years and six years later, the same respondents would again serve as data sources. Through this panel design, we could obtain estimates of gross or total change in key variables in contrast to the more limited net change figures that independent samples taken over time provide. A more important advantage is that this design allows us to make rather strong tests of cause and effect relationships through the application of cross-lagged correlational analysis. While the basic cross-lagged techniques have been known for some time it is only in recent years that more rigorous techniques of design and analysis have been worked out (Heise, 1970; Pelz and Lew, 1970; Kenny, 1971; and Neale, 1971).

Many people may prefer explanations of communication behavior that are simpler than the complex socialization model presented here. Others of us may believe that it is only through such complicated multivariate models that the complexities of the communication process can be understood.

REFERENCES

ABERLE, D. F., A. K. COHEN, A. K. DAVIS, M. J. LEVY, and F. X. SUTTON (1950) "The functional prerequisites of a society." Ethics 60 (January): 100-111.

ADELSON, J. and R. P. O'NEIL (1966) "Growth of political ideas in adolescence: the sense of community." J. of Personality and Social Psychology 4 (November): 295-306.

ADORNO, T. W., E. FRENKEL-BRUNSWIK, D. J. LEVINSON, and R. N. SANFORD (1950) The Authoritarian Personality. New York: Harper.

ALLEN, T. (1968) "Mass media use patterns in an urban ghetto." Journalism Q. 45 (Autumn): 525-528.

ARNDT, J. (1968) "A test of the two-step flow in diffusion of a new product." Journalism Q. 45 (Autumn); 457-465.

BALES, R. F. (1950) Interaction Process Analysis: A Method for the Study of Small Groups. Cambridge, Mass.: Addison-Wesley.

BAUER, R. A. (1964) "The obstinate audience: the influence process from the point of view of social communication." American Psychologist 19 (May): 319-328.

BECHTEL, R. B., C. ACHELPOHL, and R. AKERS (1971) "Correlates between observed behavior and questionnaire responses on television viewing," pp. 274-344 in E. A. Rubinstein, G. A. Comstock, and J. P. Murray (eds.) Television and Social Behavior. Washington, D.C.: National Institute of Mental Health 4.

BENEDICT, R. (1934) Patterns of Culture. Boston: Houghton Mifflin.

BERELSON, B. (1949) "What 'missing the newspaper' means," pp. 111-124 in P. Lazarsfeld and F. Stanton (eds.) Communications Research 1948-1949. New York: Harper.

BERGER, S. M. and W. W. LAMBERT (1968) "Stimulus-response theory in contemporary social psychology," pp. 81-178 in G. Lindzey and E. Aronson (eds.) Handbook of Social Psychology. Reading, Mass: Addison-Wesley 1.

BLALOCK, H. M. (1969) Theory Construction. Englewood Cliffs, N.J.: Prentice-Hall.

——— (1964) Causal Inferences in Nonexperimental Research. Chapel Hill: Univ. of North Carolina Press.

BLAU, P. M. (1962) "Patterns of choice in interpersonal relations," American Sociological Rev. 27 (February): 41-56.

BOGART, L. (1968-1969) "Changing news interests and the mass media." Public Opinion Q. 32 (Winter): 560-574.

BOTTORFF, A. (1970) "Television, respect and the older adolescent." Master's thesis, University of Wisconsin.

BREED, W. (1955) "Social control in the newsroom." Social Forces 33 (May): 326-335.

BRIM, O. G. and S. WHEELER (1966) Socialization After Childhood: Two Essays. New York: Wiley.

BRONFENBRENNER, U. (1961) "Some familial antecedents of responsibility and leadership in adolescents," pp. 239-271 in L. Petrullo and R. Bass (eds.) Leadership and Interpersonal Behavior. New York: Holt.

CARTER, R. F. and B. S. GREENBERG (1965) "Newspapers or television: which do you believe?" Journalism Q. 42 (Winter): 29-34.

CHAFFEE, S. H. (1971) "Television and adolescent aggression (overview)," pp. 1-34 in G. A. Comstock and E. A. Rubinstein (eds.) Television and Social Behavior. Washington, D.C.: National Institute of Mental Health 3.

——— and J. M. McLEOD (1971a) "Adolescents, parents and televised violence." Presented to American Psychological Assn., Washington, D.C.

——— (1971b) "Adolescent television use in the family context," pp. 149-172 in G. A. Comstock and E. A. Rubinstein (eds.) Television and Social Behavior. Washington, D.C.: National Institute of Mental Health 3.

——— (1970) "Coorientation and the structure of family communication." Presented to International Communication Assn., Minneapolis, Minn.

——— J. M. McLEOD and C. K. ATKIN (1971) "Parental influences on adolescent media use." American Behavioral Scientist 14 (3): 323-340.

CHAFFEE, S. H., J. M. McLEOD and J. L. GUERRERO (1969) "Origins and implications of the coorientation approach in communication research." Presented to Assn. for Education in Journalism, Berkeley, Calif.

CHAFFEE, S. H., J. M. McLEOD and D. B. WACKMAN (1972) "Family communication patterns and adolescent political participation," in J. Dennis (ed.) Explorations of Political Socialization. New York: Wiley.

——— (1966) "Family communication patterns and political participation." Presented to Assn. for Education in Journalism, Iowa City, Iowa.

CHAFFEE, S. H., L. S. WARD and L. P. TIPTON (1970) "Mass communication and political socialization." Journalism Q. 47 (Winter): 647-659.

CHAFFEE, S. H., K. R. STAMM, J. L. GUERRERO, and L. P. TIPTON (1969) "Experiments on cognitive discrepancies and communication." Journalism Monographs 14.

CLARKE, P. (1971) "Some proposals for continuing research on youth and the mass media." American Behavioral Scientist 14 (3): 313-322.

——— (1969a) "Parental print use, social contact about reading and use of the print media by teenage boys." Presented to Pacific chapter, American Assn. for Public Opinion Research, Napa, Calif.

——— (1969b) "Identification with father and father-son similarities in reading behavior." Presented to Assn. for Education in Journalism, Berkeley, Calif.

——— (1968) "Does teen news attract boys to newspapers?" Journalism Q. 45 (Spring): 7-13.

——— (1965) "Parental socialization values and children's newspaper reading." Journalism Q. 42 (Autumn): 539-546.

——— (1963) "An experiment to increase the audience for educational television." Ph.D. dissertation, University of Minnesota.

——— and L. RUGGELS (1970) "Preferences among news media for coverage of public affairs." Journalism Q. 47 (Autumn): 464-471.

COLEMAN, J. S. (1958) "Relational analysis: the study of social organization with survey methods." Human Organization 17 (Winter): 28-36.

COLDWELL, T. (1970) "Professionalization and performance among newspaper photographers." Master's thesis, University of Wisconsin.

DeFLEUR, M. L. (1970) Theories of Mass Communication. Second edition. New York: McKay.

DONOHEW, L. (1967) "Newspaper gatekeepers and forces in the news channel." Public Opinion Q. 31 (Spring): 61-68.

——— and R. THORP (1966) "An approach to the study of mass media within a state." Journalism Q. 43 (Summer): 264-268.

DUNCAN, O. D. (1966) "Path analysis: sociological examples." American J. of Sociology 72 (July): 1-16.

EASTON, D. and J. DENNIS (1965) "The child's image of government." The Annals of the American Academy of Political and Social Science 361: 41-57.

ELLIOTT, W. R. (1972) "Religion, family communication and political socialization." Ph.D. dissertation, University of Wisconsin.

FLEGEL, R. C. and S. H. CHAFFEE (1971) "Influence of editors, readers and personal opinions on reporters." Journalism Q. 48 (Winter): 645-651.

FOULKES, D., E. BELVEDERE, and T. BRUBAKER (1971) "Televised violence and dream content," pp. 59-119 in E. A. Rubinstein, G. A. Comstock, and J. P. Murray (eds.) Television and Social Behavior. Washington, D.C.: National Institute of Mental Health 5.

[164] Current Perspectives in Mass Communication Research

GANS, H. J. (1968) The Uses of Television and Their Educational Implications. New York: Center for Urban Education.

GRAF, W. S. (1971) "Professionalism: a case study of its effects on newspaper performance." Master's thesis, University of Wisconsin.

GREENBERG, B. S. and B. DERVIN (1970) Uses of the Mass Media by the Urban Poor. New York: Praeger.

——— and J. R. DOMINICK (1969a) "Race and social class differences in teenagers' use of television." J. of Broadcasting 13 (Fall): 331-344.

——— (1969b) Television Behavior Among Disadvantaged Children. E. Lansing, Mich.: Department of Communication, Michigan State University.

GREENBERG, B. S. and T. F. GORDON (1971a) "Social class and racial differences in children's perceptions of television violence," pp. 185-210 in E. A. Rubinstein, G. A. Comstock, and J. P. Murray (eds.) Television and Social Behavior. Washington, D.C.: National Institute of Mental Health 5.

——— (1971b) "Children's perceptions of television violence: a replication," pp. 211-230 in E. A. Rubinstein, G. A. Comstock, and J. P. Murray (eds.) Television and Social Behavior. Washington, D.C.: National Institute of Mental Health 5.

GREENBERG, B. S. and H. KUMATA (1968) "National sample predictors of mass media use." Journalism Q. 45 (Winter): 641-646.

HAZARD, W. (1967) "Anxiety and preference for television fantasy." Journalism Q. 44 (Autumn): 461-469.

HEISE, D. R. (1970) "Causal inference from panel data," pp. 3-27 in E. F. Borgatta (ed.) Sociological Methodology 1970. San Francisco: Jossey-Bass.

HERZOG, H. (1944) "What do we really know about daytime serial listeners?" pp. 3-33 in P. Lazarsfeld and F. Stanton (eds.) Communications Research 1942-1943. New York: Duell, Sloan and Pearce.

HIMMELWEIT, H. T., A. N. OPPENHEIM, and P. VINCE (1958) Television and the Child. London: Oxford Univ. Press.

HOVLAND, C. I. (1959) "Reconciling conflicting results derived from experimental and survey studies of attitude change." American Psychologist 14 (January): 8-17.

——— and W. WEISS (1951) "The influence of source credibility on communicator effectiveness." Public Opinion Q. 15 (Winter): 635-650.

ISRAEL, H. and J. P. ROBINSON (1971) "Demographic characteristics of viewers of television violence and news programs," pp. 87-128 in E. A. Rubinstein, G. A. Comstock, and J. P. Murray (eds.) Television and Social Behavior. Washington, D.C.: National Institute of Mental Health 4.

JEFFRES, L. W. (1968) "A study of similarities in the use of print media by fathers and sons." Master's thesis, University of Washington.

KATZ, E. (1968) "On reopening the question of selectivity in exposure to mass communications." In R. Abelson, E. Aronson, W. J. McGuire, T. M. Newcomb, M. J. Rosenberg, and P. Tannenbaum. (eds.) Theories of Cognitive Consistency: A Sourcebook. Chicago: Rand McNally.

——— and P. F. LAZARSFELD (1955) Personal Influence. New York: Free Press.

KENNY, D. A. (1971) "Threats to internal validity of cross-lagged panel inference, as related to 'television violence and child aggression: a followup study'," pp. 136-140 in G. A. Comstock and E. A. Rubinstein (eds.) Television and Social Behavior. Washington, D.C.: National Institute of Mental Health 3.

KLAPPER, J. T. (1960) The Effects of Mass Communication. New York: Free Press.

KLINE, F. G. (1971) "Media time budgeting as a function of demographics and life style." Journalism Q. 48 (Summer): 211-221.

——— N. CHRISTIANSEN, D. K. DAVIS, R. OSTMAN, L. VUORI, and S. GUNARATNE (1970a) "Family communication patterns, family autonomy, and peer autonomy: a theoretical model of socialization." Presented to International Sociological Assn., Varna, Bulgaria.

——— D. K. DAVIS, R. OSTMAN, L. VUORI, N. CHRISTIANSEN, S. GUNARATNE, and L. KIVENS (1970b) "Family and peer socialization and autonomy related to mass media use, mass institution evaluation and radical political activism: a descriptive analysis." Presented to International Assn. for Mass Communication, Constance, Germany.

LAING, R., H. PHILLIPSON, and A. R. LEE (1966) Interpersonal Perception: A Theory and a Method of Research. New York: Springer.

LANE, R. E. and D. O. SEARS (1964) Public Opinion. Englewood Cliffs, N.J.: Prentice-Hall.

LANZETTA, J. T. and J. M. DRISCOLL (1968) "Uncertainty and importance as factors in information search." J. of Personality and Social Psychology 10 (December): 479-486.

LEFKOWITZ, M. M., L. E. ERON, L. O. WALDER, and L. R. HUESMANN (1971) "Television violence and child aggression: a followup study," pp. 35-135 in G. A. Comstock and E. A. Rubinstein (eds.) Television and Social Behavior. Washington, D.C.: National Institute of Mental Health 3.

LEIFER, A. D. and D. F. ROBERTS (1971) "Children's responses to television violence," pp. 43-180 in J. P. Murray, E. A. Rubinstein, and G. A. Comstock and E. A. Rubinstein (eds.) Television and Social Behavior. Washington, D.C.: National Institute of Mental Health 3.

LERNER, D. (1958) The Passing of Traditional Society. New York: Free Press.

LINTON, R. (1945) The Cultural Background of Personality. New York: Appleton-Century-Crofts.

LoSCIUTO, L. A. (1971) "A national inventory of television viewing behavior," pp. 33-86 in E. A. Rubinstein, G. A. Comstock, and J. P. Murray (eds.) Television and Social Behavior. Washington, D.C.: National Institute of Mental Health 4.

LYLE, J. (1971) "Television in daily life: patterns of use (overview)," pp. 1-32 in E. A. Rubinstein, G. A. Comstock, and J. P. Murray (eds.) Television and Social Behavior. Washington, D.C.: National Institute of Mental Health 4.

——— and H. R. HOFFMAN (1971a) "Children's use of television and other media," pp. 129-256 in E. A. Rubinstein, G. A. Comstock, and J. P. Murray (eds.) Television and Social Behavior. Washington, D.C.: National Institute of Mental Health 4.

——— (1971b) "Exploration in patterns of television viewing by preschool-age children," pp. 257-273 in E. A. Rubinstein, G. A. Comstock, and J. P. Murray (eds.) Television and Social Behavior. Washington, D.C.: National Institute of Mental Health 4.

MACCOBY, E. (1954) "Why do children watch television?" Public Opinion Q. 18 (Fall): 239-244.

MARTIN, R., G. O'KEEFE, and O. NAYMAN (1972) "Newspaper editors and their readers: a coorientational approach." Journalism Q. In press.

McGUIRE, W. (1968) "The nature of attitudes and attitude change," pp. 136-314 in G. Lindzey and E. Aronson (eds.) Handbook of Social Psychology. Reading, Mass.: Addison-Wesley.

McINTYRE, J. J. and J. J. TEEVAN (1971) "Television violence and deviant behavior," pp. 383-435 in G. A. Comstock and E. A. Rubinstein (eds.) Television and Social Behavior. Washington, D.C.: National Institute of Mental Health 3.

McLEOD, J. M. (1971a) "Issues and strategies in coorientation research." Presented to Assn. for Education in Journalism, Columbia, S.C.

——— (1971b) "Research on professionalization." Presented to Assn. for Education in Journalism, Columbia, S.C.

——— and S. H. CHAFFEE (1972) "The construction of social reality," pp. 50-99 in J. Tedeschi (ed.) The Social Influence Processes. Chicago: Aldine-Atherton.

McLEOD, J. M., C. K. ATKIN, and S. H. CHAFFEE (1971a) "Adolescents, parents, and television use: adolescent self-report measures from Maryland and Wisconsin samples," pp. 173-238 in G. A. Comstock and E. A. Rubinstein (eds.) Television and Social Behavior. Washington, D.C.: National Institute of Mental Health 3.

——— (1971b) "Adolescents, parents, and television use: self-report and other-report measures from the Wisconsin sample," pp. 239-313 in G. A. Comstock and E. A. Rubinstein (eds.) Television and Social Behavior. Washington, D.C.: National Institute of Mental Health 3.

McLEOD, J. M., L. B. BECKER, and W. R. ELLIOTT (1972) "Communication and political change during the college years." Mass Communications Research Center: University of Wisconsin.

McLEOD, J. M., S. H. CHAFFEE, and H. S. ESWARA (1966) "Family communication patterns and communication research." Presented to Assn. for Education in Journalism, Iowa City, Iowa.

——— S. H. CHAFFEE, and D. B. WACKMAN (1967) "Family communication: an updated report." Presented to Assn. for Education in Journalism, Boulder, Colo.

McLEOD, J. M., G. J. O'KEEFE, and D. B. WACKMAN (1969) "Communication and political socialization during the adolescent years." Presented to Assn. for Education in Journalism, Berkeley, Calif.

McLEOD, J. M., R. R. RUSH, and K. FRIEDERICH (1968-1969) "The mass media and political information in Quito, Ecuador." Public Opinion Q. 32 (Winter): 575-587.

McLEOD, J. M., L. S. WARD, and K. TANCILL (1965-1966) "Alienation and uses of the mass media." Public Opinion Q. 29 (Winter): 583-594.

McLEOD, J. M., D. B. WACKMAN, W. H. HURT, and H. W. PAYNE (1965) "Political conflict and communication behavior in the 1964 political campaign." Presented to Assn. for Education in Journalism, Syracuse, N.Y.

MEAD, G. H. (1934) Mind, Self and Society. Chicago: University of Chicago Press.

MENDELSOHN, H. (1968) Radio in Contemporary American Life. Denver: Communication Arts Center, University of Denver.

MILLER, D. and G. SWANSON (1958) The Changing American Parent. New York: Wiley.

MURRAY, J. P. (1971) "Television in inner-city homes: viewing behavior of young boys," pp. 345-394 in E. A. Rubinstein, G. A. Comstock, and J. P. Murray (eds.) Television and Social Behavior. Washington, D.C.: National Institute of Mental Health 4.

NEALE, J. M. (1971) "Comment on 'television violence and child aggression: a followup study'," pp. 141-148 in G. A. Comstock and E. A. Rubinstein (eds.) Television and Social Behavior. Washington, D.C.: National Institute of Mental Health 3.

NEWCOMB, T. M. (1953) "An approach to the study of communication acts." Psychological Rev. 60 (November): 393-404.

O'KEEFE, G. J. and H. T. SPETNAGEL (1972) "Patterns of college undergraduate usage of selected media." Department of Mass Communications, University of Denver.

PARSONS, T. (1955) "Family structure and the socialization of the child," in T. Parsons and R. F. Bales (eds.) Family, Socialization and Interaction Process. New York: Free Press.

PELZ, D. C. and R. A. LEW (1970) "Heise's causal model applied," pp. 28-37 in E. F. Borgatta (ed.) Sociological Methodology 1970. San Francisco: Jossey-Bass.

RILEY, M. W. and J. W. RILEY (1951) "A sociological approach to communication research." Public Opinion Q. 15 (Fall): 445-460.

ROBINSON, J. P. (1971a) "Toward defining the functions of television," pp. 568-603 in E. A. Rubinstein, G. A. Comstock, and J. P. Murray (eds.) Television and Social Behavior. Washington, D.C. National Institute of Mental Health 4.

——— (1971b) "Television's impact on everyday life: some cross-national evidence," pp. 410-431 in E. A. Rubinstein, G. A. Comstock, and J. P. Murray (eds.) Television and Social Behavior. Washington, D.C.: National Institute of Mental Health 4.

ROGERS, E. M. and D. K. BHOWMIK (1970-1971) "Homophily-heterophily: relational concepts for communication research." Public Opinion Q. 34 (Winter): 523-538.

RUBINSTEIN, E. A., G. A. COMSTOCK, and J. P. MURRAY (1971) Television and Social Behavior. Five volumes. Washington, D.C.: National Institute of Mental Health.

SAMUELSON, M., R. F. CARTER, and W. L. RUGGELS (1963) "Education, available time and use of the mass media." Journalism Q. 40 (Autumn): 491-496.

SCHEFF, T. J. (1967) "Toward a sociological model of consensus." American Sociological Rev. 32 (February): 32-46.

SCHRAMM, W., J. LYLE, and E. B. PARKER (1961) Television in the Lives of Our Children. Stanford, Calif.: Stanford University Press.

SEARS, D. and J. FREEDMAN (1967) "Selective exposure to information: a critical review." Public Opinion Q. 31 (Summer): 194-213.

SIGEL, R. (1965) "Assumptions about the learning of political values." The Annals of the American Academy of Political and Social Science 361: 1-9.

STEIN, A. H. and L. K. FRIEDRICH with F. VONDRACEK (1971) "Television content and young children's behavior," pp. 202-317 in J. P. Murray, E. A. Rubinstein, and G. A. Comstock (eds.) Television and Social Behavior. Washington, D.C.: National Institute of Mental Health 2.

STEINER, G. A. (1963) The People Look at Television. New York: Knopf.

STEPEHENSON, W. (1967) The Play Theory of Mass Communication. Chicago: University of Chicago Press.

STONE, V. A. and S. H. CHAFFEE (1970) "Family communication patterns and source-message orientation." Journalism Q. 47 (Summer): 239-246.

TANNENBAUM, P. H. (1963) "Public communication of science information." Science 140 (May 10): 579-583.

TROLDAHL, V. and D. E. COSTELLO (1966) "Media exposure patterns and interpersonal communication behavior of teenagers." Presented to Assn. for Education in Journalism, Iowa City, Iowa.

WAPLES, D., B. BERELSON, and F. BRADSHAW (1940) What Reading Does to People. Chicago: University of Chicago Press.

WARD, L. S. (1971) "Effects of television advertising on children and adolescents," pp. 432-451 in E. A. Rubinstein, G. A. Comstock, and J. P. Murray (eds.) Television and Social Behavior. Washington, D.C.: National Institute of Mental Health 4.

——— G. REALE, and D. LEVINSON (1971) "Children's perceptions, explanations, and judgments of television advertising: a further exploration," pp. 468-490 in E. A. Rubinstein, G. A. Comstock, and J. P. Murray (eds.) Television and Social Behavior. Washington, D.C.: National Institute of Mental Health 4.

WATT, J. and R. KRULL (1972) "An information theory measure of television content." Mass Communications Research Center, University of Wisconsin.

WEISS, W. (1971) "Mass communications." Annual Review of Psychology 22, 309-336.

WESTLEY, B. H. and M. S. MacLEAN (1957) "A conceptual model for communication research." Journalism Q. 34 (Winter): 31-38.

WILENSKY, H. L. (1964) "Mass society and mass culture." American Sociological Rev. 29 (April): 173-197.

WOLFE, K. and M. FISKE (1949) "The children talk about comics," pp. 3-50 in P. Lazarsfeld and F. Stanton (eds.) Communication Research 1948-1949. New York: Harper.

ZIGLER, E. and I. L. CHILD (1969) "Socialization," pp. 450-589 in G. Lindzey and E. Aronson (eds.) Handbook of Social Psychology. Reading, Mass.: Addison-Wesley.

Chapter 6

MASS COMMUNICATION IN POLITICAL CAMPAIGNS: INFORMATION, GRATIFICATION, AND PERSUASION

Maxwell E. McCombs

IN THE POPULAR VIEW mass communication exerts tremendous political influence. The ability of television, newspapers, and the other mass media to mold voters' minds and to significantly influence, even alter, the outcomes of elections is a widely ascribed power. Joe McGinnis' *The Selling of the President, 1968* was on the bestseller lists for weeks. His book especially attributes a decisive political role to television and to a relatively new kind of political/mass communication creature—the image-maker.

Although pioneer image merchants Whitaker and Baxter began in a pre-TV political age (Kelley, 1956), popular concern with image-making seems most strongly associated with television (Mendelsohn and Crespi, 1970; Chester, 1969; Hiebert et al., 1971; Fuchs and Rose, 1968; Rubin, 1967). It is ironic that at the same time television fascinates millions of Americans, it simultaneously engenders a number of suspicions. Foremost among these is the devious manipulation of the voting public.

Among behavioral scientists this jaundiced view of mass communication's role in politics dates even well before television. A benchmark study for both political behavior and mass communication research was the 1940 Erie County survey (Lazarsfeld et al., 1948). The central question probed during that presidential election campaign study in Ohio was the effect of mass communication—newspapers and radio in that day—on a voter's choice at the polls. Erie County was the first significant attempt to document the effects of the ubiquitous mass media on political affairs. Such effects were widely suspected even in 1940. Numerous observers have commented on the powerful influence of radio as Franklin D. Roosevelt used it for his "fireside" chats (Sharon, 1949; Becker, 1961). And the effects of fictitious radio images had been devastatingly demonstrated by Orson Welles' broadcast about the invasion from Mars, a broadcast that panicked hundreds of Americans on the night of October 30, 1938 (Cantril et al., 1940). In politics it was Adolf Hitler who gave radio the Orson Welles treatment for real (McLuhan, 1965: 262).

Similar suspicions about the manipulative effects of mass communication have sustained a long tradition of content analyses of newspaper political coverage (Stene, 1937; Millspaugh, 1949; Batlin, 1954; Kobre, 1953; Klein and Maccoby, 1954; Kelley, 1959; Stempel, 1961a, 1965, 1969) Becker and Fuchs, 1967; Repass and Chaffee, 1968; Bishop and Brown, 1968; Nollet, 1968; Rucker, 1960; Higbie, 1961; Westley et al., 1963; Hart, 1965). More recently this tradition has incorporated studies of television news content (Goralski, 1971; Lichty et al., 1965; Bartley, 1969; Harney and Stone, 1969; Efron, 1971; Topping and Lichty, 1971). These studies of "bias" typically compare the treatment of political candidates in the news, frequently noting the inequality of coverage devoted to Democrats and Republicans and the significant correlation between political endorsements and news coverage. However, unequal coverage in the news (the operational definition of bias in most of these content analyses) does not, per se, establish any behavioral effect or influence of mass communication. But where such an effect is assumed—as media influence on politics frequently has been—only the stimulus need be described. However, such single-variable descriptions are normative, not theoretical, studies.

WINNING CONVERTS

While public and some scientific opinion seems inclined to attribute sweeping political power to mass communication, empirical evidence gathered by journalists and behavioral scientists suggests a more circumspect approach. There are few documented instances of real political or ideological conversion. Paul's experience on the Damascus road was a true conversion, a spectacular change in deep-seated beliefs and attitudes. But even among the more diffuse political attitudes of twentieth-century Americans, the mass media can claim few such conversions. Only 3 percent of the respondents in the Elmira study of the 1948 presidential campaign shifted parties between August and October (Berelson et al., 1954: 23, Table 3). Even then it is not clear that these "conversions" can be attributed to the mass media.

Nor is there any significant evidence of a bandwagon effect (Carter, 1959) on election day. There have been assertions that television broadcasts of presidential election returns and projections from the eastern seaboard before polls closed in the West caused many voters either to shift to the winner or to stay home. So far the null hypothesis has prevailed (Fuchs, 1965, 1966; Mendelsohn, 1966; Lang and Lang, 1968b; Coffin and Tuchman, 1969; Tuchman and Coffin, 1971).

Reviewing the campaign performances of five "image makers," the *Washington Post* (1970) found an even split. Their efforts produced 13 winning candidates and 13 losers. Three decades of behavioral science also has concluded that mass communication effects few political conversions (Weiss, 1969). The benchmark Erie County study concluded that informal personal influence was far more decisive than radio or newspapers in shaping voting behavior. The second major voting study focusing on the impact of mass communication—Elmira, New York in 1948—again assigned mass media a secondary role in influencing political behavior. Conversion is not a significant function of the media. "It [mass communication] crystallizes and reinforces more than it converts" (Berelson et al., 1954: 248; also see Harrison, 1965: 156).

REINFORCEMENT AND CRYSTALLIZATION

Reinforcement means buttressing existing attitudes and opinions. The content of the mass media supply the evidence and perhaps social support to back up a position already taken by the voter. The overall attitude may become more intensely held, more polarized. Or the saliences of individual items in a liberal, conservative, pro-Democratic, or pro-Republican attitude cluster may shift as the voter casts about for his best evidence and best ego defenses. But the general position of the overall cluster on the attitude continuum remains largely unchanged.

On the other hand, crystallization refers to the evolution or learning of an attitude. In the extreme, this means acquisition of an attitude where none previously existed. More frequently it means strengthening and shaping some previously vague predilection. In any event, the mass media are cast more in the role of teaching and defining than of advocating, as is the case in conversion or reinforcement.

Partisan Predispositions

Since behavioral scientists commonly consider reinforcement and crystallization to be the primary outcomes of exposure to mass communication during political campaigns (Berelson and Steiner, 1964: ch. 13), each should be considered in some detail. One mediating variable determining which of these alternatives is the most likely response to mass communication is the *partisan predisposition* of the voter. If a voter approaches a political campaign undecided or as a neutral—either a true neutral who sees merit on both sides or indifferently neutral because he knows and/or cares little about the political questions at hand—then crystallization is the likely response, if any. (In many cases, of course, the neutral ends up as the nonvoter.)

This crystallization resulting from exposure to the mass media during political campaigns may, in turn, explain the increasing instability of partisan attitudes in recent presidential elections. More voters now split their ticket, supporting one party's candidate for President and the other party's candidate for governor or senator (DeVries and Torrance, 1972). And more voters vacillate between parties during the campaign (Converse, 1962). Converse explains this partisan instability—and, indirectly, the declining importance of party identification as a locator variable—in terms of information flow. It is the person with high political interest and strong partisan identification who makes the most use of mass communication during a political campaign (Lazarsfeld et al., 1948: 124; Greenberg, 1965; Becker and Preston, 1969). At the opposite end of the continuum—no exposure to mass communication—partisan stability also is high. But the overall relationship is curvilinear. Voters with minimal mass media exposure—most often to the widely available and easily used broadcast media—fluctuate rather widely in their ballot decisions, splitting their ballots far more often than zero or high media users and/or changing their minds during the campaign.

Voting and Ticket Splitting

A very different image of ticket splitting is presented by DeVries and Torrance. They describe the ticket splitter as a highly involved, well-informed voter, not the peripherally involved voter described by Converse. Part of the discrepancy may arise from focusing on two different kinds of political neutrals, voters with low partisan involvement; DeVries and Torrance seem to focus on the *true neutral* who sees strong merit and demerit in both major parties. If he votes, this neutrality cannot be maintained; so it is typically abandoned in favor of the Republican candidate for one office and the Democratic candidate for another office. The true neutral, above all, is a ticket splitter. On the other hand, Converse's data may consist largely of *indifferent neutrals,* voters with little involvement or partisan concern. Impelled primarily by a sense of civic duty, these voters may change their minds during the campaign and /or split their ballot on election day. Converse's data focus on the discrepancy between early voting intention and final vote, and on the correlation between party identification and final vote. In any event, the crystallization of attitudes resulting from the flow of information during the campaign—especially television news and newspaper articles—is crucial to these neutral voters' behavior at the polls.

While the partisan makes far heavier use of political communication channels than the voter with little or no identification with a political party (Greenberg, 1965; Lazarsfeld et al., 1948: 124), he also tends to use these channels selectively, to extract from the plethora of campaign messages more of those which reinforce his existing partisan orientation (Grupp, 1970; Lazarsfeld et al., 1948: 125). If the messages of a political campaign, then, convert few and mostly reinforce the partisans of each side, does this mean that the hundreds of millions of dollars spent on political communications during a presidential campaign—fortunes by the candidates and parties plus vast sums by the press to observe and report the campaign—are wasted dollars? No, not really.

While a presidential campaign in the United States, or a parliamentary election in Britain, really does not follow the model of a rational intellectual dialogue between voters and candidates (Graber, 1971), it is useful (Barabba, 1971). A political campaign does not succeed in mass conversion, but it must succeed in mustering out the party faithful to vote. To win, a political party must rally its followers and those latently predisposed to follow it (Nimmo, 1970).

Plus, it must win over a sizeable number of the vacillators and ticket-splitters (DeVries and Torrance, 1972). For the politician the campaign is the communication package devised to achieve this goal (Glaser, 1965). For the public the campaign provides a motivating force, a civic ritual—if not a source of information—for ratifying at least the general sweep of government activity (Campbell, 1960).

REINFORCEMENT AND SELECTIVE PERCEPTION

Quantitatively, reinforcement has been adjudged the dominant effect of political mass communication. And selective exposure and selective perception are the concepts commonly used to explain this outcome (Klapper, 1960; Froman and Skipper, 1962; Star and Hughes, 1950).

Selective exposure and selective perception refer to a pattern of human behavior—actually a series of patterns at different levels of behavior—that results in maximum congeniality between an individual's existing attitudes and the communication allowed into his life space.

This matching of communication input with existing attitudes may occur at the time of exposure: only congenial, supportive messages (or at least a preponderance of such messages) are attended to. Or attention is directed only toward supportive elements of the message.

At the level of perception and interpretation, messages may be cognitively manipulated to be supportive of existing attitudes. Or, across time, only supportive elements of the message may be recalled.

Implicit in these concepts of selective exposure and perception are the idea of motivation, that voters are actively *motivated* to attend to supportive messages. Conversely, this view suggests that voters also are motivated to avoid contradictory, nonsupportive political messages.

Typical of the support for at least the first portion of this idea—selective attention to supportive messages—is Schramm and Carter's (1959) study of a political telethon in the 1958 California gubernatorial election. Interviews with voters indicated that twice as many Republicans as Democrats (proportionately) had viewed the Republican candidate's telethon. More viewers watched the program in Republican homes than in Democrat homes, and the average

Republican viewer watched the program for about an hour longer than did the average Democratic viewer. Similarly, results from at least six studies of the Kennedy-Nixon debates in the 1960 presidential campaign indicate that individuals with a party affiliation or specific voting intention declared their own candidate the winner more often than they chose the opposition candidate (Katz and Feldman, 1962).

The concepts of selective exposure and selective perception are subsumed by the theory of cognitive dissonance. This middle-range theory (Festinger, 1957) asserts that the juxtaposition of two contradictory cognitions—beliefs, attitudes, facts, or whatever—creates dissonance. Because dissonance is psychologically uncomfortable, the existence of very much dissonance *motivates* the individual to reduce it, and seeking out reinforcing cognitions is one way. Also the perceived likelihood of dissonance will motivate individuals to avoid threatening, nonconcurring messages. Or, at least, so says the theory. But selective exposure and selective perception have been the Achilles heel of dissonance theory. While numerous predictions derived from the theory have strong empirical support, predictions of selective exposure and selective perception, especially avoidance of nonsupportive messages, frequently have not been borne out by the empirical studies (Brodbeck, 1956; Rosen, 1961; Feather, 1962; Sears, 1965; Freedman, 1965).

Furthermore, in considering selective exposure a careful distinction must be made between de facto selectivity and actual selective exposure. "The observation of an empirical correlation between attitudes and exposure has rarely been distinguished from an active psychological preference for supportive information . . . " (Sears and Freedman, 1967: 195). Close matches between attitudes and communication exposure patterns abound in the research literature (Berelson and Steiner, 1964: ch. 13; Stempel, 1961b). Documentation is much rarer for any functional relationship suggesting an active psychological defense mechanism.

LAW OF MINIMAL CONSEQUENCES

Selective exposure and selective perception are not the only factors believed to mediate the effect of mass communication on voters. There are numerous others, all tending to attenuate whatever political influence the mass media might have. First, the media themselves are not a monolith. While most of the mass media represent the "establishment" point of view, there is still diversity and disagreement within this frame of reference. There are multiple Republican and Democrat versions of establishment policy. Sometimes there is a third party version—George Wallace's American Independent Party in 1968. All this is reflected in the mass media. Political communication in the press and on television is a melange of information and views on our proper place in the political spectrum. In recent years, the underground press (Glessing, 1970) has made strides toward widening the political spectrum presented in the popular press. There always have been the specialized political media of the far right (Lipset, 1970; Wilcox, 1962).

Even when the media have approached a near monolithic position, however, numerous mediating social and personal factors have attenuated their impact. From 1932 to 1952 the proportion of daily newspapers endorsing GOP presidential candidates increased from half to two-thirds of the dailies taking stands. The Democrats' share of the endorsements dropped from 39 percent to 15 percent in the same period (Blumberg, 1954). Obviously, there is no positive correlation between the trend in newspaper endorsements and the outcome at the polls during those decades.

Beyond the fact that there are media expressing almost all political viewpoints—a situation which contributes to, even requires, some selective exposure and perception phenomena—other social factors must be considered. Mass communication does not take place in a social vacuum. Each member of the audience is not an isolated individual waiting for a hypodermic injection by the mass media. Individuals live their lives in social groups—families, neighbors, fellow workers, and formal associations (Lane and Sears, 1964: ch. 4). Beyond these membership groups are others which function as reference groups (Atkin, 1969). All these groups have social norms, some of them relevant to political questions. Elaborate networks of interpersonal communication—sometimes even mass communication—maintain these norms. Unlike mass communication, interpersonal communication enjoys a high level of feedback. Political messages flowing in interpersonal channels can quickly be adjusted to each recipient and often enjoy the bonus of group endorsement.

Summing up the immediate impact of mass communication—in all areas, not just politics—Klapper (1960: 8) said: "Mass communication *ordinarily* does not serve as a necessary and sufficient cause of audience effects, but rather functions among and through a nexus of mediating factors and influences." He emphasized "ordinarily" because there are exceptions: the most frequent being those situations in which the recipient has no established attitude and/or the communicator enjoys a monopoly, i.e., is the only source of information. Since voter decisions at the national level are greatly influenced by party identification, which has its origins in childhood, political mass communication seldom has this advantage. Campbell et al. (1960) view the voter's decision as the end point of a funnel that sweeps backward through time encompassing a vast behavioral repertoire. This nexus of mediating factors then becomes central to any description or explanation of the political impact of mass communication. Many times the presumed political effects of the mass media disappear when this full set of variables is brought under observation. The general failure of political behavior studies to support a *1984* theory of communication effects has led to the assertion of its antithesis, the *law of minimal consequences* (Lang and Lang, 1968a; Nimmo, 1970). Since election surveys on the political role of mass communication have focused on voter behavior when party identification and politically relevant social norms are at the height of their salience, it is not surprising that such small changes attributable to mass communication have been found.

This outcome also results from the set with which observers have approached mass communication and political behavior. Often expecting mass conversions, surveys looked for shifts from negative to positive attitudes, pro-Democrat to pro-Republican, liberal to conservative. Finding few such changes in attitudes, reinforcement and the law of minimal consequences were offered as conclusions. But this initial expectation led the research to emphasize one aspect of political attitudes—*affect,* the individual's feeling of being for or against a particular political element. While, as we shall see, research has examined voters' images and their store of information, study of the cognitive component of political attitudes has been relatively neglected.

COGNITIVE EFFECTS OF POLITICAL COMMUNICATION

Voters acquire vast amounts of information from the mass media. Although mass communication has been characterized as a classroom where the students continuously come and go—often with little motivation to attend closely to any of the political messages—it is, nevertheless, a powerful teacher. The Elmira study (Berelson et al., 1954) found that those with the greatest mass media exposure are most likely to know where the candidates stand on different issues. Trenaman and McQuail (1961) found the same thing in the 1959 General Election in England.

But again this effect of mass media must be considered in the context of numerous mediating variables. Exposure to political news in the newspaper and news magazines differs significantly among demographic groups. Education, income, and occupation, these especially, discriminate between the heavy and light users of print media. While these same demographic patterns hold for television—college graduates, for example, make greater regular use of TV for political information than do high school graduates—all demographic groups do make substantial use of TV during presidential campaigns (Wade and Schramm, 1969).

Numerous other variables also mediate this public affairs learning process. Those with the greatest initial amount of information (Berelson et al., 1954: ch. 11) and greater interest in politics (Becker and Preston, 1969) make greater use of the mass media during political campaigns. What is learned during a campaign may often reinforce or simply further detail what is already known or believed. Those who make their vote decision early in the campaign—during or after the conventions and before the fall campaign gets under way—make greater use of the media than the voter who enters the campaign period uncommitted or undecided (Lazarsfeld et al., 1948: 124; for a contradictory view see DeVries and Torrance, 1972).

But despite the assertions of the law of minimal consequences, a good deal of incidental learning does occur. Even the person with little interest in politics inadvertently acquires some political information (Converse, 1962). And everyone acquires a great deal of peripheral information. Brinton and McKown (1961) compared the level of knowledge among newspaper subscribers and nonsubscribers about an "irrelevant" political issue, fluoridation of the water supply in an adjacent county. (The newspaper was published in that adjacent county.) Despite its irrelevancy or low salience, subscribers had, largely inadvertently, acquired more information on the topic. But even here part of the difference may be attributable to the higher educational level of the subscribers. Intellectual curiosity among the more educated may lead them to actively seek out political information, even information on peripheral, "irrelevant" issues.

But the mass of voters probably accept uncritically whatever the media offer (Danielson and Adams, 1961). The rational impact of what the candidates say may be a minimal part of the sentiment they arouse in voters (Wyckoff, 1968: 212). Image-making does involve the transmission of information to voters. But its central concern is not rational dialogue, but rather manipulating the salience of attributes favorable to the candidate. Even straight news reporting seems more concerned with personal qualities than with substantive issues (Graber, 1971). The proper criticism for both is not their lack of truthfulness, but rather their at least occasional lack of relevance.

COGNITIVE CHANGE

Voters do learn from the media. New cognitions are acquired, especially around election time. Although the usual sequence of attitude change is cognitive change—affective change (Rosenberg 1960; Krugman, 1965), the cognitive inputs of the media do not show up immediately in affective attitude change (Carlssen, 1965). Since cognitive sets are characterized by consistency and stability (Maccoby and Maccoby, 1961) extreme cognitive change among large numbers of people is unlikely to turn up in surveys of political behavior where a variety of factors buttress each other. The cognitive aspects of political attitudes typically are built up slowly over time. Mass communication during a political campaign is more likely to further differentiate existing cognitions rather than effect basic change or reorganization.

Research on the affective and cognitive components of attitude (Rosenberg et al., 1960; Sherrod, 1969) indicates that the two are often inextricably bound together. The stability of the cognitive component—often sizeable cognitive sets able to absorb a number of inconsistencies without undergoing fundamental change—acts as a brake on affective attitude change. A shift in affect, if it does occur, is likely to be very gradual over time—what Berelson et al. (1954) termed *canalization*.

Cognitions and "Second-hand Reality"

A fruitful strategy, then, for understanding the significant political role of mass communication lies in the observation of long-term cognitive change and the media content contributing to changes in orientation toward parties, political leaders, and issues (Field and Anderson, 1969; Sarratt, 1960).

> In filtering, structuring, and spotlighting certain public activities, the media content is not confined to conveying what party spokesmen proclaim and what the candidates say. All news that bears on political activity and beliefs—and not only campaign speeches and campaign propaganda—is somehow relevant to the vote. Not only during the campaign *but also in the periods between,* the mass media provide perspectives, shape images of candidates and parties, help highlight issues around which a campaign will develop, and define the unique atmosphere and areas of sensitivity which mark any particular campaign [Lang and Lang, 1959: 226] ;

In short, the mass media create a second-hand reality, the pseudo-environment to which political behavior is a response. The plausibility of this view is reinforced by the fact that while the usual demographic predictors of political behavior—education, sex, party identification—do not change significantly in the American population from election to election, our own recent history witnesses the ebb and flow of party votes. The succession of Eisenhower/Stevenson, Kennedy/Nixon, Johnson/Goldwater, and Nixon/Humphrey elections do not demonstrate the stable voting patterns that the demographic analyses might suggest. In respect to the role of the media in shaping perspectives on a smaller scale, the Elmira study reports an interesting trend among voters not subject to the political norms of social groups. In a campaign where a clear Democratic trend developed, those voters unaware of their three closest friends' voting intentions were much more likely to move with this national trend than those in the population subject to the social controls of informal groups (Berelson et al., 1954: 138).

Descriptions of these individual and changing political perspectives, such as Lippmann's (1922) "pseudo-environment" and "pictures in our heads," are what behavioral scientists call the "cognitive world" of the individual (Kessel, 1965): not a photograph of reality, but rather a map of the world that is peculiar to each individual. No two individuals possess the same cognitive map of politics—or set of political cognitive images—because of the numerous combinations resulting from: (a) the physical and social environment; (b) personality, values, and goals; (c) previous experience, ranging from formal education to casual observations.

Striving for Meaning

Nevertheless, some common principles describing the organization of this cognitive world have emerged from behavioral research. These principles suggest the psychological fate of information contained in political mass communication. The central premise under which all these principles of cognitive behavior can be subsumed is that man lives in an organized world. As Bartlett (1932) remarked, "It is fitting to speak of every human cognitive reaction—perceiving, imagining, thinking, and reasoning—as an effort after meaning."

This effort after meaning has been conceptualized as a need for orientation (Maslow, 1963; Westley and Barrow, 1959). Each individual feels some need to be familiar with his surroundings. To satisfy this need, to fill in the missing details of a cognitive map, individuals engage in information-seeking behavior. Lippmann's pseudo-environment, Lang and Lang's second-hand reality are the end products of this information-seeking behavior, this striving for orientation.

Mueller (1970) investigated a Los Angeles junior college board election with 133 candidates where the usual orienting cues of party affiliation and incumbency were unavailable. But four cues, including endorsement by the *Los Angeles Times,* were used by voters for orientation. Other studies (McDowell, 1965; McCombs, 1967; Hooper, 1969) also have found editorial endorsements to be key sources of orientation for many voters. It often has been hypothesized (Pool, 1963; Gregg, 1965) that the influence of newspaper endorsements is greatest at the local level and progressively declines as we move to the state and national level. But the empirical evidence does not provide consistent support for this hypothesis (Blume and Lyons, 1968; Rarick, 1970). McCombs (1967) found greater influence on votes for governor and secretary of state than for local state senator and tax board member. For local offices party identification may be the only salient attribute of each candidate and therefore, may be sufficient orientation. But for a decision between incumbent Democrat Pat Brown and Republican challenger Ronald Reagan, or for a decision on a popular Democrat incumbent secretary of state, a newspaper endorsement may have had great utility in resolving cognitive conflict. Among all six ballot decisions studied by McCombs, the greatest impact occurred for a ballot measure involving taxation of insurance companies. For this kind of obscure, technical political issue the newspaper editorial may be the only real source of orientation available. To the extent there is a geographic pattern of editorial influence, it results from the varying number of orienting cues available for ballot decision.

An Agenda-Setting Function

These cues are not always as explicit as editorial endorsements. As the Langs (1959) suggested, the day-to-day selection and play of the news by the mass media may influence voters' frame of reference for viewing politics, especially the perceived ebb and flow of political issues. While attitudes about public issues lack the potency of party identification as a predictor (and presumably, determinant) of voting, they may be the crucial "swing" element in many elections. In 1968, for example, Vietnam and the law-and-order issue seemed to swing many Democrats away from Humphrey. The mass media by emphasizing some issues and downplaying or ignoring others may set the agenda in voters' minds for a political campaign.

This notion of an *agenda-setting function of the press* is succinctly summed up by Cohen (1963: 13): "It [the press] may not be successful much of the time in telling people what to think, but it is stunningly successful in telling its readers what to think *about.*" In other words, mass communication may have little effect on the affective component of attitudes, but it has a significant cumulative effect on the cognitive aspects of attitudes, especially their salience. As Arora and Lasswell (1969: 11) remark "the mere fact of publication begins to modify current perspectives . . . " Evidence of an agenda-setting function of the press and its relation to cognitive aspects of attitudes is found also in the Erie County study: "insofar as mass media of communication led to conversion at all, it was through a redefinition of the issues . . . issues about which people had previously thought very little or had been little concerned, took on a new importance as they were accented by campaign propaganda" (Lazarsfeld et al., 1948: 98). Berelson (1941) found that the mass media influence voters' judgments about the importance of issues and Atkin (1971) found similar effects on the exposure patterns of undecided voters.

Among undecided voters in a college community high correlations also were found between what voters cited as major issues and the attention of the mass media to those issues (McCombs and Shaw, 1972). Furthermore, while the three presidential candidates placed widely divergent emphasis upon different issues, the judgments of those voters seemed to reflect the composite of the mass media campaign coverage.

The data from that 1968 election study also were analyzed separately for each news medium. High agreement between voters and individual news media on the relative importance of the issues was found for seven of the nine news media studied. The exceptions were *Newsweek* and *Time* whose condensed formats allow less variance in the selection and display of political issues. Voters also were stratified according to their party preference. Comparisons then were made of two correlations: voter emphasis/total news coverage (the agenda-setting relationship); voter emphasis/congruent partisan news coverage (the selective perception relationship). Three groups of partisans and four news media yielded 12 comparisons. Of these, eight supported agenda-setting; three demonstrated selective perception; and one showed no difference. In brief, the preponderance of evidence supported the concept of an agenda-setting function of the press in politics. Additional evidence of agenda-setting is reported in a *Charlotte Observer* study of the 1970 election (November 8, 1970). Typical among those surveyed was a voter who said she was worried about "whether the economy is going to collapse, law and order, and the *things that come up in the papers.*"

Mass Media and Political Socialization

Evidence of agenda-setting among undecided voters suggests a similar study of cognitive effects among children and adolescents. Agenda-setting, especially considered in terms of long-term cognitive change, could be a fruitful approach to the study of political socialization. Generally, the mass media have been assigned a secondary role in political socialization. Yet, note Chaffee et al. (1970) empirical research has demonstrated little evidence of any direct socialization effect by parents and school (Jennings and Niemi, 1968a, 1968b; Langton and Jennings, 1968, 1969). Their review at least implies that the usual positive correlation between party preference of parents and children is not really a functional relationship. And the usual explanation for the secondary effect of mass communication—the law of minimal consequences with emphasis on selective perception and reinforcement—is suspect on several grounds. First, the socialization process is concerned with the *formation* of cognitions and opinions, so there are few predispositions to reinforce. Furthermore, the emphasis of communication scientists on attitude change has overlooked the fundamental question—creation of any opinion at all. From the point of view of socialization, the distribution of attitudes (or attitude change) along a positive/negative continuum is irrelevant.

A simple beginning for the study of political socialization is replication of the adult media use/cognitive change studies among children and adolescents. Schramm et al. (1961) found considerable public affairs TV viewing among adolescents, but not among younger children. However, this study, like others (e.g., McCombs, 1968a), really treats media use as a form of political participation. Such participation does increase with age, even through the undergraduate college years. McCombs (1968b) also found that this increased media usage resulted in greater political interest. Following the work on family communication patterns of McLeod and Chaffee (Chaffee et al., 1966; McLeod et al., 1967), Kline et al. (1970a, 1970b) found relationships between socialization patterns and radical political activism, mass media use, and public affairs knowledge.

A direct comparison of amount of media use and change in political cognitions was made among Wisconsin junior and senior high students during the 1968 presidential campaign (Chaffee et al., 1970). Their analysis indicated a significant link between public affairs media use and increased political knowledge. In fact, "high media use during the campaign predicted a large relative *future* gain in knowledge better than it explained current knowledge," a finding which Chaffee et al. interpret as indicating the causal role of mass communication in the political socialization process. They also report student ratings for sources of *information* and *personal opinion* on two specific current issues. On both, the junior and senior high students rated the mass media above parents, teachers, or friends. But when Hess and Torney (1967) asked fourth through eighth graders where they would search for advice about whom to vote for, if they could vote, the media were ranked far below parents. Overall, the patterns of pre-adult use of mass communication and their relationship to political cognitive development are only dimly outlined. The importance of filling in this area is underscored by Byrne's (1969) intriguing finding that children with primarily television (rather than newspaper) news exposure felt more favorably about the government and thought that the government is more effective. Since television use dominates among Negro, lower SES, and rural groups, these variables may mediate the relationships found by Byrne. If not spurious, his findings suggest a major political cognitive effect of mass communication. The implications for new communication technologies such as CATV (Smith, 1970; Slattery, 1971; Woods, 1971) which promise a plethora of public affairs communication are intriguing.

USES AND GRATIFICATIONS APPROACH

These demographic variables relevant to Byrne's findings are only a few of the variables describing the plethora of individual differences within mass communication audiences. A voter does not come to the mass media as a tabula rasa to be written upon. The potency of preexisting attitudes brought to the mass communication setting was among the first major findings of mass communication/ voter research. Social status and its numerous concomitants also are strongly related to mass communication exposure (Schramm and White, 1949). Even among individuals of similar demographic and ideological backgrounds, the motivations to attend to various media—and particular messages within them—and the gratifications obtained from exposure vary widely (McQuail, 1969).

"Seeking" vs. "Effects" Approaches

Because of all these factors antecedent to exposure, there has been increased emphasis by communication scientists in the past decade or so on a *uses-and-gratifications approach* to mass communication research (Katz, 1959; Klapper, 1963; Blumler, 1964). This work often is referred to as the study of *information-seeking behavior* (Troldahl, 1965). The contrast between this approach and the long dominant *communication effects* approach (Klapper, 1960; Higbie, 1961; Halloran, 1964; Schramm and Roberts, 1971) is easily illustrated with Schramm's (1954) structural model of communication. In that model the key elements are a Communicator, Message, and Audience with arrows indicating that the major flow is from Communicator to Message to Audience. With the question in mind, "What are the effects of mass communication?" this is a logical sequence for the model. But from the information-seeking, or uses-and-gratifications, point of view the arrow between Message and Audience should be reversed to indicate movement from Audience to Message. Rather than asking what mass communication does to people, we instead ask about what people do with mass communication. Descriptively, this is a more realistic depiction of mass communication where a plethora of messages abound, but only a relative few are selected by any individual. At the level of explanation, it suggests asking *why* certain attributes of individuals, such as the traditional locator variables level of education and sex, are related to communication behavior patterns.

Blumler and McQuail (1969) followed a uses-and-gratifications approach to locate variables mediating the political effects of television during the 1964 British general election. If television and the other mass media have no real political impact—as so many investigators have concluded—why, they asked, do voters follow the media at all? Is the seeking of reinforcement the only significant motive for using mass communication, as the concepts of selective perception and selective exposure emphasize? Analysis of the reasons given by British voters for watching party TV broadcasts yielded a typology of motivations, including reinforcement seeking and vote-guidance seeking. And the ratio of the reasons for viewing to reasons for *not* viewing yielded a useful measure of the strength of motivation. Both motivational variables recast the overall survey finding—often replicated—that both initial levels of knowledge and information gain are positively associated with level of exposure to mass communication. Among vote-guidance seekers, for example, information gain was generally high and quite independent of amount of exposure to mass communication.

In the Blumler and McQuail survey, exposure to political television could be assumed for most respondents because party broadcasts in Britain appear simultaneously on all channels. In such a situation individual voter motivations were crucial in mediating voter responses to the television stimulus. The effect of TV depended on what the voter brought to the TV situation. Much political communication takes place under such circumstances. The voter does not actively seek it out. He simply tolerates accidental or inadvertent exposure.

But under some circumstances the voter does seek out political communication, at least some kinds of voters seek out communication. In such cases, individual variables such as need for orientation or type of political motivation are the critical independent variables and communication exposure plays a mediating role (Vinyard and Sigel, 1971).

Sequence of Effects

A study of UCLA students' use of mass communication (McCombs, 1968b) illustrates a simple merger of the *effects* and *uses-and-gratifications* approaches. Preliminary analysis indicated strong, nonspurious relationships between year in college, exposure to mass communication, and political interest. Causal analysis subsequently indicated that the sequence was exactly in that order. Personal cognitive needs, indexed by year in college, led individuals to seek out or expose themselves to varying amounts of mass communication. This link is a simple illustration of information-seeking behavior. As exposure to mass communication increased, the effect was increased political interest. In the effects tradition of mass communication research, here was good evidence of a significant social effect resulting from mass communication. And this effect—a change in a personal characteristic—in turn generated a new pattern of information seeking, greater attention to news magazines and newspaper editorials.

Concern for mass communication audiences' uses-and-gratification also is central to the growing body of coorientation research (McLeod, 1971). This approach, building on Newcomb's (1953) A-B-X model, conceptualizes communication in *interpersonal* terms. This interpersonal exchange of information quite often functions as an independent variable, preceding any selection of messages from the mass media. When used in this manner, it represents the information-seeking tradition in communication research. But other studies examine coorientation processes as the dependent variable, a kind of effects question.

Communication scientists typically have fragmented the ongoing process of communication, most often looking at fragments involving communication effects. Consideration of personal characteristics and intrapersonal communication behavior has often been relegated to a concern with simple demographic locator or predictor variables. The distinction suggested by the existence of two broad approaches, or guiding points of view (communication effects/information-seeking behavior), is artificial and must be eliminated. We must consider what factors bring each individual to the mass media, what happens both while he is there and subsequently—intentionally and incidentally—and what contribution mass communication makes to the ultimate outcome.

To be fruitful this consolidated approach must be presented in theoretical terms. What has passed for mass communication theory has been, in reality, a loose collection of orientations toward data and a few empirical generalizations. While our knowledge has high empirical import, it has little of theoretical import to contribute to an explanation of mass communication and its role in political behavior. The few concepts that exist should be clarified and linked with new insights. Descriptions cast in primitive terms abound about *what there is,* but explanations of *why it is* are missing.

REFERENCES

ARORA, S. K. and H. D. LASSWELL (1969) Political Communication. Holt, Rinehart and Winston.

ATKIN, C. K. (1969) "The impact of political poll results on candidate and issue preferences." Journalism Q. 46 (Autumn): 515-521.

ATKIN, C. K. (1971) "How imbalanced campaign coverage affects audience exposure patterns." Journalism Q. 48 (Summer): 235-244.

BARABBA, V. P. (1971) "Practical use of political research." Paper presented to the American Association of Political Consultants.

BARTLETT, F. C. (1932) Remembering: An Experiment and Social Study. Cambridge, England.

BARTLEY, R. L. (1969) "Searching for that bias in TV news." Wall Street J. 174 (December 18, 1969): 14.

BATLIN, R. (1954) "San Francisco newspapers' campaign coverage: 1896-1952." Journalism Q. 31: 397-303.

BECKER, J. D. and I. L. PRESTON (1969) "Media usage and political activity." Journalism Q. 46 (Spring): 129-134.

BECKER, J. and D. FUCHS (1967) "How two major California dailies covered Reagan vs. Brown." Journalism Q. 44: 645-653.

BECKER, S. L. (1961) "Presidential purpose: the influence of broadcasting." Q. J. of Speech 47 (February): 10-18.

BERELSON, B. (1941) "Content emphasis, recognition and agreement: an analysis of the role of communications in determining public opinion." Ph.D. dissertation, University of Chicago.

——— and G. STEINER (1964) Human Behavior: An Inventory of Scientific Findings. New York, Harcourt, Brace and World.

BERELSON, B., P. LAZARSFELD, and W. McPHEE (1954) Voting. University of Chicago Press.

BISHOP, R. and R. BROWN (1968) "Michigan newspaper bias in the 1966 campaign." Journalism Q. 45: 337-338.

BLUMBERG, N. (1954) One Party Press? Lincoln: University of Nebraska Press.

BLUME, N. and S. LYONS (1968) "The monopoly newspaper in a local election: the Toledo Blade." Journalism Q. 45 (Summer): 286-292.

BLUMLER, J. G. (1964) "British television: the outlines of a research strategy." British J. of Sociology 15: 223-233.

――― and D. McQUAIL (1969) Television in Politics: Its Uses and Influence. Chicago: University of Chicago Press.

BRINTON, J. E. and L. N. McKOWN (1961) "Effects of newspaper reading on knowledge and attitude." Journalism Q. 38 (Spring): 187-195.

BRODBECK, M. (1956) "The role of small groups in mediating the effects of propaganda." J. of Abnormal and Social Psychology 52: 166-170.

BYRNE, G. C. (1969) "Mass media and political socialization of children and pre-adults." Journalism Q. 46: 140-142.

CAMPBELL, A. (1960) "Surge and decline: a study of electoral change." Public Opinion Q. 24: 397-418.

――― P. E. CONVERSE, W. E. MILLER, and D. E. STOKES (1960) The American Voter. New York: John Wiley.

CANTRIL, H., H. GAUDET, and H. HERTZOG (1940) The Invasion from Mars. Princeton, N.J.: Princeton University Press.

CARLSSEN, G. (1965) "Time and continuity in mass attitude change: the case of voting." Public Opinion Q. 29: 1-15.

CARTER, R. F. (1959) "Bandwagon and sandbagging effects: some measures of dissonance reduction." Public Opinion Q. 23: 279-287.

CHAFFEE, S. H., J. McLEOD, and D. B. WACKMAN (1966) "Family communication and political socialization." Paper presented to the Association for Education in Journalism, Iowa City, Iowa.

――― L. S. WARD, and L. P. TIPTON (1970) "Mass communication and political socialization." Journalism Q. 47 (Winter): 647-659.

CHESTER, E. W. (1969) Radio, Television and American Politics. New York: Sheed & Ward.

COFFIN, T. E., and S. TUCHMAN (1969) "The influence of television election broadcasts in a close election." Public Opinion Q. 33 (Fall): 445-446.

COHEN, B. C. (1963) The Press, the Public and Foreign Policy. Princeton, N.J.: Princeton University Press.

CONVERSE, P. (1962) "Information flow and the stability of partisan attitudes." Public Opinion Q. 26 (Winter): 578-599.

DANIELSON, W. A. and J. B. ADAMS (1961) "Completeness of press coverage in the 1960 campaign." Journalism Q. 38 (Autumn): 441-452.

DeVRIES, W. and V. L. TORRANCE (1972) The Ticket-Splitter. Grand Rapids, Michigan: W. B. Eerdmans.

EFRON, E. (1971) The News Twisters. Los Angeles: Nast Publishing.

FEATHER, N. T. (1962) "Cigarette smoking and lung cancer: a study of cognitive dissonance." Australian J. of Psychology 14: 55-64.

FESTINGER, L. (1957) A Theory of Cognitive Dissonance. Stanford: Stanford University Press.

FIELD, J. O. and R. E. ANDERSON (1969) "Ideology in the public's conceptualization of the 1964 election." Public Opinion Q. 33: 380-398.

FREEDMAN, J. L. (1965) "Preference for dissonant information." J. of Personality and Social Psychology 2: 287-289.

FROMAN, L. A. and J. K. SKIPPER, Jr. (1962) "Factors related to misperceiving party stands on issues." Public Opinion Q. 26: 265-271.

FUCHS, D. A. (1966) "Election day radio-television and Western voting." Public Opinion Q. 30 (Spring): 226-236.

――― (1965) "Election newscasts and their effects on Western voter turnout." Journalism Q. 42 (Winter): 22-28.

――― and E. D. ROSE (1968) "Reagan vs. Brown: a TV image playback." J. of Broadcasting 12 (Summer): 247-260.

GLASER, W. A. (1965) "Television and voting turnout." Public Opinion Q. 29: 71-86.

GLESSING, R. J. (1970) The Underground Press in America. Bloomington, Indiana: Indiana University Press.

GORALSKI, R. (1971) "Agnew and the networks revisited." Johns Hopkins Magazine 22 (Spring): 19-22.

GRABER, D. (1971a) "The press as opinion resource during the 1968 presidential campaign." Public Opinion Q. 35 (Summer): 168-182.

――― (1971b) "Press coverage patterns of campaign news: the 1968 presidential race." Journalism Q. 48: 502-512.

GREENBERG, B. S. (1965) "Voting intentions, election expectations and exposure to campaign information." J. of Communication 15 (September): 14-19.

GREGG, J. E. (1965) "Newspaper editorial endorsements and California elections 1948-1962." Journalism Q. 42 (Autumn): 532-538.

GRUPP, F. W., Jr. (1970) "Newscast avoidance among political activists." Public Opinion Q. 34 (Summer): 262-266.

HALLORAN, J. D. (1964) The Effects of Mass Communication: with Special Reference to Television. Leicester: Leicester University Press.

HARNEY, R. F. and V. A. STONE (1969) "Television and newspaper front page coverage of a major news story." J. of Broadcasting 13 (Spring): 181-188.

HARRISON, M. (1965) "Television and radio," ch. 10 in D. E. Butler and A. King, The British General Election of 1964. London: Macmillan.

HART, J. A. (1965) "Election campaign coverage in English and U.S. daily newspapers." Journalism Q. 42: 213-217.

HESS, R. D. and J. V. TORNEY (1967) The Development of Political Attitudes in Children. Chicago: Aldine.

HIGBIE, C. E. (1961) "1960 election studies show broad approach, new methods." Journalism Q. 38 (Spring): 164-170.

HIEBERT, R. E. et al. [eds.] (1971) Political Image Merchants: Strategy in New Politics. Washington, D.C.: Acropolis.

HOOPER, M. (1969) "Party and newspaper endorsement as predictor of voter choice." Journalism Q. 46 (Summer): 302-305.

JENNINGS, M. K. and R. NIEMI (1968a) "The transmissions of political values from parent to child." Amer. Pol. Sci. Rev. 62 (March): 169-184.

――― (1968b) "Patterns of political learning." Harvard Educational Rev. 38 (Summer): 443-467.

KATZ, E. (1959) "Mass communication research and the study of culture: an editorial note on a possible future for this journal." Studies in Public Communication 2: 1-6.

――― and J. J. FELDMAN (1962) "The Kennedy-Nixon debates: a survey of surveys," in S. Kraus (ed.) The Great Debates. Bloomington: Indiana University Press.

KELLEY, D. (1959) "Press coverage of two Michigan congressional elections." Journalism Q. 35: 447-449.

KELLEY, S. (1956) Professional Public Relations and Political Power. Baltimore: John Hopkins Press.

KESSEL, J. H. (1965) "Cognitive dimensions and political activity." Public Opinion Q. 29: 377-389.

KLAPPER, J. T. (1963) "Mass communication research: an old road surveyed." Public Opinion Q. 27: 515-527.

——— (1960) The Effects of Mass Communication. New York: Free Press.

KLEIN, M. and N. MACCOBY (1954) "Newspaper objectivity in the 1952 campaign." Journalism Q. 31: 285-296.

KLINE, F. G., D. K. DAVIS, R. OSTMAN, L. VUORI, N. CHRISTIANSEN, S. GUNARATNE, and L. KIVENS (1970a) "Family and peer socialization and autonomy related to mass media use, mass institution evaluation and radical political activism: a descriptive analysis." Paper presented to the International Association for Mass Communication Research, Constance, Germany.

KLINE, F. G., N. CHRISTIANSEN, D. K. DAVIS, R. OSTMAN, L. VUORI, and S. GUNARATNE (1970b) "Family communication patterns, family autonomy and peer autonomy: a theoretical model of socialization." Paper presented to the Research Committee on the Sociology of Mass Communication of the International Sociological Association, Varna, Bulgaria.

KOBRE, S. (1953) "How Florida dailies handled the 1952 presidential campaign." Journalism Q. 30: 163-169.

KRUGMAN, H. E. (1965) "The impact of television advertising: learning without involvement." Public Opinion Q. 29 (Fall): 349-356.

LANE, R. E. and D. O. SEARS (1964) Public Opinion. Englewood Cliffs, N.J.: Prentice-Hall.

LANG, K. and G. E. LANG (1959) The Mass Media and Voting. New York: Free Press.

——— (1968a) Politics and Television. Chicago: Quadrangle Books.

——— (1968b) Voting and Nonvoting. Waltham, Mass.: Blaisdell Publishing.

LANGTON, K. P. and M. K. JENNINGS (1969) "Acquisition of political values in the schools." Amer. Pol. Sci. Rev. 63 (March): 51-56.

——— (1968) "Political socialization and the high school civics curriculum." Amer. Pol. Sci. Rev. 62 (September): 852-867.

LAZARSFELD, P., B. BERELSON, and H. GAUDET (1948) The People's Choice. New York: Columbia University Press.

LICHTY, L. W., J. M. RIPLEY, and H. B. SUMMERS (1965) "Political programs on national television networks: 1960 and 1964." J. of Broadcasting 9 (Summer): 217-229.

LIPPMANN, W. (1922) Public Opinion. New York: Macmillan.

LIPSET, S. M. (1970) The Politics of Unreason: Right Wing Extremism in America 1790-1970. New York: Harper & Row.

MACCOBY, N. and E. E. MACCOBY (1961) "Homeostatic theory in attitude change." Public Opinion Q. 25 (Winter): 538-545.

MASLOW, A. H. (1963) "The need to know and the fear of knowing." J. of General Psychology 68: 11-24.

McCOMBS, M. E. (1968a) "Negro use of television and newspapers for political information." J. of Broadcasting 12 (Summer): 261-266.

––– (1968b) "Consequences of education: media use and political interest." Presented to the annual convention of the Association for Education in Journalism, August 1968.

––– (1967) "Editorial endorsement: a study of influence." Journalism Q. 44 (Autumn): 545-548.

––– and D. L. SHAW (1972) "The agenda-setting function of the mass media." Public Opinion Q. 36: 176-187.

McDOWELL, J. L. (1965) "The role of newspapers in Illinois at-large elections." Journalism Q. 42 (Spring): 281-284.

McLEOD, J. M. (1971) "Issues and strategies in coorientational research." Presented to the annual convention of the Association for Education in Journalism, August 1971.

––– S. H. CHAFFEE, and D. B. WACKMAN (1967) "Family communication: an updated report." Presented to the Association for Education in Journalism, Boulder, Colorado.

McLUHAN, M. (1965) Understanding Media. New York: McGraw-Hill.

McQUAIL, D. (1969) Toward a Sociology of Mass Communication. London: Collier Macmillan.

MENDELSOHN, H. (1966) "Election day broadcasts and terminal voting decisions." Public Opinion Q. 30: 212-225.

––– and I. CRESPI (1970) Polls, Television and the New Politics. Scranton: Chandler Publishing.

MILLSPAUGH, M. (1949) "Baltimore newspapers and the presidential election." Public Opinion Q. 13: 122-123.

MUELLER, J. E. (1970) "Choosing among 133 candidates." Public Opinion Q. 34 (Fall): 395-402.

NEWCOMB, T. M. (1953) "An approach to the study of communicative acts." Psych. Rev. 60: 393-404.

NIMMO, D. (1970) The Political Persuaders. Englewood, N.J.: Prentice-Hall.

NOLLET,M. (1968) "The Boston Globe in four presidential elections." Journalism Q. 45: 531-532.

POOL, I. D. (1963) "The effect of communication on voting behavior," ch. 10 in W. Schramm (ed.) The Science of Human Communication. Basic Books.

RARICK, G. R. (1970) "Political persuasion: the newspaper and the sexes." Journalism Q. 47 (Summer): 360-364.

REPASS, D. and S. CHAFFEE (1968) "Administrative vs. campaign coverage of two presidents in eight partisan dailies." Journalism Q. 45: 528-531.

ROSEN, S. (1961) "Post-decision affinity for incompatible information." J. of Abnormal and Social Psychology 63: 188-190.

ROSENBERG, M. J. et al. (1960) Attitude Organization and Change. New Haven: Yale University Press.

ROSENBERG, M. J. (1960) "An analysis of affective-cognitive consistency," ch. 2 in M. J. Rosenberg et al., Attitude Organization and Change. New Haven: Yale University Press.

RUBIN, B. (1967) Political Television. Belmont, Calif.: Wadsworth Publishing.

RUCKER, B. W. (1961) "News services' crowd reporting in the 1956 presidential campaign." Journalism Q. 37 (Spring): 195-198.

SARRATT, R. (1960) "Newspaper influence." American Editor 3 (January): 7-14.

SCHRAMM, W. (1954) "How communication works," pp. 3-26 in W. Schramm (ed.) The Process and Effects of Mass Communication. Urbana: University of Illinois Press.

――― and R. F. CARTER (1959) "Effectiveness of a political telethon." Public Opinion Q. 23: 121-126.

SCHRAMM, W., J. LYLE and E. PARKER (1961) Television in the Lives of our Children. Stanford: Stanford University Press.

SCHRAMM, W. and D. P. ROBERTS (1971) The Process and Effects of Mass Communication. Urbana: University of Illinois Press.

SCHRAMM, W. and D. M. WHITE (1949) "Age, education and economic status as factors in newspaper reading," pp. 438-450, in W. Schramm (ed.) Mass Communications. Urbana: University of Illinois Press.

SEARS, D. O. (1965) "Biased indoctrination and selectivity of exposure to new information." Sociometry 28: 363-376.

――― and J. L. FREEDMAN (1967) "Selective exposure to information: a critical review." Public Opinion Q. 31: 194-213.

SHARON, J. H. (1949) "The fireside chat." The FDR Collector. I (November): 3-20.

SHERROD, D. R. (1969) "A balance theory approach to candidate perception." American Association of Public Opinion Research, May, 1969. Lake George, New York.

SLATTERY, W. J. (1971) "Do you know what's going to happen to cable TV?" TV Guide 19 (April 3, 1971).

SMITH, R. L. (1970) "The wired nation." The Nation 210 (May 18): 582-606.

STAR, S. A. and H. M. HUGHES (1950) "Report on an educational campaign: the Cincinnati plan for the United Nations." Amer. J. of Sociology 55: 389-400.

STEMPEL, G. (1969) "The prestige press meets the third party challenge." Journalism Q. 46: 712-719.

――― (1965) "The prestige press in two presidential elections." Journalism Q. 42: 15-21.

――― (1961a) "The prestige press covers the 1960 presidential campaign." Journalism Q. 38: 157-163.

――― (1961b) "Selectivity in readership of political news." Public Opinion Q. 25 (Fall): 400-404.

STENE, E. (1937) "Newspapers in the campaign." Social Science 12: 213-215.

TOPPING, M. C. and L. W. LICHTY (1971) "Political programs on national television networks: 1968." J. of Broadcasting 15: 161-179.

TRENEMAN, J. and D. McQUAIL (1961) Television and the Political Image. London: Menthuen.

TROLDAHL, V. C. (1965) "Studies of consumption of mass media content." Journalism Q. 42 (Autumn): 596-603.

TUCHMAN, S. and T. E. COFFIN (1971) "The influence of election night television broadcasts in a close election." Public Opinion Q. 35 (Fall): 315-326.

VINYARD, D. and R. S. SIGEL (1971) "Newspapers and urban voters." Journalism Q. 48: 486-501.

WADE, S. and W. SCHRAMM (1969) "The mass media as sources of public affairs, science, and health knowledge." Public Opinion Q. 33: 197-209.

Washington Post (1970) "Image-makers and how they did." by Bernard Nossiter. Thursday, November 5: 1.

WEISS, W. (1969) "Effects of the mass media of communication," in G. Lindzey and E. Aronson (eds.) Handbook of Social Psychology. Reading, Mass.: Addison-Wesley.

WESTLEY, B. H. and L. C. BARROW, Jr. (1959) "An investigation of news seeking behavior." Journalism Q. 36 (Fall): 431-438.

WESTLEY, B. H., C. E. HIGBIE, T. BURKE, D. J. LIPPERT, L. MAURER, and V. A. STONE (1963) "The news magazines and the 1960 conventions." Journalism Q. 40 (Autumn): 525-532, 647.

WILCOX, W. (1962) "The press of the radical right: an exploratory analysis." Journalism Q. 39 (Spring): 152-160.

WOODS, W. C. (1971) "When the boob on the tube is you." Washington Post (April 30).

WYCJIFF, G. (1968) The Image Candidates: American Politics in the Age of Television. New York: Macmillan.

Chapter 7

THE COMMUNICATION ENVIRONMENT OF THE URBAN POOR

Brenda Dervin and Bradley S. Greenberg

INTRODUCTION

The social scientist often is caught running in an attempt to keep up with his society. When the "war on poverty" was joined in the 1960s, little empirical ammunition was available to guide the poverty worker. This was particularly true in the area of communication. While there was a large volume of research available on communication per se and on poverty per se, the intersection of the two was almost nil. Yet, one of the major "war cries" of the poverty practitioner was for evidence on which to plan action strategies.

By the early 1970s, the situation has improved somewhat. A growing body of literature focuses on poverty and communication jointly. The purpose of this chapter is to review that literature, assess it and posit directions for future work.[1] In all, some 4,000 different studies were examined to develop an overview of the communication environment of the urban poor. No more than 200 had some relevance to poverty-communication; only some 30 studies were directly related to the issue, and most of these were research products of the last four or five years.[2] The work available provides an adequate baseline picture of the communication behaviors of the poor and shows surprising agreement on findings.

Authors' Note: Preparation of this manuscript was facilitated by the British Broadcasting Corporation, London, during Professor Greenberg's sabbatical.

Let us place the recent emergence of a poverty-communication focus within the context of research on poverty as it has been conducted in the past decade.

Research on Defining "Poverty"

Prior to and during the early 1960s, a large and tedious volume of literature focused on defining the poor and their demographic characteristics. While some researchers still continue to belabor the general issue of defining poverty, most social scientists have come to accept a relativistic definition: the poor are those with low incomes. More specifically, the poor are that one-fifth of the nation's families living below income standards developed by the Office of Economic Opportunity.

What does poverty mean in terms of money? For a nonfarm family of four, the poverty income level in 1959 was just under $3,000, and in 1970, the figure was $3,800. The Office of Economic Opportunity estimates that 40 million people lived at or below such levels in 1959, and 26 million in 1970.

Using this relativistic definition of poverty, considerable literature agrees on a strongly supported capsule picture of the demographic context of poverty (e.g., Orshansky, 1965; U.S. Department of Labor, 1965). The urban poor are more likely than the nonpoor to be: (1) unskilled and unprepared for jobs; (2) low in education; (3) living in large, often extended families; (4) living in split families; (5) living in one-parent-only households, often matriarchal; (6) unemployed or employed in low-paying, hard-labor jobs; and (7) highly mobile. The individuals within this group called "poor" are of all racial and ethnic groups. However, blacks, Puerto Ricans and similar minority groups are more likely to be poor and, indeed, to be *poorer* on any available measures of poverty.

In this first stage of poverty research, communication received only incidental focus.

Research on Poverty Life Styles

When talking about the poor, both scientific and lay literature bandy about two key cliches—the "vicious cycle of poverty" and "the dysfunctional subculture of poverty." The second stage of poverty research during the early 1960s focused almost solely on documenting this cyclical nature of poverty. Briefly, researchers in this period suggested that the poor remain poor because of environmental and psychological factors which deter the possibility of escape and inhibit meaningful changes in their life style.

Some social scientists and much of the nonpoor public tended to attribute cause and effect to such findings. The poor remained poor because they were lazy. The poor lacked achievement. The poor emphasized family and friends over work. Increasingly, however, researchers began to acknowledge the problems of their own middle-class biases and the poverty life style was reinterpreted from a "vicious, dysfunctional trap" to a "functional response." [3]

The American poor more currently are portrayed as being poor in an affluent, middle-class society. The society assumes skill, literacy, motivation, education and information-seeking abilities. The cycle of poverty has received a second interpretation. In this reinterpretation the poor are seen as badly equipped to deal with a highly educated, affluent society. The society is poorly prepared to deal with its poor. In response, the poor have developed a subculture and psychological orientations which middle-class observers agree are dysfunctional to operation in the major society. The subculture emphasizes family, friendship and kin relationships. It is less achievement-oriented. It is, in many respects, a closed system. Yet, it appears to be a functional response to the realities of a life of poverty.

The major portion of the available poverty-communication research has this life-style emphasis. The typical methodology is to compare the communication behaviors of the poor to the nonpoor and then to interpret these behaviors within the context of the "poverty life style."

The research in this stage has been descriptive primarily. It has intended to fully describe the poverty life style and differentiate it from the middle-class life style. Built solely on field surveys, this research emphasizes statistical averages and statistical differences between the poor and nonpoor. Its weakness, of course, is that statistical portraits cloak many differences. Little of this research has differentiated between subgroups of the poor. In addition, while such enquiry has acknowledged poverty life styles as a response to a societal context, only recently have studies begun to focus on the society portion of the problem.

Research on the Total Society

Underlying most early work was an implicit assumption that if somehow the poor could be changed, poverty could be eliminated. A growing number of investigators (Rainwater, 1970a, 1970b; Miller, 1970; Pearl, 1969) are suggesting a shift in concentration to the social system and how that system must be altered. Thus, while we have learned that the poor lack achievement in the middle-class sense, researchers are beginning to ask what the society is doing to prevent achievement. Although communication scholars have demonstrated that the poor lack information on which to base decisions, they are beginning to ask whether the society prevents the poor from getting certain kinds of information.

It would be useful, if, at this point, we could synthesize the major theoretical strains in the poverty-communication area. However, the first interest of most studies has been to describe the unknown, to compare the poor to the nonpoor, and not to exceed greatly that level of explication. Little theory has yet come about, although that complaint is not confined to this area of communication research. Perhaps the material in this chapter can serve to evoke theoretical insights about poverty and communication.

The major portion of this chapter reviews and analyzes the work of the past decade on poverty-communication, with particular emphasis on adults. Some interesting areas are excluded for lack of space, e.g., communication during riots, analyses of media content, and others are omitted because they are dealt with comprehensively elsewhere, e.g., language and poverty.

In addition, this chapter includes original findings from a recent large-scale study of the communication behaviors of low-income black adults. The study, conducted by Greenberg, Dervin and Bowes consisted of interviews with 366 low-income black adults in Cleveland.[4] Data on the communication and information processing behaviors of that sample will be presented, in part. Much of the data presented throughout this review are comparative in the sense that findings are available for the poor and the nonpoor. Such comparisons are not available for the findings from this most recent study which dealt solely with low-income blacks.

THE MASS MEDIA

Mass Media Availability

Research workers agree on one point: while the poor may be poor in dollars, they are not poor in media access. Media levels are generally high across all sampled low-income groups (Allen, 1968; Block, 1970; Caplovitz, 1963; Greenberg and Dervin, 1970; Greenberg et al., 1970; Shosteck, 1969; Singer, 1968). A capsule picture of the media availability of low-income urban families as drawn from these studies suggests:

- 95 percent of low-income households have at least one TV set. Almost 40 percent own two or more sets. These percentages are very similar for both low-income and general population adults. Low-income household ownership of color TV sets, however, is lower than that of the general population—about 10 percent compared to 22 percent in one study. By the end of 1971, general population ownership of color sets was 40 percent.

- Almost 100 percent of the households have at least one radio with most having multiple sets. The average number of radios owned, however, is less than that of the general population.

- 50-75 percent of the households have at least one daily newspaper available regularly. In general the poor have less newspaper availability than the nonpoor. One study also found that low-income whites were significantly more likely than low-income blacks to have a daily newspaper available.

- Movie attendance is rare according to the few studies which have assessed this behavior. In one, 70 percent of the low-income adults last went to a movie over a month ago.

- At least 75 percent of the households own at least one phonograph with one study showing higher phonograph ownership among low-income blacks than low-income whites. Phonograph ownership by the poor is significantly less than that of the nonpoor.

- The average low-income black family has two black periodicals available regularly.

Some researchers have been surprised at these high media availability levels, particularly with such durable media products as TV sets, phonographs, and radios. Two researchers (Block, 1970; Frazier, 1965) inferred that these high ownership levels are a symptom of "conspicuous" or "compensatory consumption"—an attempt to compensate for other deprivations. Others (Caplovitz, 1963; Tussing, 1970) suggest that such consumption is a *necessity* in our highly media-oriented society.

Mass Media Exposure

Marshall McLuhan's "electronic village" (McLuhan, 1964) is, perhaps, the best descriptive term of the media environment of the poor. The media research all converges: the poor are heavy users of television and radio and, in comparison with the nonpoor, low users of magazines and newspapers. While the studies vary on absolute media use levels, this general picture of media use by the poor can be drawn. [5]

- Most low-income adults watch television from 4 to 6 hours a day. Low-income blacks watch more TV than low-income whites. One study indicated an average of 2.0 hours of TV viewing on a weekday for general population adults, 4.8 for low-income whites and 5.7 for low-income blacks. That study tapped TV viewing during winter and spring months in the midwest. Recent evidence shows an average of 2.9 hours viewing on a weekday for low-income blacks during the hottest part of July.

- At any given time of the day, the low-income population has a higher proportion of viewers than the general population. In fact, during some morning and afternoon hours when general population viewing ranges at around 5-10 percent, low-income viewing is at 25-40 percent.

- The poor listen to the radio as much or more than the general population with the average adult listening about two hours. Most evidence agrees on this level of radio use. One study found considerably higher radio usage with low-income black adults listening an average of 5½ hours on a weekday.

- The low-income population uses newspapers less than that general population and generally reads less of all print media. Low-income blacks make less use of daily newspapers than low-income whites. The specific newspaper use figures vary, although these generalizations hold regardless of usage level. As examples one researcher found that 40 percent of his low-income adult sample read less than one hour a week in any print medium. A recent study of low-income blacks found the average respondent scanned or read three sections of the daily newspaper every day.

- The poor read fewer magazines than the nonpoor. Non-magazine reader figures among the poor range from 10 percent in one study to 33 percent in another. Low-income blacks, however, show more use of magazines than low-income whites. This difference is accounted for by the reading of black periodicals.

- Low-income families are significantly higher users of phonographs than general population respondents (despite lower ownership of phonograph sets). For example, 59 percent of low-income adults used phonographs yesterday compared to 23 percent of general population adults. Low-income blacks reported significantly higher usage than low-income whites (71 percent compared to 46 percent).

- The average low-income adult spends almost one-half of a 16-hour waking day on electronic media compared to one-fourth a waking day for general population respondents.

The major force of these findings centers on the high use of the electronic media by the poor. The findings also pinpoint some essential differences in the media environments of low-income blacks and whites. Blacks use newspapers less but black periodicals and phonographs more.

Low-income blacks are going to specialized media to get subcultural materials which are not available to them in the majority media.

Reasons for Watching TV

Why does one person watch more TV than another? Given that the poor watch more TV, researchers are addressing this general question specifically to that subgroup.

Early (pre-poverty era) research tended to focus on alienation, anxiety, and self-images as possible predictors of greater television exposure. Most found no relationship. Some found the more alienated used TV more, others obtained the opposite.

When the studies turned their attention to the content of television viewing, there was more parsimony. A sizable set of studies found some basis for agreement.[6] The more under stress an individual (the more frustrated, the more fatalistic, the more isolated, the more alienated), the more likely he is to turn to media content which is high in fantasy orientation. Since the poor are higher on any of these measures, one reason for greater television use is identified—if we accept the premise that TV fare fills a high fantasy viewing function.

Meyersohn (1968) summarized previous approaches to the general issue of "Why more TV?" into two propositions:

- the less, the more theory which states that the fewer the resources an individual has and the more isolated he is, the more his viewing; and

- the less, the less theory which states that the fewer the resources an individual has and the more isolated he is, the less his viewing.

Using national sample data, he found that the first proposal fit best for middle-class respondents. However, for low-income respondents, both theories fit depending on what resources were used as the predictor of TV viewing. Respondents with less leisure time equipment (e.g., games) available to them, watched TV more. Respondents with less other mass media available to them, watched TV less. He concluded that one cannot make the general statement that the poor watch more TV because they lack resources.

Further explanation is offered by some recent work which looks not so much at personality and resource predictors of television viewing but at uses made of television. These studies generally agree that the poor use TV for different reasons than the nonpoor.[7] Results indicate the poor use TV for *stimulation* (because it is exciting) and as a *school of life* (to learn how to solve problems, to learn about people, to learn things not learned in school). The middle class, on the other hand, use TV more to overcome boredom. For children and teenagers, these three dimensions of TV usage order by race and class. Low-income blacks say that it is more exciting, more is learned, and there is less use for relief of boredom than for low-income whites. Middle-class respondents label it least exciting, least instructive, and more for relief (Greenberg and Dominick, 1969a, 1969b). While these last findings have not yet been replicated with adult respondents, a recent study asked a sample of 366 low-income black adults why "people watch TV". Results in Table 1 indicate that from 52 percent to 73 percent of the respondents agreed that "excitement" and "school of life" statements were reasons why people watch TV. In contrast, only 39 percent agreed that people watch TV because they "have nothing better to do."

Another aspect not much researched is the use of TV as a basis for post exposure social interaction. Bogart (1955) suggested that the media provide an impersonal means of developing bonds between people. Two recent studies (Greenberg and Dervin, 1970; Greenberg

TABLE 1

REASONS FOR WATCHING TV GIVEN BY CLEVELAND
LOW-INCOME BLACK ADULTS

People watch TV because . . .	Percentage of respondents who agreed with this item (n=366)
it's exciting	57
they can learn from the mistakes of others	69
it shows how other people solve the same problems they have	61
it shows what life is really like	52
it keeps their minds off other things	65
they can learn a lot	73
they have nothing better to do	39

et al., 1970) suggest that television content is a major topic of conversation among the poor. For example, 57 percent of a low-income black adult sample talked with others about TV two or more times a week with 37 percent indicating regular talk about soap operas and 23 percent regular talk about shows which feature black stars. While data are available on the poor respondent's perceptions of why he uses TV, no data are available on how talk about TV is used in actual social interactions. We do not know, for example, if talk about soap operas provides a bond between women in cross-racial communication situations, or in discussing domestic problems among same-race viewers. Nor are there comparable data on the use of talk about TV from nonpoor respondents.

Mass Media Content Preferences

One of the most active areas of attention in the poverty-communication focus has been the media content preferences of the poor. Particular emphasis has been placed on the viewing preferences of blacks as compared to whites. Much of this work is confounded by lack of adequate controls for economic status, varying use of sample controls, and differing variable operationalizations. However, from some 18 studies on this question, it is possible to extract certain generalizations. [8] They will be presented by medium.

Television

The most documented of the content-preference research areas, this issue is also the most contradictory. Given the higher overall viewing of the poor, a natural consequence is that for any one type of television content their viewing is higher than that of the general population. Thus, for example, 69 percent of the low-income adults in the Greenberg and Dervin (1970) study regularly watched five or more of the 12 top-rated shows compared with 42 percent of the general population. Because of overall higher low-income viewing, it is fruitless to try to make general statements on the order of "the poor watch more soap operas." The answer will always be "yes." The poor watch more soap operas and more of almost every entertainment content category.

More meaningful insights came, however, from answers to questions such as "what are your favorite TV programs." The data here suggest that the poor, particularly women (who, unfortunately, constitute a far too great proportion of most poverty study samples), name "soap operas" or "my stories" as their favorites. Also frequently named by both males and females are westerns, mysteries, and suspense dramas.[9]

The most recent evidence on favorite TV shows comes from our study of low-income black adults as summarized in Table 2.

Another meaningful question is whether the television preferences of the poor are the same or different from those of the general population. Most of the evidence on this question is confounded by lack of control for overall viewing. Greenberg and Dervin (1970) converted the proportion of low-income and general population viewers for the 12 top-rated TV shows of the season to ranks (thereby controlling for differential amounts of viewing). The correlation (Rho) between low-income and general population preferences was .03, indicating almost no agreement in those TV show preferences.

More attention has been focused on black versus white viewer program preferences. Unfortunately, many of these data are confounded by lack of control for the lower income of blacks. Thus, Carey (1966) found little correlation between black and white viewer program preferences. When income controls were introduced (Fletcher, 1969; Greenberg and Dervin, 1970), results were contradictory. Fletcher found little correlation between the program

TABLE 2

TYPES OF FAVORITE TV SHOWS NAMED BY CLEVELAND
LOW-INCOME BLACK ADULTS

Television show type	Percentage of respondents who named one or more favorite TV shows in this category[a] (n=366)
Mystery and suspense drama	57
Soap operas	46
Westerns	36
Situation comedies	36
News, information, and education	30
Audience participation (quiz) shows	16
Talk and variety shows	20
Musical shows	12
Feature films and movies	18
Science fiction	9
Sports	5
Adventure	4

a. Each respondent was asked to name all of his favorite TV shows. Only 3 percent of the respondents named seven or more shows. This analysis is derived from a content analysis of the first six shows named by all respondents. The content analysis scheme is based on the categorization of TV shows used by A. C. Nielson (1969). The average respondent named 4 favorite TV shows.

preferences of black and white children. Greenberg and Dervin, however, found a high and significant correlation between the program preferences of low-income black and low-income white adults.

From the entire group of 18 studies in this area come some indications of what might be the kinds of program preference differences of blacks and whites without an income control. The findings suggest that blacks like and view comedy and general variety shows less than whites. Blacks choose country music, middle-class romantic music shows (e.g., Lawrence Welk) and news less than whites. However, blacks prefer conflict drama shows, shows depicting the life of family units, and shows with a central hero without a mate. In addition, the most recent evidence (Greenberg et al., 1970) found that the four most popular shows for a sample of low-income black adults all featured a black actor or actress. *"Mod Squad"* and *"Julia"* were the top shows for those respondents.

Newspaper

Far fewer studies have focused on this question. The four available (Allen, 1968; Greenberg and Dervin, 1970; Greenberg et al., 1970; Lyle, 1967) generally agree that the breadth of low-income readership within a newspaper is low. Greenberg and Dervin, for example, found that only 17 percent of their adult, poor respondents reported reading "all" of the newspaper compared with 39 percent of the general population respondents. Top-rated sections of the newspaper for low-income readers included headlines, classified ads, and ads in general. In comparison with general population adults, the low-income adult respondents less frequently reported regular readership of the front page, comics, and sports. As with television content preferences, no correlation was found between general population and low-income newspaper section preferences. However, there was found a high correlation (as with TV preferences) between black and white low-income adult newspaper content preferences.

Radio

Five studies (Allen, 1968; Greenberg and Dominick, 1969b; Larson, 1968; Lyle, 1967; Sargent and Stempel, 1968) give information on radio content preferences. Generally, findings show that the preferred radio content is music, which is what radio mainly offers. Little has been done, yet, on use of radio stations directed to black audiences. Larson (1968) found that in his sample of Chicago adults, radio stations appealing to black audiences drew more black listeners than those appealing to mass audiences.

Magazines

Little attention has been focused on the content of magazines preferred by low-income readers. Again, most of the focus has been on black and white reader differences. Two semi-quantitative studies (Gerbner, 1958; Rainwater et al., 1959) suggest that among lower-income women, confessional or *True Story* type magazines are the most popular. This lead is supported by Allen (1968) who found three confessional magazines among the favorites of his black low-income adult sample.

In those studies focusing on blacks, the preferred magazines from the "establishment" are *Reader's Digest* (read by 80 percent of Detroit blacks according to Ingram, 1969), *Life,* and *Look.* Of the black magazines, *Ebony* is the top favorite, cited by 50 percent of both Lyle's (1967) and Allen's (1968) black samples. The most recent evidence from a low-income black sample (Greenberg et al., 1970) supports this finding. More than 58 percent of their respondents indicated they read *Ebony.* The Ingram study found more blacks reading *Ebony* than its "establishment" counterpart, *Life.* In addition, *Jet* was named by 30 percent of Lyle's Los Angeles sample and 48 percent of Greenberg's Cleveland sample as a magazine getting regular readership.

Allen (1968) and Ingram (1969) give the only evidence of actual content preferences within magazines. They found their low-income black respondents preferred reading about personalities, particularly in black magazines. Nonquantitative observations by other social scientists (e.g., Frazier, 1965) support this finding.

Perceptions of the Media

A growing number of studies have gone beyond a concern with the amount and content of viewership and have begun to look at perceptions of the media by the poor.

In one of the classic media research traditions, a number of studies have asked "which medium" is most credible? And, from the preferences of the poor they get a resounding and almost unanimous "TV" as the answer, no matter how or by whom the question is phrased. TV comes out on top as the most reliable medium, the most important, the most preferred for world news, and the most believable. As would be expected, the poor are much more favorable to TV than the nonpoor, who more often cite newspapers as their most credible medium. And, as would be predicted from the media trends cited earlier, low-income blacks are more favorable to television than low-income whites.[10]

These studies do show some interesting exceptions, however. When asked what is the preferred source for local news, most low-income respondents cited radio and television about equally (30 percent for each). Whereas 7 percent of the low-income whites cited people, 22 percent of the blacks made that their first choice.

Such findings as these suggest, as did the Kerner Commission Report (1968), that television does less to serve the needs of isolated individuals in our society. The poor (blacks in particular) must go to interpersonal and nonestablishment channels for a substantial portion of the local news they need or find interesting.

A number of studies have dealt with specific criticisms of the media made by the poor. These studies have dealt mainly with black perceptions of the media and, not surprisingly, find blacks critical. [11]

At one extreme, the Kerner Commission charged that ghetto blacks distrust the mass media, particularly the press, and see the media as instruments of the white power structure and the police. Most blacks (regardless of income) agree that the majority media do not give enough attention to blacks. In a recent study, about 25 percent of the low-income black adults sampled thought blacks were treated fairly on TV "most" or "all of the time," and a similar proportion said "rarely" or "never." The respondents reacted almost identically to newspaper treatment of blacks. Specific criticisms by the respondents were that the media featured too few blacks or featured blacks in "bad" images. In addition, the respondents saw the press as giving too much emphasis to ghetto crimes.

The two studies which have dealt with criticisms of the black print media (Ingram, 1969; Lyle, 1967) present an interesting paradox. Ingram found that while militant blacks charged that *Ebony* was aimed at middle-class blacks, poor black respondents said they liked reading about the glamor and accomplishments of blacks in *Ebony*. Lyle reported that the highest readers of the black newspaper (blacks living in the ghetto) saw themselves as less represented by the paper; they saw the black paper as covering news of more educated blacks.

"TV tells it like it is" fairly well sums up low-income respondent perceptions of the "reality" of TV content according to the findings of four studies (Greenberg and Dominick, 1969a, 1969b; Greenberg and Hanneman, 1970; Greenberg et al., 1970) which have explored a relatively untapped area of media behavior. Using a series of agree-disagree statements on the order of "The people I see on TV are like those I see in real life," results showed a consistent trend across three age levels—childhood, adolescence, and adulthood. Poor blacks saw TV as more real than poor whites. The poor, in general, saw TV as more real-to-life than the general population. In the most

TABLE 3

BELIEF IN REALITY AS PORTRAYED BY TV OF CLEVELAND
LOW-INCOME BLACK ADULTS

	Percentage of respondents who said this item was "true" (n=366)
Your favorite TV show tells about life the way it really is	50
The people in your favorite TV show are like people you meet in real life	63
The same things that happen on TV often happen to you in real life	60
Families on your favorite TV shows are pretty much like families you see in real life	63

recent study more than 50 percent of 366 low-income black respondents agreed with all four statements indicating that TV presents an accurate portrayal of reality. These are in Table 3.[12]

An extension of this work (Greenberg and Hanneman, 1970) makes an interesting intersection between actual changes in television presentation and treatment of blacks (using content analysis) and viewer perceptions of those changes. They found that in a recent viewing season, blacks were more likely than whites to view the five top-rated shows which featured black actors in central roles. However, they found no difference between the races in perceptions of the frequency of minority group appearance on television.

When they separated white viewers in terms of their degree of antagonism toward black militants, they found that the more antagonistic the whites, the more likely they were to watch shows without blacks as central characters, to see TV as fairer to minorities, and to see TV as less realistic in its portrayal of minority group members.

Such studies raise the general (and little-researched) issue of the correspondence between viewer perceptions of media content, media portrayal of reality, and descriptive data on "reality" itself. Singer (1969) asked the question when he reported that his sample of participants in the Detroit riot saw much more violence in television reports of the riot than content analysis suggested was actually in the TV coverage.

THE SOCIAL COMMUNICATION MATRIX

This section outlines the social matrix of the low-income community—the relationship of the low-income adult to the environment outside his family. This is the context of friends, neighbors, school, job, merchants, social welfare agencies, and the establishment. Much of the literature is confusing if not contradictory, particularly when attempts are made to mesh findings from different geographic regions. Nevertheless, we shall suggest, from these data, that the state of being poor makes that person's social communication world more alike than racial, ethnic, or regional characteristics make for differences. This section highlights the generalizations which appear to hold despite subgroup differences.

Peers and Friends: The Interpersonal Network

Energy in the low-income community is little focused on individual activities. Indeed, the very concept of individual achievement is somewhat meaningless since the poor typically see little or no possibility for individual gain or improvement. The important center of low-income life is the kinship and peer network and group life. Whatever the low-income person's racial or ethnic background, this generalization appears to hold.[13]

A number of researchers have found that visiting family and friends, gossiping, talking about neighborhood and family events are among the major activities in the low-income community. While contacts extend to employer, landlord, teacher, policeman, and so on, the kinship and peer contacts form the major (for some, the entire) portion of the low-income person's interpersonal ties. Within these informal limits, gregariousness is high.

The most comprehensive and most recent data on the nature of low-income interpersonal contacts comes from our study of 366 low-income black adults in Cleveland. An in-depth analysis of the characteristics of all interpersonal contacts made "yesterday" by these respondents supports the generalization of a tight kin-peer network in the ghetto. Table 4 summarizes these findings.

Of all interpersonal contacts "yesterday," 85 percent were with people in the peer-kinship network (family or friends). In addition, 93 percent of the contacts were black and 66 percent of the contacts took place in the respondents' homes. Only 18 percent of the topics talked about in these contacts were related to subjects other than home, family or friends.

Such findings suggest that the interpersonal contacts within the low-income community are highly homogeneous. Social scientists with a psychological bent have suggested that this strong emphasis on the kin-peer net is a means of raising self-esteem which has been deterred by lack of success in the major society. While individual

TABLE 4

DESCRIPTION OF PEOPLE TALKED TO YESTERDAY BY
SAMPLE OF CLEVELAND LOW-INCOME ADULTS

Average number of people talked to yesterday	3.46
Total contacts yesterday for entire sample (n=366)	1266
Total contacts on whom characteristic data were gathered[a]	1020
Percentage of contacts who	
lived outside respondent home	68
met with respondent in respondent's home	66
were of the opposite sex	19
were in the peer-kinship net (friends or family)	85
had jobs	38
were black	93
Analysis of topics of conversation	
Average topics talked about with each contact	1.32
Average number of topics talked about with all contacts	4.18
Percentage of different topics talked about by each respondent which were not related to home, family, friends[a]	18

a. Detailed background information was collected on only six of the contacts made by each respondent "yesterday." This procedure meant that 13 percent of the contacts "yesterday" were not analyzed.

b. In all, the 366 respondents talked about 111 different topics "yesterday." These topics were content analyzed into categories. The categories which were judged as not relating solely to home, family, and friends were: jobs and employment, crime, education, mass media, news, city and neighborhood problems, welfare, black unity, prejudice, race hatred, politics and government.

achievement may be the criterion for success in middle-class society, the low-income kinship and peer network is a strong mutual aid society where the criterion for success is not such achievement.

Despite the strength of this kinship and peer network, however, researchers agree on an underlying core of weakness. Ghetto life is such that emergencies are frequent and interpersonal mistrust is high. The idealized image of a tight-knit lower-class community may have applied to communities of several decades ago. Contemporary lower-class communities have high mobility caused by job layoffs, home repossession, and other frequent economic crises. Friendships have little depth or history and are uprooted frequently.

Unfortunately, the strength of the interpersonal network in the low-income community also provides the grounds for exploitation of the poor by outsiders. Caplovitz (1963) documented well how the seller of shoddy merchandise on high credit terms uses the strong interpersonal net to his advantage. Caplovitz also found some evidence suggesting that peddlers are passed from family member to family member and friend to friend.

The nature of the low-income interpersonal net, therefore, is pointed to by researchers as part of the poverty cycle. Lack of individual success means greater emphasis on group life. In turn, this means that the low-income person places less importance on individual achievement and has less opportunity to develop an expansive repertoire of role behaviors and more flexible social skills. It has been suggested that this lack of role flexibility leaves the low-income person unprepared for dealing in the primarily middle-class oriented job world (Gans, 1962; Henry, 1965; Roach and Gursslin, 1965).

Voluntary Organizations and Leadership

Beyond the informal kinship-peer system, the research agrees that low-income communities show little organization.[14] Participation in voluntary organizations is low, club-going is considered a middle-class and, often, snobbish activity. Little gain is seen to be had from participation. This generalization cuts across ethnic and racial groups.

Given minor participation in voluntary organizations, indigenous formal leadership is also weak. The poor have few bargaining agents.

Those that they do have often lack power within the major society. This seems particularly true of black communities (Clark, 1967; Frazier, 1965). Leaders, on the other hand, who gain influence in the major society do so at the cost of losing influence within the low-income community.

Unfortunately, virtually no research has been done on opinion leadership within U.S. low-income communities. As will be indicated later in the section on sources of information, most poor people get most of their information on most topics either from television or from family and friends.

Yet, the large body of opinion leadership research in other societies and in U.S. rural areas would suggest opinion leadership as a lucrative area for study. [15]

Despite the general picture presented above of low involvements and participation, recent results suggest a potential for involvement and leadership. Kurtz (1968) found a cluster of poor people actively serving a Spanish-American community with information for solving housing, health, and other problems. The characteristics of these "opinion leaders" were not disclosed. A recent nationwide study by O'Shea and Gray (1966) supported the general picture of low involvement for low-income adults. But, they found that 16 percent of their very lowest income respondents considered themselves leaders or active nonleaders in community activities, and 30 percent indicated they had been involved in some type of community activity such as signing petitions or collecting money. These data suggest a core of potential leadership. One study (Cloward and Jones, 1963) found that involvement did bring a payoff. Low-income parents in his study who were more active in the PTA expressed higher value for education but more dissatisfaction toward the actual practices of the schools and teachers. This dissatisfaction, the researchers suggested, might lead to involvement.

Another study compared the use of indigenous leaders in welfare programs to that of professionals (Grosser, 1966) and found that indigenous leaders were better able to predict the views of clients toward the current state of affairs in the community and the possibilities for improvement. Only 26 percent of the professionals got high prediction scores compared to 52 percent of the indigenous leaders. Interestingly, however, the indigenous leader responses were still closer to those of the professionals than they were to the clients.

That suggests the "opinion leaders wear out" notion expressed by two observers of black ghettos (Clark, 1966; Frazier, 1965) and often shown by classic opinion leadership research.

A key to community involvement for the poor seems to relate back to the strength of the family and peer group. While participation in nonfamily and establishment-connected organizations (labor unions, political parties, etc.) is low across all studies, participation in organizations based on the peer-family linkage is higher. Thus, the church and school organizations receive stronger support in low-income communities and, in particular, low-income black communities (Frazier, 1955; Gans, 1962; Greenberg et al., 1970; Kurtz, 1968). Forty percent of 366 Cleveland low-income black adults reported memberships in church groups, 30 percent in school organizations. These two types of organizations received highest membership mentions. Others were: unions, 25 percent; political groups, 20 percent; civil rights and community action groups, 18 percent; social groups, 11 percent; neighborhood groups, 10 percent; and sports groups, 6 percent.

Caretakers, Establishment, and Information Sources

In addition to the electronic media (the low-income person's major sources of information on the outside world), the low-income community is also serviced by a number of establishment representatives—"caretakers" as Gans (1962) called them. The brunt of the research evidence suggests that these caretakers (social workers, teachers, policemen, politicians) are underused and little trusted by low-income residents. [16] While middle-class respondents use professionals and the print media more often as their sources of information and help, the poor more often use interpersonal, in-ghetto contacts. The evidence also suggests that low-income blacks put even greater emphasis on these personal sources than low-income whites.

The most comprehensive evidence available on the use of information sources by the poor comes from our recent study of low-income black Cleveland adults. The use of sources for information was approached from two perspectives. The first asked respondents what sources they had used for help or information in any area in the past. The second asked respondents to name potential sources in ten hypothetical problem areas.

Responses as to general sources approached indicated higher reported usage of nonfamily and friends than prior research suggested. Table 5 shows that the most frequently used source type were lawyers or the legal aid society, mentioned by 64 percent of the 366 respondents. Relatives received the next highest mention (55 percent). All other source types were named by less than half the respondents. Teachers, for example, were reported to be used by 25 percent, civil rights leaders by 16 percent, social workers by 30 percent, and the public housing agency by 30 percent. There is, unfortunately, no such comprehensive evidence available on the middle-class for comparison purposes. These recent data, however, suggest that the gloomy picture of almost no establishment source use, as attested to by prior work, is not quite so prevalent.

More telling, perhaps, are the respondent answers to what sources they would go to for help or information in ten hypothetical problem areas. Tables 6 and 7 summarize the results. Across these ten problem areas, the typical respondent named only one source for each problem. Of the total sources named, 17 percent were in-ghetto sources (family, friends, or relatives), 28 percent were service organizations (nonprofit help organizations) or professionals, and 9

TABLE 5

USE OF SOURCES FOR HELP OR INFORMATION IN THE PAST BY
A SAMPLE OF CLEVELAND LOW-INCOME BLACK ADULTS

Sources	Percentage of respondents (n=366) who used sources at least a little in the past
Neighbors	40
Friends	28
Relatives not living in home	55
Pastors or preachers	31
Teachers	25
Civilrights or black leaders	16
Lawyers or legal aid society	64
Doctors	40
Public housing agency	21
Social worker/welfare dept.	30
Fellow employee	29
Public health/dental clinic	40

TABLE 6

SOURCES OF HELP OR INFORMATION NAMED IN TEN PROBLEM
AREAS BY CLEVELAND LOW-INCOME BLACK ADULTS

Problem area	Average number of sources named	Percentage of the total sources named who were. . . .[a]		
		in-ghetto network sources	service organ- zations and professionals	print media sources
Buying a TV set	1.23	16	1	6
Getting a car fixed	1.19	18	1	1
Finding a place to live	1.32	16	7	25
Finding a good place to buy groceries	1.43	10	0	28
Finding the best place to borrow money	1.30	38	16	1
Buying a stove	1.21	5	2	8
Finding a job	1.38	14	56	15
Finding a new doctor	1.21	42	52	6
Helping a friend who was picked up by police	1.55	11	73	0
Helping a family whose father is out of work	1.67	7	50	0
TOTAL ACROSS PROBLEMS	13.50	17	28	9

a. Percentages do not add to 100 because this analysis focused only on specific classes of responses. Omitted were answers designating commercial sellers as sources and all references to "I'd do it myself." See Table 7 for the former.

TABLE 7
MOST FREQUENTLY NAMED SOURCES OF HELP OR INFORMATION IN
TEN PROBLEM AREAS BY CLEVELAND LOW-INCOME BLACK ADULTS

Problem area	Sources named by 10% or more of the 366 respondents	Percentage of respondents who named this source
Buying a TV set	Store or salesman	72
Getting a car fixed	Garage or car dealer or service station	74
Finding a place to live	Realtor	47
	Newspaper	25
Finding a good place to buy groceries	Newspaper	31
	Grocery or supermarket	36
	Comparison shopping	12
Finding the best place to borrow money	Bank	31
	Friend or relative	29
	Finance company	10
Finding a job	Employment service	52
	Newspaper	11
Buying a stove	Store	78
Finding a new doctor	Friend or relative	38
	Hospital	32
	Medical association	12
Helping a friend who was picked up by police	Lawyer	66
	Councilman	14
	Friend or relative	14
Helping a family whose father is out of work	Give material help myself	72
	Welfare department	39

percent were print media sources. The remaining 46 percent of the sources named were commercial sellers or "I'd do it myself" responses.

An analysis of the sources named for specific problems provides some insights. For the six areas concerned with specific consumer behavior (buying a TV set, getting a car fixed, finding a place to live, finding a place to buy groceries, finding a place to borrow money, and buying a stove), the major source types named were commercial sellers, in-ghetto friends and neighbors, or "I'd do it myself," responses. For three of these problems—a place to live, borrow money and groceries—there were a substantial number of mentions given to the media or service organization sources. For finding a place to live, 25 percent mentioned the print media, for finding a place to buy groceries, 31 percent mentioned the print media. In both cases, newspapers were the chosen medium.

For the remaining four problem areas (finding a job, finding a doctor, helping a friend who was picked up by the police, and helping a family whose father is out of work) the most frequently mentioned source (50 percent to 80 percent) was a service or professional organization. Interestingly, each of these involved naming a very specific source: the employment service, hospitals or the medical association, lawyers or legal aid, and the welfare department.

Again, there are no comprehensive data available on the middle-class for comparison. These findings do suggest, however, that for crisis problems (such as finding a job or helping a friend picked up by the police), very specific establishment sources are well known and sought out.

On noncrisis problems (consumer buying), the major source type named are commercial sellers with the in-ghetto network also having an important role (see Table 7). Nonprofit service organizations receive very few mentions for these problem types

Perhaps, the major import of these findings is that in most problem areas, 50 percent or more of the respondents indicated they would use only commercial or in-ghetto sources or their own resources in problem-solving. This evidence agrees with findings from prior work. Mendelsohn (1968) found that 60 percent of his low-income respondents lacked information on where to get help for everyday problems. Block (1970) found that 60 percent of his respondents would not ask anyone for advice on where to buy a television set.

Much of the emphasis in recent poverty programs has been to reach clients on a fuller range of their life problems than only crisis issues. However, the interpretation of evidence suggests that a major reason for the low use of "establishment" and professional sources in the ghetto is the viewing of these sources with suspicion and hostility.

The poor often believe that professional assistance sources simply attempt to get their clients to adjust to the status quo (Clark, 1967).

The law, police, and government agencies are viewed as exploiters of the low-income community (Gans, 1962; Lewis, 1966; McIssac and Wilkinson, 1965; Kerner Commission, 1968). Welfare recipients in one study (McIssac and Wilkinson, 1965) had only a vague idea of the purpose of regular caseworker visits. The most usual reaction was that caseworkers visited in order to verify that the family was still eligible for welfare. The perception of the caseworker as a resource for problem-solving was rare. Dordick (Dordick et al., 1969) found that clients erroneously saw job-training centers only as employment agencies and not as possible sources of skill improvement help. The researchers suggested inadequate communication by the caretakers as the reason for these faulty perceptions.

Several researchers suggest that the caretaker system is inefficient.[17] These establishment agencies were developed by the middle class and are based on the premise of client self-help and motivation for improvement. Thus, the caretakers share a kind of colonialistic view towards their clients, judging them through middle-class values, approaching them through middle-class orientations. Gleanings from the literature, for example, suggest the caretakers assume their clients understand bureaucratic operation and work on middle-class time schedules. Few poverty programs have used advertising in order to reach their clients, assuming that the very existence of an available resource will bring people to that resource. Yet, evidence shows, the poor often do not know that caretaking agencies exist and have little if any available means for getting the information that would lead them to these resources.

Others present an even dimmer picture by suggesting that even those agencies established with the explicit objective of serving the poor often neglect those clients with the greatest need for services.

Thus, for example, Levin and Taube (1970) found that of 452 female public housing tenants, those tenants who were black, less educated, on welfare, or without male adults at home were less likely to obtain adequate housing services. These same tenants were also less knowledgeable about the bureaucratic power structure of the housing authority. Levin and Taube (among others, e.g. Sjoberg, Brymer, and Farris, 1966; Scott, 1967) suggest that bureaucratic service agencies are concerned primarily with self-maintenance. The problems of their hard-core clients are not easily solved. In order to maintain a record of successes, the agencies not only may ignore the most needy clients, they also may prevent those clients from obtaining information about the bureaucratic structure.

Some experimental caretaking programs have been launched although data on the success of such programs are not readily available. Birney (1968) reported on the success of job opportunity TV programs in four cities, finding generally low turn-out and response. Among the problems he uncovered were incapability of the resource agencies (state employment centers) to handle responses from the programs, inefficient job-referral procedures leading to failures to hire, bad timing of the TV programs, and middle-class TV formats. The most successful of the programs (in terms of response) combined entertainment with information-giving and were aired just before sports events on Saturday afternoons.

Another television information-giving experiment tested the use of different incentives to get the poor to watch a series of eight television programs giving information on everyday problems. Money proved to be the best incentive, the one used by 44 percent of the viewers. Interpersonal communication was used by 17 percent of the viewers and printed leaflets by 16 percent.

Communication and Development

Surprisingly, few have looked at the relationship between communication variables and development in United States urban settings. Yet, a large body of research on development in peasant societies confirms a strong relationship.[18] Modernization—the improvement of life conditions—is an interactive behavioral system in which improvement must occur simultaneously in a number of areas for progress to be made, the research suggests. Increased media use leads to increased vicarious participation in society. This indirect participation, in turn, leads to increased actual participation and more media use. Interpersonal communication also plays a major role in development. Most agree that the mass media are more important in creating awareness of possible societal changes while interpersonal communication is more important in persuasion and actual change. Many development efforts abroad are trying to make judicious use via television clubs and radio forums of combining both mass media and interpersonal channels.

But what role does communication play in the "modernization" of the U.S. urban poor?

The available evidence suggests an interesting paradox. For the urban poor in the U.S., communication—both media and interpersonal—may be dysfunctional to development. The one hard-data study available deals with the Appalachian poor (Donohew, 1967; Donohew and Singh, 1969) and finds the most isolated persons were the higher adopters of poverty program services. The mass media users were not high adopters. Indeed, while they showed higher aspirations than other poverty types, they also showed more social isolation and a greater sense of powerlessness.

This study concurs with leads from other social scientists.[19] These researchers give some hints that the high use of television (with its homogeneous, non-means-oriented content) and the high use of in-ghetto interpersonal ties (also homogeneous and nonachievement-oriented) leave the American urban poor in an information void.

Wade and Schramm (1969) suggest that television and radio are not the media in our society which impart understanding, new concepts, and interpretive ability to people. Rather, the print media do this task. Thus, they found general population respondents had more accurate information in a number of areas if they were print media users. Block (1970) confirms this by finding that his low-income respondents had more functional criteria for shopping (prices more important than convenience) if they were higher readers.

Thus, it appears, that given high TV viewing and high in-ghetto contacts as the main information sources, the resulting information may turn out to be little information. Several development theorists (Eisenstadt, 1955; Etzioni, 1969; Frey, 1963) term this situation an information imbalance.

Dervin explicitly asked about the relationship of the communication behaviors of the poor to their use of information ("information control") in solving problems. She (Dervin, 1971) posited that there are varying levels or types of information needed if an individual is to make better decisions in the "nitty-gritty" problem areas of modern society. These problem areas include consumer activities (buying goods and services), employing, education, and community action.

Taking the area of consumer credit as an example, it was posited that an individual needs five types of information in order to make a "better" decision on where to get credit:

(1) he needs to be aware of sources of information in the problem area;
(2) he needs to be aware of means of getting credit;
(3) he needs to be aware of criteria on which means could be evaluated;
(4) he needs data which allow him to use the criteria in evaluating means; and
(5) he needs to have information which allows him to implement the results of his decision-making.

Respondents were 366 low-income black adults. The relationship of four communication variables to these types or levels of information control were analyzed. The communication variables were: use and dependency on television; use and dependency on newspapers; gregariousness; and diversity of interpersonal contacts. The last variable tapped the extent to which the respondent belonged to different organizations, the extent to which the respondent's daily contacts showed divergence from the ghetto-norm, and his daily life took him outside the ghetto.

All four communication behaviors predicted awareness of sources of information and awareness of means to achieve outcomes. Respondents who were higher TV users, higher newspaper users, high in gregariousness, and high in diversity of contacts were all more lively to be aware of sources of information. High gregarious respondents were more aware of all types of sources—both in-ghetto and out, both expert and nonexpert, both professional and nonprofessional. Respondents who were either high TV or high newspaper users were more aware of professional, institutional, and media sources. Respondents who were high in interpersonal diversity also were more aware of professional sources.

At the more complex levels of information control, however, the picture changed somewhat. While gregariousness related to better control at the "awareness of source" level, at higher levels it related to less expert use of information in decision-making. More gregarious respondents, for example, used less expert criteria for evaluating means. At these more complex levels, television seemed to play no role, either functional or dysfunctional. High use of newspapers and diversity of contact related to more expert use of information.

Three major inferences come from these findings. First, while some research suggested that high television use was "dysfunctional" to the ghetto resident, these findings show TV use related to greater awareness of more expert sources.

Secondly, the findings posit that an "information mix" is at work. While all four communication variables relate to greater awareness of information sources, each variable predicts best those sources most relevant to that variable. Gregariousness predicts the use of in-ghetto sources; newspapers and television the use of institutional and media sources. This suggests the "information control" mix might necessarily involve some optimum combination of exposure to various information systems. Thirdly, the respondents who achieved the highest level of information control were those who were more diverse in their interpersonal contacts, who had more opportunity to make contacts *outside* the closed ghetto system. If verified in future work, these results should have great impact on the kinds of recommendations made for poverty programs by the communication researcher.

DIRECTIONS FOR FUTURE RESEARCH

The preceding review well documents the fact that there is now a sizeable body of evidence available describing the communication behaviors of the poor. It demonstrates that these behaviors differ from those of the middle class and that these behaviors may, indeed, be part of the cycle of poverty.

Certainly, theoretical frames are necessary before the research can be applied well to actual problems. And as yet, the cry from the practitioner for help in planning programs is still unanswered. Little of the research has focused on the application of findings to real-world cases.

In one sense, the poverty-communication research focus is ready for a "take-off." A good baseline core of descriptive data is available. What is needed now are well-thought-out theoretical and applied studies. In addition, research is needed which does not avoid or ignore the larger societal question of the effect of the nonpoor majority on the poor minority.

The number of researchable questions generated by this review is large. A brief attempt will be made in the remainder of this chapter to delineate a few of them.

Diffusion of Information

Over the past 15 years, mass communication researchers have generated a sizeable body of evidence on the diffusion of information process in the overall society. Much of this research has been tied to a middle-range theory on the diffusion of news. Yet, little research has focused on this issue as it applies to the low-income communities in the United States. Little is known about the diffusion of information either within the ghetto or between the major society and the ghetto. Spokesmen for the growing core of ghetto-run information agencies claim that the major society purposively tries to withhold information from ghetto residents. Little concrete evidence is available to support this challenge. Many question could be asked. Does the in-ghetto diffusion of news curve mirror that of the major society? For what type of news or information does it differ? What major-society news does not reach the ghetto? Who facilitates the flow of information into the ghetto? Who retards the flow? Is there a relationship between the operating assumptions of differing "caretaking agencies" working within the ghetto and the flow of information from that agency to ghetto residents?

Functions of the Mass Media

A classic question for the mass communication researcher has been "what are the functions of the mass media?" This question is particularly appropriate to the poverty-communication focus. Specific studies might focus on the increased attention being given in the media to poverty and racial issues. Does vicarious integration via television make actual integration seem more natural to now isolated whites? What are white perceptions of the new black "heroes" on television? Does white viewing of black TV heroes change white perceptions of real-life blacks? What do blacks think of the new black TV "heroes"? Are black heroes boosting black self-images and serving as role models? Would increased television surveillance of the environment (reporting on the problems of blacks) make whites more or less emphathic with the poor? Does increased information on the discontents of blacks make whites more or less fearful?

Studies might focus on questions relating to the informational content of the media as such information applies to everyday problems. What information in the media is applied by the poor to everyday problems? What happens when a high believer in TV reality receives information on problem-solving from TV which directly conflicts with information given by family and peers? Do both the poor and nonpoor adapt the modes of conflict resolution seen in TV drama to their own lives? What social values are picked up from the media? Do children and adolescents learn about family behavior and interaction that is foreign to them? To what extent are these models of interpersonal interaction applied to their own lives?

Development and Change

Implicitly, the goal of most poverty programs has been to allow the poor to achieve "better" life styles. This question has been the major focus of a large body of development-communication research in foreign countries. Yet, little of the research on poverty in the United States has focused on this question. While a great deal of evidence is available on the role of change agents in developing countries, almost none is available on change agents (e.g., social workers, community action workers, etc.) in the United States. Among the questions which might be asked are these. What strategies are used by change agents working in U.S. ghettos? How do the poor assess source credibility? Who are the innovators and opinion leaders in the ghetto? Does the diffusion of innovation model developed for peasant cultures in foreign countries and for agricultural innovations with farmers apply to the U.S. ghetto? Can communication strategies used in developing countries be applied in the United States? would tele-clubs work in the manner that radio forums worked overseas? What communication strategies merely raise motivation levels and which ones stimulate change?

Conclusion

In many senses, the poverty-communication focus is a vital test case for the communications researcher. Poverty is a real-world problem. The discontent of the poor and the loss of credibility in the caretaking system are real-world problems. The poverty-communication area is seminal for the researcher who is socially aware and ready to tackle theoretical questions which could well have direct application to a current social problem. This kind of attention by the communications researcher is long overdue for the problem will not go away.

NOTES

1. This chapter emerges from a six-year research project on communication and poverty conducted in the Department of Communication at Michigan State University. For readers who want a longer overview of the area, the bulk of the project output is in *Use of the Mass Media by the Urban Poor* (Greenberg and Dervin, 1970), and in 14 research monographs, some of which are available from that department.

2. References cited in this chapter include only the more relevant ones. For a more complete annotated bibliography, see Greenberg and Dervin (1970).

3. See, for example, Caplovits, 1963; Clark, 1967; Drake, 1965; Gans, 1962; Herzog, 1963; Irelan and Besner, 1965; Lewis, 1966; Roach and Gursslin, 1965; Tussing, 1970.

4. Readers interested in more complete findings from this comprehensive study are directed to Greenberg et al., 1970; Dervin, 1971; Bowes, 1971.

5. See for example, Allen, 1968; Block, 1970; Friedman, 1957; Gans, 1962; Greenberg and Dervin, 1970; Greenberg et al., 1970; Greenberg and Kumata, 1968; Keller, 1963; McCombs, 1968; Sargent and Stempel, 1968; Shosteck, 1969.

6. Anast, 1964; Hazard, 1967; Katz and Lazarsfeld, 1955; Maccoby, 1951; McLeod et al., 1966; Middleton, 1963; Pearlin, 1959; Riley and Riley, 1951; Sargent and Stempel, 1968; Schramm et al., 1961;

7. Cassata, 1968; Gerson, 1966; Greenberg et al., 1970; Greenberg and Dominick, 1969a, 1969b; Mendelsohn, 1968.

8. See, in particular, Allen, 1968; Block, 1970; Carey, 1966; Dervin, 1971; Fletcher, 1969; Gerbner, 1958; Greenberg and Dervin, 1970; Greenberg et al., 1970; Greenberg and Dominick, 1969a, 1969b; Ingram, 1969; Larson, 1968; Lyle, 1967; Mendelsohn, 1968; Runciman, 1960; Sargent and Stempel, 1968; Shosteck, 1969; Singer, 1968; Williams, 1969.

9. A caution is necessary in interpreting these findings. The general content preferences of the poor, given their overall high viewing, might simply reflect what the networks offer. If Westerns occupy more TV hours, Westerns may more frequently be cited as "favorite TV shows." This point needs to be studied.

10. Allen, 1968; Block, 1970; Greenberg and Dervin, 1970; Greenberg and Dominick, 1969a, 1969b; Lyle, 1967; Westley and Severin, 1964.

11. Columbia Broadcasting System, 1968; Feagin and Sheatsley, 1968; Greenberg and Hanneman, 1970; Greenberg et al., 1970; Lyle, 1967; Shosteck, 1969; Kerner Commission, 1968.

12. In one of the studies, the questions were worded negatively for a subsample of the respondents. It was concluded that the results reported were not a function of an acquiescence set by the respondents.

13. See, for example, Caplovitz, 1963; Cohen and Hodge, 1963; Chilman, 1966; Gans, 1962; Gottlieb, 1967; Henry, 1965; Irelan and Besner, 1965; Lewis, 1966; Liebow, 1967; Minuchin et al., 1967; Muir and Weinstein, 1962; Rainwater, Coleman, and Handel, 1959; Riesman, 1964.

14. Cohen and Hodge, 1963; Foskett, 1955; Gans, 1962; Irelan and Besner, 1965; Lewis, 1966; Mendelsohn, 1968; Rainwater, Coleman, and Handel, 1959; Singer, 1968.

15. Katz, 1957; Katz and Lazarsfeld, 1955; Lazarsfeld, Berleson, and Gaudet, 1948; Merton, 1957; Rogers, 1962.

16. See, for example, Allen, 1968; Block, 1970; Caplovitz, 1963; Donohew and Singh, 1969; Dordick et al., 1969; Greenberg and Dervin, 1967; Greenberg et al., 1970; Hibbarb, 1967; Mendelsohn, 1968; Singer, 1968; Shosteck, 1969; Tussing, 1970; Kerner Commission, 1968.

17. Cloward and Epstein, 1964; Cohen, 1967; Cohen and Hodge, 1963; Dordick et al., 1969; Epstein, 1968; Grossner, 1966; Irelan and Besner, 1965; Mellinger, 1956; Rein, 1965.

18. See, for example, Beltran, 1968; Berlo, 1968; Borra, 1970; Farace, 1968; Lerner, 1963; McNelly, 1968; Pye, 1963; Rogers, 1966; Rogers, 1962.

19. Block, 1970; Caplovitz, 1963; Chilman, 1965; Dordick et al., 1969; Lasswell, 1959; Lazarsfeld and Merton, 1949; Mendelsohn, 1968; Rotter, 1966; Wade and Schramm, 1969.

REFERENCES

ALLEN, T. H. (1968) "Mass media use patterns in a Negro ghetto." Journalism Q. 45 (Autumn): 525-531.
ANAST, P. (1964) "Self-image as a determinant of vicarious need." Psychology 1: 8-10.
BELTRANS, L. R. (1968) Radio Forums and Radio Schools in Rural Mass Education for National Development. East Lansing, Michigan: Michigan State University. (mimeo).
BERLO, D. (1968) Mass Communication and the Development of Nations. East Lansing, Michigan: The International Communications Institute, Michigan State University. (mimeo).
BIRNEY, J. (1968) "Opportunity line presentations across the nation." New York: Project Labor Market, New York University Graduate School of Business Administration. (mimeo).
BLOCK, C. E. (1970) "Communicating with the urban poor: an exploratory inquiry." Journalism Q. 47 (Spring): 3-11.

BOGART, L. (1955) "Adult talk about newspaper comics." Amer. J. of Sociology 61: 26-30.

BORRA, R. (1970) "Communication through television: UNESCO adult education experiments in France, Japan, and India." J. of Communication 20: 65-83.

BOWES, J. (1971) The Relationship of Information Control Behaviors to the Political Effectiveness of Low-Income Urban Black Residents. Ph.D. dissertation, Michigan State University.

CAPLOVITZ, D. (1963) The Poor Pay More. New York: Free Press.

CAREY, J. W. (1966) "Variations in Negro-white television preference." J. of Broadcasting 10: 199-211.

CASSATA, D. M. (1968) A Study of the Mass Media Habits of Denver's Tri-Ethnic Populations: An Ethnic Comparison. University of Denver. Master's thesis.

CHILMAN, U. S. (1966) Growing Up Poor. U.S. Department of Health, Education, and Welfare, Welfare Administration Publication No. 13, Washington, D.C.: Government Printing Office.

CLARK, K. B. (1967) Dark Ghetto: Dilemmas of Social Power. New York: Harper.

CLOWARD, R. A. and I. EPSTEIN (1964) "Private social welfare's disengagement from the poor: the case for family adjustment agencies," in A. Pearl and F. Riessman, Poverty and Low Income Cultures: Ten Views. National Institute for Mental Health, Washington, D.C.

CLOWARD, R. A. and J. A. JONES (1963) "Social class: educational attitudes and participation," pp. 190-216 in A. H. Passow, Education in Depressed Areas. New York: Teachers College Press, Columbia University.

COHEN, J. (1967) "A descriptive study of the availability and usability of social services in the south central area of Los Angeles." Los Angeles Riot Study MR-85: Institute of Government and Public Affairs, UCLA.

COHEN, K. and H. M. HODGE, Jr. (1963) "Characteristics of the lower blue collar class." J. of Social Problems 10 (Spring): 103-134.

CBS (1968) White and Negro Attitudes Towards Race Related Issues and Activities. Princeton, New Jersey: Public Opinion Research Corp.

DERVIN, B. (1971) Communication Behaviors as Related to Information Control Behaviors of Black Low-Income Adults. Ph.D. dissertation, Michigan State University.

DONOHEW, L. (1962) "Communication and readiness for change in Appalachia." Journalism Q. 44: 679-687.

DONOHEW, L. and B. K. SINGH (1969) "Communication and life styles in Appalachia." J. of Communication 19: 202-216.

DORDICK, H. S., L. G. CHESLER, S. I. FIRSTMAN, and R. BRETZ (1969) Telecommunications in Urban Development. Santa Monica, Calif.: RAND Corporation.

DRAKE, St. C. (1965) "The social and economic status of the Negro in the United States." Daedalus 94 (Fall): 771-814.

EINSESTADT, S. N. (1955) "Communication systems and social structure: An exploratory comparative study." Public Opinion Q. 19 (Summer): 153-167.

EPSTEIN, I. (1968) "Social workers and social action: attitudes towards social action strategies." Social Work 13: 101-108.

ETZIONI, A. (1969) "Toward a theory of guided societal change." Social Science Q. 50: 749-754.

FARACE, R. (1968) "Mass communication and national development: some insights from aggregate analysis," in D. Berlo, Mass Communication and the Development of Nations. East Lansing, Michigan: The International Communication Institute, Michigan State University, Chapter 5 (mimeo): V (1)-v(17).

FEAGIN, J. R. and P. B. SHEATSLEY (1968) "Ghetto resident appraisals of a riot." Public Opinion Q. 32 (Fall): 352-362.

FLETCHER, A. D. (1969) "Negro and white children's television program preferences." J. of Broadcasting 13: 359-366.

FOSKETT, J. M. (1955) "Social structure and social participation." Amer. Soc. Rev. 20: 431-438.

FRAZIER, E. F. (1965) Black Bourgeoisie. New York: Collier (original ed. in French, published in 1955).

FREY, F. (1963) "Political development, power, and communications in Turkey," ch. 17 in L. W. Pye, Communication and Political Development. Princeton: Princeton University Press.

FRIEDMAN, M. (1957) Television Program Preference and Televiewing Habits of Children as Related to Their Socio-Economic Status. Yeshiva University: Doctoral Thesis.

GANS, H. J. (1962) The Urban Villagers: Group and Class in the Life of Italian Americans. New York: Free Press.

GERBNER, G. (1958) "The social role of the confession magazine." Social Problems 6: 29-41.

GERSON, W. (1966) "Mass media socialization behavior: Negro-white differences." Social Forces 45: 40-50.

GOTTLIEB, D. (1964) "Goal aspirations and goal fulfillments: differences between deprived and affluent American adolescents." Amer. J. of Orthopsychiatry 34: 934-941.

GREENBERG, B. S. and B. DERVIN (1967) Communication and Related Behaviors of a Sample of Low-Income Urban Adults Compared with a General Population Sample. Project CUP, Report 1, Mass Communication Among the Urban Poor: Michigan State University.

——— with J. BOWES and J. DOMINICK (1970) Use of the Mass Media by the Urban Poor. New York: Praeger.

GREENBERG, B. S. and J. R. DOMINICK (1969a) "Racial and social class differences in teen-agers use of television." J. of Broadcasting 13 (Fall): 331-344.

——— (1969b) Television Behavior Among Disadvantaged Children. Project CUP, Report No. 9: Michigan State University.

GREENBERG, B. S. and G. J. HANNEMAN (1970) "Racial attitudes and the impact of TV blacks." Educational Broadcasting Rev. 4: 27-34.

GREENBERG, B. S. and H. KUMATA (1968) "National sample predictors of mass media use." Journalism Q. 45 (Winter): 641-646, 705.

GREENBERG, B., J. BOWES, and B. DERVIN (1970) Communication and Related Behaviors of a Sample of Cleveland Black Adults. Project CUP, Report No. 13, Communication Among the Urban Poor. Michigan State University.

GROSSER, R. (1966) "Local residents as mediators between middle class professional workers and lower class clients." Social Service Rev. 40: 56-63.

HAZARD, R. (1967) "Anxiety and preference for television fantasy." Journalism Q. 44 (Autumn): 461-469.

HENRY, J. (1965) "White people's time, colored people's time." Transaction 2.

HERZOG, E. (1963) "Some assumptions about the poor." Social Service Rev. 38: 389-402.

HIBBARD, W. F. (1967) Transportation: Role in the Urban Problem. Transportation Employment Project: Sacramento, Calif.

INGRAM, J. (1969) "What blacks read—and who they believe." Detroit Scope Magazine 1: 6-8.

IRELAN, L. and A. BESNER (1965) "Low income outlook on life." Welfare in Rev. 3: 13-19.

JONSTONE, J. and E. KATZ (1959) "Youth and popular music: a study in the sociology of taste." Amer. J. of Sociology 62: 563-568.

KATZ, E. (1957) "The two-step flow of communication: an up-to-date report on an hypothesis." Public Opinion Q. 21 (Spring): 61-78.

——— and P. F. LAZARSFELD (1955) Personal Influence. New York: Free Press.

KELLER, S. (1967) "The social world of the urban slum child: some early findings." Amer. J. of Orthopsychiatry 33: 823-831.

Kerner Commission (1968) Report of the National Advisory Commission on Civil Disorders. New York: Bantam.

KURTZ, R. (1968) "Gatekeepers: agents in acculturation." Rural Sociology 33: 63-70.

LARSON, C. M. (1968) "Racial brand usage and media exposure differentials," pp. 208-215 in K. Cox and B. Enis, A New Measure of Responsibility for Marketing. 1968 June Conference Proceedings, Series no. 27, American Marketing Association, Philadelphia.

LASSWELL, H. D. (1949) "The structure and function of communication in society," pp. 102-115 in W. Schramm, Mass Communications. Urbana: University of Illinois Press.

LAZARSFELD, P. F., B. BERELSON, and H. GAUDET (1948) The People's Choice. New York: Columbia University Press.

LERNER, D. (1963) "Toward a communication theory of modernization," in L. W. Pye, Communications and Political Development. Princeton, New Jersey: Princeton University Press.

——— (1958) The Passing of Traditional Society: Modernization in the Middle East. New York: Free Press.

LEVIN, J. and G. TAUBE (1970) "Bureaucracy and the socially handicapped: a study of lower-status tenants in public housing." Sociology and Social Research 54: 209-219.

LEWIS, O. (1966) "The culture of poverty." Scientific American 215: 19-25.

LIEBOW, E. (1967) Tally's Corner: A Study of Negro Streetcorner Men. Boston: Little, Brown.

LYLE, J. (1967) "The Negro and the news media," ch. 9, pp. 163-182 in J. Lyle, The News Megalopolis. San Francisco, California: Chandler.

MACCOBY, E. E. (1951) "Why children watch TV." Public Opinion Q. 15: 421-444.

McCOMBS, M. E. (1968) "Negro use of television and newspapers for political information, 1952-1964." J. of Broadcasting 13 (Summer): 261-266.

McISSAC, H. and H. WILKINSON (1965) "Clients talk about their caseworkers." Public Welfare 23: 147-154.

McLEOD, J., S. WARD, and K. TANCILL (1965-1966) "Alienation and uses of mass media." Public Opinion Q. 29 (Winter): 583-594.

McLUHAN, M. (1964) Understanding Media: The Extension of Man. New York: McGraw-Hill.

McNELLY, J. T. (1968) "Perspective on the role of mass communication in the development process," pp. 1-11 in D. Berlo, Mass Communication and the Development of Nations. East Lansing, Michigan: The International Communications Institute, Michigan State University. (mimeo)

MELLINGER, G. D. (1956) "Interpersonal trust as a factor in communication." J. of Abnormal and Social Psychology 52: 304-309.

MENDELSOHN, H. (1968) Operation Gap-Stop: A Study of the Application of Communication Techniques in Reaching the Unreachable Poor. University of Denver: Communication Arts Center.

MERTON, R. (1957) "Patterns of influence: local and cosmopolitan influentials," in R. Merton, Social Theory and Social Structure. New York: Free Press.

MIDDLETON, R. (1963) "Alienation, race, and education." Amer. Soc. Rev. 28: 973-977.

MILLER, S. M. (1970) "Poverty research in the seventies." J. of Social Issues 26: 169-173.

MINUCHIN, S., B. MONTALUO, B. GUERNEY, Jr., B. ROSMAN, and F. SCHUMER (1967) Families of the Slums: An exploration of Their Structure and Treatment. New York: Basic Books.

MUIR, C. E. and E. A. WEINSTEIN (1962) "The social debt: an investigation of lower class and middle class norms of social obligation." Amer. Soc. Rev. 27: 532-539.

MYERSOHN, R. (1968) "Television and the rest of leisure." Public Opinion Q. 32 (Spring): 102-112.

ORSHANSKY, M. (1965) "Who's who among the poor: a demographic view of poverty." Washington, D.C.: Social Security Bulletin: 3-33.

O'SHEA, R. M. and S. B. GRAY (1966) "Income and community participation." Welfare in Rev. 4: 10-13.

PEARL, A. (1970) "The poverty of psychology—an indictment," pp. 348-363 in V. L. Allen (ed.) Psychological Factors in Poverty. Chicago: Markham.

PEARLIN, L. I. (1959) "Social and personal stress and escape television viewing." Public Opinion Q. 23 (Summer): 255-259.

PYE, L. W. (1963) Communications and Political Development. Princeton, New Jersey: Princeton University Press.

RAINWATER, L. (1970a) "The problem of lower class culture." J. of Social Issues 26 (Spring): 133-148.

——— (1970b) "Neutralizing the disinherited: some psychological aspects of understanding the poor," ch. 1, pp. 1-27 in V. L. Allen (ed.) Psychological Factors in Poverty. Chicago: Markham.

——— R. P. COLEMAN, and G. HANDEL (1959) Workingman's Wife. New York: Oceana Publications.

REIN, M. (1965) "The strange case of Dependency." Transaction 2.

RIESMAN, F. (1964) "Low-income culture: the strengths of the poor." J. of Marriage and the Family 26: 417-421.

RILEY, M. W. and J. W. RILEY, Jr. (1951) "A sociological approach to mass communications research." Public Opinion Q. 15: 444-450.

ROACH, L. and O. R. GURSSLIN (1965) "The lower class, status frustration, and social disorganization." Social Forces 43: 501-510.

ROGERS, E. M. (1965-1966) "Mass media exposure and modernization among Columbian peasants." Public Opinion Q. 29 (Winter): 614-625.

——— (1962) Diffusion of Innovations. New York: Free Press.

ROTTER, J. B. (1966) "Generalized expectancies for internal versus external control of reinforcement." Psych. Monographs: General and Applied 80: 1-28.

RUNCIMAN, A. P. (1960) "A stratification study of television programme." Sociology and Social Research 44: 257-261.

SARGENT, W. and G. H. STEMPLE III (1968) "Poverty, alienation, and mass media use." Journalism Q. 45 (Summer): 324-326.

SCHRAMM, W., J. LYLE and E. PARKER (1961) Television in the Lives of our Children. Stanford: Stanford University Press.

SCOTT, R. A. (1967) "The selection of clients by social welfare agencies: the case of the blind." Social Problems 14 (Winter): 248-257.

SHOSTECK, H. (1969) "Some influences of television on civil unrest." J. of Broadcasting 23: 371-385.

SINGER, B. D. (1968) Television and the Riots. Department of Sociology, University of Western Ontario, London, Ontario. (mimeo)

SJOBERG, G., R. A. BRYMER and B. FARRIS (1966) "Bureaucracy and the lower class." Sociology and Social Research 50: 325-337.

SMYTHE, D. W. (1954) "Reality as presented by television." Public Opinion Q. 18: 143-156.

TUSSING, A. D. (1970) "Framework: economics of poverty." Presented to the American Council on Consumer Interest, Columbia, Missouri.

U.S. Department of Labor, Office of Policy Planning and Research (1965) The Negro Family: The Case of National Action. Washington, D.C.: Government Printing Office.

WADE, S. and W. SCHRAMM (1969) "The mass media as sources of public affairs, science, and health knowledge." Public Opinion Q. 33 (Summer): 197-209.

WESTLEY, B. H. and W. J. SEVERIN (1964) "Some correlates of media credibility." Journalism Q. 41 (Summer): 325-355.

WILLIAMS, F. (1969) "Social class differences in how children talk about television." J. of Broadcasting 13 (Fall): 345-367.

Chapter 8

MASS MEDIA PORTRAYAL—SEX AND VIOLENCE

Douglas A. Fuchs and Jack Lyle

INTRODUCTION

Sensation has always been a part of the mass media. This is unavoidable, given the functions of the media within society. These functions have been summarized by the political scientist Harold D. Lasswell (1948) as: surveillance of the environment, correlation of response to the environment and the transmission of culture from one generation to the next. And, as the pioneer American sociologist Charles Cooley (1956) observed, surveillance—or news—does often concentrate on the titillating aspects of the environmental events. To use his words, news is basically "organized gossip."

If we examine the earliest printed news reports in the English language, the broadsides and "newsbooks" issued in England in the seventeenth century—we find that they largely focused on events involving violence and sex. And very early in the development of the printed medium, entrepreneurs like Addison saw the opportunity to develop journals which would not only inform, but also entertain. So the *Spectator* came into being. In colonial Boston this example was followed by James Franklin, who began to publish a paper with the announced function of providing entertainment and diversion as well as news.

One of the fruits of the industrial revolution was the expansion of leisure time. This expansion could be measured both in terms of the amount of "free time" available and the number of persons enjoying it. And as leisure time and the leisure market has increased, the balance of mass media content seems to have shifted increasingly in favor of entertainment at the expense of "information."

The modern press, in effect, came into being with the establishment of the "penny papers" of the mid-nineteenth century. These papers were founded on the belief that there was a "mass audience" for papers among the working class as well as among the elite. To attract this audience, the editors of these penny papers shifted the emphasis from politics to the police beat, to stories of human interest, sensation and scandal. The culmination of this trend was the period of "yellow journalism" in the 1890s.

Book publishing as an industry in this country can be traced to the Civil War when federal government subsidized publication of cheap volumes. These were distributed to Union troops to help them fill the empty hours between battles. Mott (1962) states that this literally created a book-reading public. Most of these books were designed only to entertain. In the years after the war they were followed by the development of the "dime novel."

As technology developed and new media have appeared, each in turn has received its share of criticism and concern. Protest over movie content led the industry to establish the "Hays Office" in the early 1930s to administer a self-imposed production code intended to stem a rising flood of criticism of movie content, particularly concerning sex and violence. Psychiatrist Fredrick Wertham's *Seduction of the Innocent* spearheaded an attack on comic books in the 1950s and led to a code in that industry; the code is primarily concerned with violence. Orson Welles' radio production, "Invasion from Mars," based on the H. G. Wells novel, triggered panic in hundreds of thousands of listeners across the nation, actually sending many into physical flight. The incident not only illustrated the vitality of the medium but also provoked demands for control of the radio content. In the 1940s radio stations voluntarily banned various phonograph recordings from the air because of sexual allusions. Today there is concern about references to sex and drugs as well in the lyrics of many recorded songs.

These scattered examples are provided to underline a basic thesis: concern about violence and sex has paralleled the development of the mass media and has involved practically every medium.

Combining the recognized role of the media as purveyors of

information and entertainment with the nature of their human audience, this concern is perhaps as inevitable as the presence of violence and sex in media which are allowed to operate without authoritarian control or censorship. Media operating freely will inevitably bring into focus the nature of the human being and of society. And since we are only human, our reflex response is to protect ourselves and blame the media without asking whether we are attacking symptom or cause.

The media are not merely reflections of the society they serve. They have dynamic impact—if for no other reason than the fact that individuals do react to the reflection. Indeed, the basic economic support of much of the American media—newspapers, magazines, radio and television—is based on the premise that they do exercise a dynamic influence upon their audience. Surely advertisers assume that their messages will stimulate action.

These points are not intended to imply that concern for violence and sex in the media is neither legitimate nor necessary. They are intended as a warning against simplistic criticism which takes such concern out of the societal context. The media may have harmful effects upon individuals and perhaps even the whole society. But the media cannot be modified without modifying other elements of the society they serve.

Concern on these issues today has risen to what is perhaps the highest level in history. But this does not necessarily mean that these are higher levels of violent and pornographic content in the media now than in the past. It may only reflect the fact that the media are today more ubiquitous than at any time in the past. Whatever the cause, the concern has helped stimulate three massive research projects by the federal government including two national commissions, one on violence and one on obscenity. The reports of both commissions have dealt in depth with the mass media. Indeed, the Violence Commission in 1969 issued a separate volume containing the staff report on mass media and violence. More recently, in 1971, there has been the Report to the Surgeon General by the Scientific Advisory Committee on Television and Social Behavior.

VIOLENCE

Most concern and complaint about mass media violence today

centers on one medium: television. This follows a historical precedent. Such complaints historically have focused on the medium of the day and certainly television is the dominant medium at the present time.

It was suggested above that there is more widespread concern about media violence today than ever. It should not be surprising if this were so because the broadcast media—first radio and now television—have made greater and more rapid demands on our time than any other medium developed to date. They come directly into our homes and provide a highly specific portrayal of events, fictitious and real. Walter Lippmann (1922) wrote of the "pictures in our heads" which we have of the world beyond our immediate experience.

The audiovisual portrayal of that world on television has certainly had impact on both the scope and the content of those "pictures." The credibility of television news has been found to rest largely on the fact that people accept the television pictures as "experiencing" an event for themselves. Further, they develop a personal relationship with the apparently human reporter they see and hear, a relationship hard to achieve with reportage presented through impersonal printed type.

Further, the broadcast media have eliminated the time barrier. Through them we receive within our homes reports—even pictures—of events as they unfold.

Another reason why complaints concerning violence tend to focus upon television is the fact that television has largely displaced older media which traditionally have featured violent content. Schramm et al. (1961), for instance, report evidence suggesting that the advent of television reduced the use of detective and mystery magazines and comic books, as well as of movies. The radio detective series are no more. Cowboy movies, once the traditional Saturday movie fare for youngsters, have all but disappeared from the movie screens.

Horror movies, mystery magazines, comic books and murder mysteries all remain, but their audience does not begin to match the scope achieved by television. There is also evidence to suggest that those who do read "true detective" magazines and the "action" comics are also most likely to watch the more violent content provided by television.

For all these reasons, the bulk of research on mass media violence done in the past decade has concentrated on television. Hence the discussion which follows will put the major emphasis on that medium.

In looking at the work done on violence in the mass media, we will deal with three major areas: content studies, use studies and studies on effects.

Content

One of the basic questions raised by concern over mass media violence is: just how much violence is there in content offered by the media? How does the present level compare with that of the past?

Turning first to the historical comparison, Clark and Blankenburg (1971) have provided data for general magazine fiction, newspaper front pages, motion pictures and network television. Generally, the period covered is from 1925-1969, varying upon the availability of the specific medium. The picture which emerges is a complex one. They state that though critics at present may speak of the excess of violence in the media now, their evidence showed that the level is actually lower at present than it has been in the recent past.

But they add, that although there has been considerable fluctuation over time in the amount of violence in the various media, there are cycles and it appears that generally the high point of each cycle in the years studied has surpassed that of the preceding one. Assuming the pattern holds, the future will see another eventual upturn in the amount of violence.

In a chapter for the Mass Media Task Force report to the Violence Commission, Greenberg (1969) reviewed the research literature on violence in mass media content. He states that because of the diversity of media and methods, it is impossible to offer a concise answer to the question: how much violence is there in the media? He does state, though, that the overriding impression "is that there is a great deal of violent content available, at all times of the day, for all manner of intended audience" (p. 442). He goes on to say that the trend indicates an even greater availability of such content, that violence is usually presented as a means of achieving virtually any type of goal and, whether sanctioned or not, it is likely to be successful. He states that, as of 1968, violence was the predominant means for resolving conflict in television drama.

The difficulty with attempting an assessment of violence in the printed media is just the sheer number of book titles, magazines, newspapers and other periodicals published each year and the great diversity of their availability from one community to another.

Television, however, is a different matter. Although the total number of program hours presented each year is enormous, most are taken up by series which follow a general format from week to week. Further, most television production is concentrated in the offerings of the three major networks and their distribution is fairly uniform nationally. The most comprehensive analysis of television content is a series of studies by George Gerbner (1971). From 1967 to 1969, he videotaped the dramatic offerings of the three networks in the prime evening hours and Saturday morning for a one-week period in the fall. The programs have been analyzed for type and frequency of violent content.

He reports that violence prevailed in eight out of every ten plays for all three years. While he found the rate of violent events remained constant at about eight per hour over the three-year period, the violence did become less gory, less lethal and involved fewer persons per event. Significantly, he found that children's cartoon programs were among the highest in violent content. In this regard, his definition of violence as "the overt expression of physical force against others or self, or the compelling of action against one's will on pain of being hurt or killed," is vital in interpreting his conclusions.

Thus there is little doubt that there is a high level of "violence" available in all the mass media and particularly in television. But are simple measures of frequency or even the level of violence sufficient? Because this problem parallels that of "what is pornography?" we will delay taking it up until the end of the chapter.

But there is another, special problem of violence in mass media content. This problem stems from the fact that one function of the media—at least of television, radio, newspapers and some magazines—is to provide news. Inescapably, many news reports are concerned with violent events. Greenberg (Baker and Ball, 1969: 430-432) summarizes a series of newspaper content studies showing that crime and accident news accounted for well over 10 percent of news content, running as high as 40 percent in some papers. War and defense news generally ran as high or higher.

This pattern has occurred in newspapers for over a century since police reporting was introduced by the "penny papers." The *New York Times,* in fact, was established in part as a reaction to what some elements of mid-nineteenth-century New York society thought was an excessive attention to violence and sensation in the press. But even the *New York Times* deals with murder, muggings, rape, and war. While some may admire the *Christian Science Monitor* for its policy of ignoring crime news, we must also ask whether or not a general circulation daily paper which followed the same policy would be fulfilling its intended function. Would the environmental surveillance provided under such a policy aid the paper's readers in adjusting to their social surroundings?

The same situation applies to television news, perhaps even more strongly since this medium has the potential for showing violent events—and their results—in far more graphic detail. It is not without significance that Israel and Robinson (1971) report from a national sample of adults that most complaints concerning violence on television focused on the content of television news, not the entertainment programs. And it is worth noting that various social commentators have suggested that the portrayal of the carnage of war on television screens in their own living rooms—something which has been possible for the first time during the Indochina conflict—has played a large role in stimulating public dissatisfaction with the United States' involvement in Vietnam.

But the fact remains that stories of violence may be newsworthy and are popular. In a national sample of adults, Haskins (1969) found that, generally, the more violence in the item, the higher the average reader interest in the item.

Having acknowledged that television and the other media do offer the public a considerable variety of violent content, the next question is: to what extent does the public avail itself of this offering?

Again we have problems in attempting to deal with some media. For instance, direct attendance figures for individual movies are seldom made public, although attendance revenues are reported in the trade journals. In the case of books, the largest share of violent content is carried by paperbacks and sales figures for individual titles are hard to come by. The same is true for comic books. Some circulation figures are available for mystery and detective magazines;

none stands among circulation leaders. With books, comic books and magazines, there is a further problem. To make a realistic assessment of the impact of these media, one needs to know the amount of duplication of content between titles. There is little firm evidence on this, but it does appear that there is considerable overlap both between titles in a given medium and between the media themselves.

With television, however, we have better data. Of particular interest is a study by Greenberg and Gordon (1971). They had newspaper television critics and a sample of nonexpert adults rate network programs on violent content. They found a general consensus between the critics and the public on the twenty most violent programs for the 1970 season. These were:

Mod Squad
Mannix
Mission Impossible
Hawaii Five-O
It Takes a Thief
The FBI
Gunsmoke
High Chaparral
Dragnet
Ironside

Bonanza
The Virginian
The Name of the Game
Land of the Giants
Lancer
Death Valley Days
The Bold Ones
Then Came Bronson
Daniel Boone
Paris 7000.

The listing here is in the order of violence according to the general public. Whereas seven of the top ten still survived in the 1971 season, only three of the next ten were still in the network schedules.

Nielsen ratings show that in the 1970 season Gunsmoke, Ironside, Hawaii Five-O, Bonanza and Mannix scored in the top twenty programs in at least one report. In the early 1971 ratings, Gunsmoke and Mannix were still in the top ten. It appears beyond dispute that in any given week the majority of the American public will watch at least some television violence. Further, this audience will include a large number of youngsters all the way down to elementary school age. For instance, Lyle and Hoffman report that three of Greenberg and Gordon's most violent programs were among the most viewed programs for sixth graders, nine were among those most viewed by tenth graders. And in a small group of black five-year-olds, Murray (1971) found that the one show seen by the most youngsters was Mod Squad.

There is considerable agreement over a number of studies that there is a category of "violence viewers," a group which watches considerably more of the violent programs than the majority of the population. Israel, for instance, reports that in a national sample of adults, 12 percent of the men and 11 percent of the women watched more than eight-and-a-half hours of "most violent" programs during a two-week period. These persons constituted one-third of the audience for all the violent programs despite the fact that they represented only one-tenth of the sample.

In analyzing these groups, Israel reports that men generally watch more violence than do women. Further, both his data and that of several other studies done under the sponsorship of the Surgeon General's Scientific Advisory Committee for Television and Social Behavior (a research group conceived in 1969 to supply policy decision-making information to Senator Pastore's Sub-Committee on Communications) provide persuasive indications that those with little education, those who are poor and disadvantaged, generally are above the norm in the amount of violence viewed on television (see Volume 5 of the series published in 1972 by the Government Printing Office). Perhaps most disturbing is the pattern of findings that viewing of violent programs is particularly high among those who have had a high rate of personal involvement with violent behavior.

Effects

This brings us to the question of cause and effects. All the findings reported above are of a correlational nature. While they have found viewing of violent programs to be strongly related to reports of personal experiences with violence, they cannot be used as evidence that either of these causes the other.

Does violence on television cause violent behavior on the part of viewers? This is the question raised by large numbers of the public, particularly parents. It is understandable that those expressing the concern are confused and perplexed by the answers they are given. The situation itself is complex as are the conflicting interests that have led to conflicting methods, results and interpretations (for a comprehensive review of the literature cited below, see Liebert, 1971).

One of the major problems with the "evidence" supporting the thesis that violence causes violence is that it has been accumulated primarily through laboratory studies. There is now an accumulation of over a decade of such experimentation, stemming primarily from the efforts of Albert Bandura and Leonard Berkowitz, their students and colleagues. Painstakingly, they have pursued a careful course of testing various combinations of stimuli and conditions.

Bandura's work is perhaps the most widely publicized, particularly those studies involving "Bobo dolls," inflated plastic clown figures which can be used as punching bags.

The typical paradigm for these studies involves children in a nursery-like setting. The experimental stimuli consist of film or television content shown on a television screen. Some contents show violent behavior toward an object-the Bobo doll, or real persons-some do not. Subsequently the subjects are placed in a play situation with a number of toys (including a Bobo doll) and in some cases experimentally frustrated. The dependent measure is aggressive behavior by the child in the post-stimulus situation, particularly behavior modelled on the television content.

Results generally have supported the hypotheses that children learn specific aggressive behavior from seeing it performed in the experimental stimulus, and that this behavior will be evoked under conditions of frustration.

Berkowitz has worked with older youngsters and young adults. The experimental stimuli usually consist of violent and nonviolent film sequences. Subjects are then asked to perform acts of puzzle solving or the like in cooperation with an unseen (and actually nonexistent) colleague to whom they can administer electric shocks. Those who have seen aggressive content administer a greater number of shocks of greater intensity than those exposed to nonaggressive stimuli.

The supporters of the Bandura/Berkowitz school contend that the cumulative import of their studies demonstrate a causal connection between exposure to violence or aggressive behavior on television and real violent or aggressive behavior. The experimenters themselves, however, made no claim to any situation outside the laboratory or the "field experimental setting."

Their critics emphasize the artificiality of the laboratory situations used in these experiments. The close time proximity of exposure and frustration, the coincidence of Bobo doll in the content and in the child's environment, the rather unrealistic nature of the "shock" measure all are cited as casting doubts about the results.

However, the Bandura/Berkowitz group have continued to accumulate data piece by piece and gradually widen the scope of the studies, including taking them out of the laboratory. (In 1969, for example, Berkowitz commenced a series of studies in the "natural" setting of a Wisconsin Juvenile Detention Facility.)

Diametrically opposed to the Bandura/Berkowitz school are those who claim evidence to support a "catharsis" effect of television violence on viewers. This school, led by Seymour Feshbach and his colleagues (1971) contends that rather than trigger violent behavior, seeing violence on television serves as a catharsis function. This is the thesis that by watching the performance of violence on the screen, we are able to sublimate our own tensions and frustrations, thus reducing the likelihood of our performing aggressive or violent acts.

Typically, the researchers of the group have studied youngsters in boarding school or foster home dormitory groups. The subjects do their television viewing in their accustomed environment and schedule. But some groups are permitted to see violent programs and others are not. Measures of subsequent interpersonal aggression are obtained by observation. Other dependent variables include verbal aggression, fantasy aggression and a series of before and after scores on personality tests measuring such things as hostility and anxiety. Feshbach and Singer (1971: 141) state that boys "exposed to aggressive TV content manifested significantly less behavioral aggression toward peers and authority than boys exposed to non-aggressive TV content." However, they go on to qualify the findings, stating that these results held only for the boys in the "homes."

While the proponents of the "catharsis school" claim that its supporting research has been done in more "natural" settings than that of the Bandura/Berkowitz school, unfortunately it has also been open to considerable methodological criticism.

Thus the battle has been joined, frequently spilling over into the popular press. The result has been increased confusion and perhaps resentment in the public and among social scientists.

Under the sponsorship of the Surgeon General's Scientific Advisory Committee on Television and Social Behavior, a considerable body of new research has been done in this area. Substantial new results have been achieved by the Bandura/Berkowitz school, but they still carry major qualifications. The catharsis school continues the fight, but it should be noted that results reported to this project by Feshbach did not achieve a clear replication of his earlier findings nor do they provide unequivocal support for the catharsis thesis. The battle continues to rage with methodological critiques, rebuttals and rejoinders.

In their report to the Surgeon General, members of the Scientific Advisory Committee state "there is a convergence of the fairly substantial experimental evidence for *short-run* causation of aggression among some children by viewing violence on the screen and the much less certain evidence from field studies that extensive violence viewing precedes some *long-run* manifestations of aggressive behavior. This convergence of the two types of evidence constitutes some preliminary indication of a causal relationship, but a good deal of research remains to be done before one can have confidence in these conclusions." They then go on to say that "the two sets of findings converge in three respects: a preliminary and tentative indication of a causal relation between viewing violence on television and aggressive behavior; an indication that any such causal relation operates only on some children (who are predisposed to be aggressive); and an indication that it operates only in some environmental contexts. Such tentative and limited conclusions are not very satisfying. They represent substantially more knowledge than we had two years ago, but they leave many questions unanswered."

But perhaps by now the battle has become a diversion, obscuring other evidence which has at least strong implications for the public's anxious question about effects.

Learning

One thing we do know: the audience does learn from television. And by this we mean that they learn from their viewing of entertainment. What they learn tends to be general and superficial. Robinson (in this volume) reports studies assessing learning among both adults and teenagers on such things as specifics of geography and concepts of weather. He found little evidence of learning in these areas.

But most parents state that they feel their children learn from television. Youngsters themselves think they learn from television and so do many adults. And there is evidence of various types of learning.

Preschool-age children can recite commercial jingles and they request things seen advertised on television. Ward (1971) reports that by the time they finish elementary school, children comprehend the basic function of commercials. The study of Schramm et al. (1961) reported evidence of accelerated vocabulary learning as a result of television and similar evidence has been found more recently by LaPlante (1968).

While the recent evidence suggests that many children even at the elementary school age have developed some discounting of television as a representation of the "real world," it still seems likely that the vast exposure to television experienced by most children must have had an incremental effect on their "picture of the world." But perhaps more important is the fact that the children who are most likely to accept television's world as realistic are those from poor and disadvantaged families. Significantly, children from such families and those who have had more personal experience with violence perceive television content as containing less violence than do their peers (Chaffee, 1971).

Pertinent to the question of social learning from television is a study by Stein and Freidrich (1971). Stein and her colleagues integrated television viewing into the activities of nursery school groups. Over a four-week period this content was systematically varied for three matched groups. One group saw a "prosocial program," *Misterogers' Neighborhood;* another saw "aggressive programs," *Batman* and *Superman* cartoons; a control group saw neutral children's films. Perhaps the most significant finding in the study was that in the aggressive program group, children who were initially above average in interpersonal aggression showed more aggressive behavior after seeing the programs. Those initially below average in aggression did not respond differentially to the three television conditions. Further, the children exposed to the aggressive programs showed less persistence, tolerance of delay and lower levels of rule obedience than children exposed to the prosocial program.

These results are highly suggestive for interpreting results from the many correlational studies now in the literature. Lyle and Hoffman (1971), for instance, report that viewing of violent programs was positively related to high levels of conflict with parents. Chaffee (1971) has carefully gone through the various correlational studies. He concludes that while the results of many of the studies individually are not impressive, the overall pattern of results is. This pattern, he states, points to a positive relationship between aggression and violence in behavior and in viewing violence on television.

It still remains debatable if television is the causal force, but it certainly appears that it can and does play a reinforcing role in the development of a repertoire of violent, aggressive actions and may contribute to a propensity to make use of those actions.

For most children and adults a variety of factors—parental guidance, peer group pressures, internalized social class norms—act as constraints. The child or adult may learn violent skills, but is constrained from using them. However, these constraints may be absent in the environment of many children. Indeed, these constraints are most likely to be missing in the home environment of children most likely to see large amounts of television violence.

In most correlational studies, the amount of variance explained by television is small. Other factors obviously are equally more important or more fundamental. But to dismiss television's impact on this ground is to beg the question of what amount of contribution is "significant" or "critical."

Perhaps the most perplexing problem is that violence on television or in any medium does not affect all the audience in the same way. Indeed, it is likely that the same stimulus may not even affect the same individual in the same way under different sets of conditions.

This brings us once more to a problem alluded to much earlier, the problem of defining violence and pornography or erotica. When is their use justified? Certainly the classics of our culture—from the Old

Testament on—are replete with both. Yet students are expected to read Shakespeare in school, encouraged to view Goya and Rubens in museums.

The results discussed above showing differential perceptions of violence in the same stimuli by different groups in the population indicate an area in which more study is needed. These results strongly suggest that individuals' definitions of violence may vary widely. Does such a possible semantic difference reflect different susceptibility to violent stimuli in the media?

The following finding of Lyle and Hoffman illustrates the type of problems which this question may represent. They found that among their very young children, nursery school and first grade ages, there was considerable overlap in the television content mentioned by children as being "scary" or "frightening" and that which was their favorite. In most of the studies that have been done on television violence and children, classification of television stimuli has been based on adult definitions of what is violent.[1] It is not inconceivable that by using adult standards and definitions we are either focusing on the wrong content of television or at least excluding some things which may have deleterious effects upon children. If we are concerned with the effects of television violence on children, perhaps we need to start by establishing better definitions using the perceptual framework of children.[2]

Almost any review of the research on the impact of television somewhere makes the plea for longitudinal research. And we must once again repeat the plea because it is still lacking. To date there is only one truly longitudinal study in the literature, a study by Lefkowitz et al. (1971). Using data on the same group over a 10-year period, from third grade through high school, Lefkowitz found results strongly suggesting a relationship between heavy viewing of television violence in the younger years and involvement in behavioral aggression in the high school years. But this study was fortuitous, and the inferences made from it are very tenuous. The data collection was designed for other purposes. That these results were obtained under such a handicap makes the need for longitudinal studies designed specifically for this purpose all the more apparent.

Granted the difficulties involved in long-term panel studies, the question remains: can we ignore the need given the scope of the possible consequences of the findings for society? Further, if we accept the contention of many developmental psychologists concerning the importance of the years of early childhood, could we not at least mount longitudinal studies encompassing these years? The work of Stein and of Lyle and Hoffman clearly indicate that children of these ages can be studied both by observation and interview.

PORNOGRAPHY

On the surface, one would expect that our society might have a mature and reasoned attitude toward the mass communication of sexually oriented material. We have, after all, had sexually explicit writing available to us since the 1400s when Gutenberg began using movable type. That the United States, at least, has anything but a consistent set of mores on human sexuality and the mass media is, perhaps a consequence of this liturgical beginning to the question.

As any insightful person might feel, the general fact seems to be that our people are widely and steadfastly ambivalent about the mass communication/sex question. It is, in other words, acceptable to look at *Playboy* magazine's monthly tonnage of bust and bottom, but it is "immoral" to allow more than a certain stipulated number of inches of decolleté on a television program (even one hosted by *Playboy*'s publisher, Hugh Heffner himself). Whether, in the end, our apparent ambivalences about publicly displayed sexuality are "right" or "wrong" and whether these values are attributable to the Puritans of 1600 or to a general scientific and communication revolution in the mid-twentieth century, is as moot as it is irrelevant. The facts are: (1) Americans do have a double standard about the issue—gross differences between attitude and behavior; (2) Americans are, presently, at least, very different in the general shape of this attitude/behavior set, from other peoples (especially the Scandinavians); and (3) Americans are undergoing a rapid change in both behavior and in expressed attitudes.

It is especially because of the latter point, we think, that the Congress and President Johnson established, in 1967, the Commission on Obscenity and Pornography. In his unreleased letter setting up the TV/violence study of 1969-1971, President Nixon too initially expressed an interest in both sex and violence on television.

The final report of the "Pornography Commission" was sent out by the Commission on September 30, 1970. It is a succinct and most thorough documentation of the relevant social science literature preceding the work of the Commission itself; it is also a good, nontechnical summary of those pieces of research that were contracted out by the Commission. The political and moral furor that followed the issuing of the report is not, of course, included in the document itself. The general outcome was that the effects of exposure to pornographic materials seem to be inconsequential; they are also negligible.

In these few pages we will present a brief overview of the volume produced by the Pornography Commission. We will do so by examining two substantive sections of relevance to this chapter; i.e., traffic patterns or audience exposure findings, and "impact" findings.

Traffic and Exposure Patterns

The observed realities of pornography traffic in this country led the Commission and the present authors to delimit the field of study in this fashion: books, periodicals, movies and various additional materials such as mailed photos, were included. Television and newspapers were excluded since there is little even faintly approaching obscenity or pornography in either medium. Also at the start of this, comes another caveat about the estimates of the amount of written pornographic material consumed by the American public. Since the publishing industry assesses volume in terms of dollar intake rather than volume of books and periodicals sold (at least the publicly released figures are such), we are at a loss to infer accurately how many units of pornography are released during a given time period. Neither is there more than anecdotal information about how much multiple readership there is of a given sexually oriented book or magazine; we would speculate that there is a great deal more of this "pass along" readership than there is on less explicitly sexual, less expensive writings.

Even if we allow that the amount of pornography and the real size of at least the reading prurient public are indeterminants, we are still left without the type of "body count" index that is available in the study of violence on television. That is, no one has reported analyzing a substantial number of the sexually oriented films and

TABLE 1[a]

DOLLAR VOLUME OF SEXUALLY ORIENTED MATERIALS

Books ("Adult Only," Retail Prices):	$45-55 Million	(of an industry total of $25 Billion in 1968).
Periodicals ("Adult Only"):	$25-35 Million	(of a total of $2.6 Billion in 1967).
Motion Pictures[b] (Box Office):	$450-460 Million	(of a total of $1.065 Billion in 1969).
Mail Order:	$12-14 Million	
Under-the-Counter:	$5-10 Million	

a. Report of the Commission on Pornography, pp. 84-85.
b. Includes "R," "X," Sex Oriented Unrated and "Exploitation" Films.

come up with the kind of data on frequency and types of sexual interactions that Gerbner (1971) did for three weeks of network television violence.

Nevertheless, the Pornography Commission's own tabular representation of sexually oriented materials is somewhat revealing.

Brief amplifications of the data on the mass media of concern to this volume are in order here. Since movies are the highest dollar volume sexually oriented medium, we will start with them. As even a non-movie-goer now can tell (from a glance at the newspaper entertainment ads) explicit sex in general films is seemingly more common and more explicit every week. It has been said, in fact, that the hard core pornography theaters are suffering greatly because of losing business to the neighborhood theater showing Hollywood films.

We do not know if the correlation has been made between a relatively recent financial resurgence (late 1960s) of the domestic film industry and the loosening of customs as to films' sexual orientation. The link is not unlikely.

The film industry's public relations arm—the Motion Picture Association of America—took cognizance of the need to present to the society the appropriate concern for this new filmed sexual revolution. In 1968 they promulgated their general film rating system.

Although the bemused critic can entertain himself by trying to fathom the judgmental criteria for these "G," "G.P.," "R" and "X" ratings, they are there nevertheless.[3] The differences in explicitness of sex between an "R" and an "X" movie may be questionable and perhaps transient, but the avowed purpose of the ratings—i.e., to allow a parent to prejudge a film's appropriateness for his children—does not seem to be working. Informal observations of movie theaters' attendance restrictions for "R" films at least indicate that any child of any age can and does attend when he wants. The ratings, as might have been expected, probably enhance a film's attractiveness to much of the audience it was nominally to have been kept from.

As an aside, we note something that is eminently obvious in the rating system operated by the MPAA. That is, their lack of concern with exposing moviegoers—especially children (whose movie going is explicitly restricted by the MPAA to "G" and "G.P." films—to intensive and extensive filmed violence.

Of the motion pictures not even under the rating aegis of MPAA, there is little worth saying. The so-called "art" films, the "exploitation films," and the "16 mm. movies" are ultimately exposed to a relatively small number of persons. The Pornography Commission reports (pp. 104-105) that some 600 theaters exhibited exploitation films weekly during 1969; industry estimates for the income from these showings were $60-70 million or some 5.9 percent of industry totals for that year. Industry sources, incidentally, were cited as estimating that 1970 revenues from exploitation films might have run as much as 20 percent behind 1969. While $60+ million dollars spent on attendance to exploitation films is not to be ignored, the most important question, as yet unanswered and perhaps not easily answerable is: who spent the money? Was it a small audience, each with high attendance rates? Was it a large number of curiosity seekers, each seeing only one presentation? An oblique approach to these questions was provided by the national sample survey to be discussed later.

Sexually Oriented Printed Materials

Like the situation in the movies in the United States today, it is difficult to classify the publishing industry into neat categories or degrees of sexual orientation. Sex is generally available in a large number of books and magazines. The volume of sales of both paperback and hardcover books in the class of *Valley of the Dolls, Everything You Always Wanted to Know About Sex, The Sensuous Woman,* etc. are indicators of a growing demand for information and entertainment of this kind. *Playboy* magazine's short history is one of phenomenal success (in its fiscal year 1971, some 74 million copies of the magazine were sold at $1.00 per copy—newsstand price); not even Hugh Heffner could accurately guess how many total readers his magazine ultimately has.

The number of "Confession," "Barber Shop," "Men's Sophisticates" or other nonclassifiable periodicals sold in this country are much more easily measured than are sexual-oriented books. The simple reason, of course, is that circulation data are the final criterion by which advertising rates are set and by which the publications either rise or fall. The Pornography Commission estimated these figures for the categories of magazines noted above:

(1) Confession Magazines (audience—young women; content usually only implicit sex); yearly sales = 110 million copies; 1969 revenue = $38.5 million.

(2) Barber Shop Magazines (male audience; contents are "action" and sex oriented; photos of the "pin-up" type, nude or partly nude women); yearly total (1969) sales for 20 selected examples of this class: 30 million copies; revenues of approximately $14 million.

(3) "Men's Sophisticates" (substantially nude female models; genitals not shown). In 1961, sales by 62 Commission selected "girlie" magazines were over 40 million copies; revenues $31+ million.

(4) Playboy, the apotheosis of "special" magazines is, as we have said, a veritable institution. In late 1970, it was, in fact, admitted to the corporate sanctum sanctorum; its shares being admitted to trading on the New York Stock Exchange.

Exposure to Erotic Materials

It has been noted that Abelson (1970) headed a survey team in a national study of exposure to written or depicted sex act descriptions. Some 84 percent of men and 69 percent of women had seen such materials. Several other limited focus studies funded by the Pornography Commission found similar data on exposure to erotica. The figures are also consistent with the findings of Kutschinsky (1970) who did his work in Copenhagen, Denmark.

The demographics of exposure to erotica are as expected: incidence is higher among young persons, urban dwellers, college educated, socially and politically active, and religiously inactive persons. Zetterberg (1970) reports similarly for his Swedish data.

The question of frequency of exposure to erotica was also handled by Abelson. Only 14 percent of men and 5 percent of women admitted to having seen visual erotica more than five times during the two years preceding the survey.

Nominally the greatest concern in the whole area of pornography is that young people will be exposed to erotica. The several studies cited in the Commission report indicate generally that the concerns are well founded. Wilson and Jacobs (1970) in a survey of sex educators and counselors said 64 percent estimated that half of the nation's teenage boys are exposed to explicit erotic materials before age 14; girls were thought to be some two years behind this schedule.

There have been some attempts to observe and classify patrons of "adult" book stores. Massey (1970) made 2,477 such observations, but found that subjects were almost all male, mostly middle-aged, white, "well" or "casually" dressed, middle class, and probably married. Various observational studies of patronage of adult movie theaters (e.g., Winick, 1970) showed generally similar results.

Impact

Neither the amount of erotic material abounding in the country nor the interest in who uses it would be of concern to government if deleterious effects were not assumed to be associated with exposure to it. The unwritten charge of the "effects panel" of the Commission seems to have been to measure the extent of the negative effects of pornography on individuals and on the society generally.

The effects panel of the Commission reviewed the scientific literature dating up to 1968; they generalize their own conclusions: "(a) Pictures and words depicting various aspects of human sexuality produce sexual arousal in a considerable proportion of the adult population; (b) materials which elicit arousal differ according to the sex of the viewer; (c) persons differ in their preference for, and response to, sexual stimuli; (d) the context in which the viewing occurs is a significant determinant of the extent to which persons will be aroused by the materials."

What the Commission did not find in the previous work was an indication of the extent or duration of arousal, how the stimulation might affect subsequent behavior, public attitudes about sexuality, or the viewer's general mental health. They subsequently set these areas as of primary importance in their own work.

The organization of the set of 1968-1970 studies funded by the Commission followed a comprehensive plan. The studies leveled their interest on both the attitudinal and behavioral dimensions of the pornography question. Abelson's (1970) national sample was surveyed to assess, among other things, the public's feelings about the severity of the erotica question. Only 2 percent of the 2,486 adults considered sex or erotica to be one of the "two or three most important problems facing the country today." An additional 9 percent cited the "general moral breakdown in society" which may subsume the direct erotica response. Public opinion about the effects of erotica varied widely. Both positive and negative effects were cited; most of those citing predominantly negative effects had relatively less personal experience with erotica.

The opinions of designated "experts" showed the expected tendency to impute erotica with either more or less negative impact—i.e., 57.6 percent of police chiefs linked reading "obscene books" with juvenile delinquency; only 12.4 percent of mental health professionals identified this relationship. Additionally, 16.8 percent of a sample of 3,423 psychiatrists and psychologists responded that they were either convinced or suspected they had had cases where pornography was a causative factor in antisocial behavior (p. 195). On balance, it is clear that most professionals agree that exposure to obscene or pornographic materials does not have deleterious effects on the individual. As Wilson and Jacobs (1970) found: 77 percent of a national sample of sex educators and counselors suggested that adolescents are interested in sexually oriented materials and that this interest stems from a "natural curiosity."

Behavioral Responses to Erotica

Citing an impressive complex of experimental studies, the Commission concludes that seeing erotica does indeed produce psychosexual stimulation. The degree of stimulation is a function of such things as presentation factors (e.g., film is more arousing than still pictures), individual sexual orientation, situational factors in the experiment, and the gender of the viewer and of the person depicted.

A satiation effect has been found to be so great as to have elicited this comment (Money, 1970): "The half life of pornography is approximately two to three hours in one's total lifetime." In discussing the research on direct sexual behavioral effects of viewing erotica, the Commission concludes that established patterns of sexuality are only slightly altered by having been shown sexual materials. Those slight changes in experimental participants' sexual lives which did occur were of a distinctly short duration. That is, only short-term (up to 48 hours after viewing erotica) effects were evidenced.

Those readers who are methodologically inclined are urged to peruse either the Commission report or the researchers' own technical reports, also published by the Government Printing Office. It will be seen that, within the constraints of the validity assumptions this sort of intrusive research must live with, the program was well done.

Attitudes Toward Sex as a Function of Exposure to Erotica

Perhaps the most amorphous claim of the anti-pornography segment of the society is that the general and individual moral fibre of our people are harmed by the very existence of sexually oriented materials. Again resorting to their major sample survey (Abelson, 1970) the Commission tried to pin down whether attitudes toward sexuality differ in those persons who have been either naturally or experimentally exposed to erotica.

The American survey and the several Scandinavian ones cited previously all find that the more recently and more widely experienced pornography consumer tends to have more liberal attitudes toward sex than does the relatively more sheltered individual. The effects panel of the Commission noted that there is more likely a "self-selection" phenomenon operating here than a causal link between viewing pornography and having liberal sex attitudes.

The several before-after attitudes tests cited (before and after *seeing* erotic stimuli) indicate that there was almost no observed change in attitudes toward sex after viewing. Combined with the data reporting little actual change in behavior after viewing erotic materials, it would seem as if much of the question about the deleterious effects of pornography on the individual has been clarified.

Erotica Exposure and Juvenile Delinquency

The effects panel made an effort to investigate allegations that recent increasing rates of juvenile delinquent behavior were traceable to increasing availability of erotic materials for young people. While all the survey and clinical data used by the Commission point out the widespread youthful experience with erotica, there seemed to be no correlational evidence at all to allow one to infer even a hint of a causal relationship.

The importance of another dimension of this same problem area is underlined by a finding of the aforementioned national sample survey. About half the adults questioned avowed that seeing sexually oriented materials "leads people to commit rape." Crime statistics and sample survey questionnaires are far from the most accurate way to attack this problem, but they seem, because of social constraints, to be the best indicators available presently. At the very least, however, cross-national comparisons—between sexually "liberated" Denmark and the United States—are possible and likely to be fruitful. Even though the validity of crime statistics may be even less sound than other social indicators, in the case of Denmark it is possible to chart the longitudinal relationship between amount of sexually oriented materials available and the number of sex and other violent crimes committed. Statistics compiled by Ben-Veniste (1970) show that over the period 1958-1969, the Copenhagen sex crime rate decreased continuously. The sharpest decline came in 1967-1969; this coincides, interestingly if not causally, with the Danish Parliament's removal of all restrictions on the distribution of erotic materials to persons over 16 years old. It was further indicated that the decreasing sex crime rates could not be attributed to either altered law enforcement practices or to the likelihood of variability in reporting of such crimes.

One obvious and well-exploited methodological approach to the question of erotica and sex crimes is to interview sex criminals. Thirty-five years of research has shown that self-report data indicate no relationships between these variables. Sex criminals are apparently "normal" in their responses to erotica (disregarding the question of the reliability of their responses for the moment). In fact, retrospective reports of exposure to erotica during adolescence find sex offenders much *less* likely to have been so exposed. The sex offenders' "recent" experience with erotica was shown, however, to be no different than either non-sex-offender criminals or control outside populations.

More negative effects evidence was uncovered when before-after questioning of sex offenders and non-sex offenders was conducted around the experimental showing of fifteen erotic depictions.

Not only the Commission researchers' direct questioning of the sex-crime/erotica-consumption relationship but the clinical data on sex offenders generally lead to a similar finding. It seems that sexual repression, and a rather strong *absence* of sexually oriented discussions, materials, or other exposure in childhood characterize the typical sex offender. The conclusion that a catharsis effect might exist here must apparently be considered.

SUMMARY

The Commision's panel concentrating on the effects and impact of pornography did a fine job. Working under severe time, resource, and implied political restraints (e.g., having a Commission partly composed of unscientific and biased individuals) they have published just what they set out to: an updating of the relevant social science literature, an analysis of the present U.S. situation regarding the traffic and content of pornography, and the results of a comprehensive research program designed to fill in some of the major gaps in the survey and experimental approaches to the study of the impact of erotica on individuals and the society.

One can hardly quarrel with the Commission's assessments of the extent of the pornography traffic in this country. It is only necessary to visit the corner newsstand to get a fair estimate of what is available and, if you stand there long enough and unobtrusively enough, you can find out who is availing himself of the materials.

Despite the political rejection of the report and its conclusions and recommendations (for removing many of the restraints on the distribution of pornography), the scientists will have had their way. The reports are publicly available and can be replicated by interested scientists. Something of importance has been added to the literature on human attitudes and behaviors.

This study of pornography may indeed have been limited in many ways; it may have been misbegotten; it may at times have been misdirected and misinterpreted. It may turn out to be the *only* major effort in this area ever to be funded by the U.S. government and, given a realistic appraisal of social science research priorities today, that may be all well and good. One thing the Commission did do, though, is to contribute to our knowledge of the things under study. And that, after all, is what science is about.

GENERAL DISCUSSION

The juxtaposition of these two types of media content and the literature concerning them is an interesting exercise. Regardless of the empirical evidence on causal effects or their lack, both violence and pornography are frequently the object of impassioned attitudes pro and con. These strong attitudes certainly color the reaction to and the evaluation of what empirical evidence does exist.

The differences of opinion regarding the report of the Pornography Commission should not have surprised anyone in view of Abelson's findings that politically conservative individuals are likely to be negatively disposed toward erotica.

However, one might suggest that this type of prejudicial reaction also carries over to the "scientific community." For instance, it is worth noting that among social scientists—who tend to be more liberal than the population at large—there is some evidence of a greater readiness to accept a "catharsis" effect for erotic material than for violent material.

When one compares the evidence on violence and on pornography, both seem to stress that whatever effects may occur vary according to individual and environmental circumstances. In the violence literature the fact that media stimulation appears to explain some 10 percent of the variance in aggressive/violent behavior is suggested as being a cause of concern. In the pornography literature the fact that *only* 16 percent of psychiatrists interviewed said they were sure they had treated cases in which erotic material and deviant behavior were connected is suggested as not being worthy of concern.

It is interesting that there appears to have been little in the way of attempts to study the two in combination. Certainly, in actual fact, violence and pornography often appear in combination in the media. Many of the new movies, with a major appeal for young adults, emphasize both violence and sex. Many of the pornographic books and magazines feature masochistic or sadistic sex.

A problem common in both lines of research is that of definition. What is the borderline between acceptable "rough-housing" and violence? What is the difference between artistic erotica and pornography? In neither field has this problem been adequately resolved. There may be a partial analogy to the phenomenon of subliminal perception in that individual differences in thresholds make simple definition impossible.

The Report to the Surgeon General on Television and Violence states:

> It is conceivable that prolonged exposure of large populations to television violence may have very little immediate effect on the crime rate, but that such exposure may interact with other influences in the society to produce increased casualness about violence which permits citizens to regard with increased indifference actual suffering in their own or other societies, and to reflect that indifference in major political and economic decisions.

One might suggest similarly that more open depiction of sex in the media over a long period (in which birth control measures are increasingly available) may help to bring about modification in basic societal mores concerning not only sex but marriage and family life. Some will say this would be good, some that it would be bad. Regardless of the point of view, one should consider the possibility of such long-range effects and their implications.

No adequate longitudinal effects studies have either been done or are presently under way in the fields we have been discussing. Whether one wants to attribute this deplorable situation to the shortsightedness of funding sources in the social sciences or to the apparent disinterest of the scientists themselves is irrelevant. Even though more work has perhaps been done in researching effects of violence and erotica than in any other mass communication field, there still remains a great deal to learn. Under the circumstances that now prevail, it is perhaps not any more unjustifiable than it is unexpected to see the TV Violence Committee presenting such an equivocal summary of its researchers' work during 1970-1971.

The final point to be made refers, by its definition, beyond the charge of the group just completing its work on "television and social behavior." That is, the inferences that the legislative branch is to make from the scientific studies done at their request. On several occasions, U.S. Senate Committees have held hearings on the issue of television's part in producing juvenile delinquency and general aggression among viewers. No legislation resulted.

The Senate Sub-Committee on Communications is to hold hearings in Spring, 1972 on the substance of the Surgeon General's Advisory group's deliberations. Again, the problem of assigning a social value to a body of largely non-generalizable data on TV and violence will face these members of the Senate. They are not to be envied the responsibility they have for determining whether the scientists' findings are now clear enough to indicate restrictive legislation.

NOTES

1. For a different approach see Murray, Cole, and Fedler (1970) in which violence was rated by a panel of students to provide a peer group difference.

2. This definitional problem is exemplified by an experience related by a female member of the Motion Picture Industry's film review board. She relates the different reactions of herself and her male colleagues—reactions which could affect the ratings accorded movies—to scenes showing the rape of women and those showing the rape of men.

3. Jack Valenti, President of MPAA, was quoted in a December 26, 1971, Los Angeles Times article, "The objective of the rating system is simple. Film ratings are given on the suitability of a movie for viewing by children."

REFERENCES

ABELSON, H., R. COHEN, E. HEATON, and C. SUDER (1970) "Public attitudes toward and experiences with erotic materials." Technical Reports of the Commission on Obscenity and Pornography. Vol. 6. Washington, D.C.: Government Printing Office.

BAKER, R. and S. BALL (1969) Mass Media and Violence: A Staff Report to the National Commission on the Causes and Prevention of Violence. Washington, D.C.: Government Printing Office.

BEN-VENISTE, R. (1970) "Pornography and sex crime: the Danish experience." Technical Reports of the Commission on Obscenity and Pornography. Vol. 7. Washington, D.C.: Government Printing Office.

BERLINGHAUSEN, D. and R. FAUNCE (1965) Some Opinions on the Relationship Between Obscene Books and Juvenile Delinquency. University of Minnesota, Graduate School. (unpublished)

CHAFFEE, S. (1971) "Television and adolescent aggressiveness," in G. Comstock and E. Rubinstein (eds.) Television and Social Behavior, Vol. 3. Washington, D.C.: Government Printing Office.

CLARK, D. and W. BLANKENBURG (1971) "Trends in violent content in selected mass media," in G. Comstock and E. Rubinstein (eds.) Television and Social Behavior, Vol. 1. Washington, D.C.: Government Printing Office.

COOLEY, C. (1956) Social Organization. New York: Free Press.

FESHBACH, S. and B. SINGER (1971) Television and Aggression. San Francisco: Jossey-Bass.

GERBNER, G. (1971) "Violence in television drama: trends and symbolic functions," in G. Comstock and E. Rubinstein (eds.) Television and Social Behavior, Vol. 1. Washington, D.C.: Government Printing Office.

GREENBERG, B. (1969) "The content and context of violence in the mass media," in R. Baker and S. Ball (eds.) Mass Media and Violence. Washington, D.C.: Government Printing Office.

——— and T. GORDON (1971) "Perceptions of violence in television: critics and the public," in G. Comstock and E. Rubinstein (eds.) Television and Social Behavior, Vol. 1. Washington, D.C.: Government Printing Office.

HASKINS, J. (1969) "The effects of violence in the printed media," in R. Baker and S. Ball (eds.) Mass Media and Violence. Washington, D.C.: Government Printing Office.

ISRAEL, H. and J. ROBINSON (1971) "Television in day-to-day life: patterns of use," in G. Comstock and E. Rubinstein (eds.) Television and Social Behavior, Vol. 1. Washington, D.C.: Government Printing Office.

KUTSCHINSKY, B. (1970) "Sex crimes and pornography in Copenhagen: a study of attitudes." Technical Reports of the Commission on Obscenity and Pornography. Vol. 7. Washington, D.C.: Government Printing Office.

LaPLANTE, W. (1968) An investigation of the sight vocabulary of pre-school children as measured by their ability to recognize words shown frequently on television. Ph.D. dissertation, Temple University.

LASSWELL, H. (1948) The structure and function of communication in society. Institute for religious and social studies of New York City.

LEFKOWITZ, M., L. ERON, L. WALDER, and C. SUDER (1971) "Television violence and child aggression: a follow-up study," in G. Comstock and E. Rubinstein (eds.) Television and Social Behavior, Vol. 3. Washington, D.C.: Government Printing Office.

LIEBERT, R. (1971) "Television and social learning: some relationships between viewing violence and behaving aggressively," in J. Murray, E. Rubinstein, and G. Comstock (eds.) Television and Social Behavior, Vol. 2. Washington, D.C.: Government Printing Office.

LIPPMANN, W. (1922) Public Opinion. New York: Harcourt, Brace.

LYLE, J. and H. HOFFMAN (1971) "Children's use of television and other media," in E. Rubinstein, G. Comstock, and J. Murray (eds.) Television and Social Behavior, Vol. 4. Washington, D.C.: Government Printing Office.

MASSEY, M. (1970) "A marketing analysis of sex-oriented materials in Denver, Colorado, August, 1969." Technical Reports of the Commission on Obscenity and Pornography. Vol. 4. Washington, D.C.: Government Printing Office.

MONEY, J. (1970) "The positive and constructive approach to pornography in general sex education, in the home, and in sexological counseling." Technical Reports of the Commission on Obscenity and Pornography. Vol. 10. Washington, D.C.: Government Printing Office.

MOTT, F. L. (1962) American Journalism: A History, 1690-1960. New York: Macmillan.

MURRAY, J. (1971) "Television in inner-city homes: viewing behavior of young boys," in E. Rubinstein, G. Comstock, and J. Murray (eds.) Television and Social Behavior, Vol. 4. Washington, D.C.: Government Printing Office.

SCHRAMM, W., J. LYLE, and E. PARKER (1961) Television in the Lives of Our Children. Stanford: Stanford University Press.

STEIN, A., and L. FREIDRICH (1971) "Television content and young children's behavior," in J. Murray, E. Rubinstein, and G. Comstock (eds.) Television and Social Behavior, Vol. 2. Washington, D.C.: Government Printing Office.

WARD, S. (1971) Effects of television advertising on children and adolescents. Cambridge, Mass.: Marketing Sciences Institute. (mimeo)

WERTHAM, F. (1954) Seduction of the Innocent. New York: Rinehart.

WILSON, C., and S. JACOBS (1970) "Survey of sex educators and counselors." Technical Reports of the Commission on Obscenity and Pornography. Vol. 10. Washington, D.C.: Government Printing Office.

WINICK, C. (1970) "A study of consumers of explicitly sexual materials: some functions of adult movies." Technical Reports of the Commission on Obscenity and Pornography. Vol. 4. Washington, D.C.: Government Printing Office.

ZETTERBERG, H. (1970) "The consumers of pornography where it is easily available: the Swedish experience." Technical Reports of the Commission on Obscenity and Pornography." Vol. 9. Washington, D.C.: Government Printing Office.

Chapter 9

ENVIRONMENT AND COMMUNICATION

Keith R. Stamm

INTRODUCTION

The environmental crisis is normally thought of as a biological problem arising from man's tampering with delicate ecological balances. Generally speaking, it is correct to say that the biological sciences have "discovered" this danger, and that they have gained much of the knowledge necessary to maintaining environmental quality. At the same time, it has often been said that while the remedies for many of our most serious environmental problems are known, recognized solutions are not being implemented.

Often, out of frustration and a desire to "do something," groups launch such activities as hanging flower boxes from the light poles on Main Street, or a cleanup of the local waterfront. The "believers" in ecology thus have the satisfaction of having done something, although it was not anything that had any great impact on the environmental crisis.

It is a lot harder to get the essential things done. Consider the futility and wasted energy when several hundred volunteers pick up litter along a lakeshore, if the municipal sewage authority or cottage owners are dumping huge quantities of harmful effluents into the same lake.

The point of departure for this chapter is that the environmental problem is in large part social (or collective) in nature. This can be readily appreciated by asking yourself "What can I, as an individual, do to resolve the environmental crisis?" Not very much, all by yourself.

For example, it would be pointless for you to recycle your old newspapers, cans and bottles if no one else did. For that matter, you could not even do it without the help of other people. Individuals must do something, all right, but to be effective they must achieve collective action based upon an exchange of thought with other individuals.

It is in this context that communication emerges as an important aspect of the environmental crisis. Joint recognition of problems and consideration of alternative courses of action are not possible without communication.

Identifying the specific role that communication, and the mass media, should play (prior to and for the duration of collective action) is not an easy task. The problem can be seen by introducing a prototype of the environmental problem and considering the many different purposes to which communication might be put.

A PROTOTYPE ENVIRONMENTAL ISSUE

The issue we will use involves an Army Corps of Engineers water management project proposed for a rich farming district in north-eastern North Dakota. The land in this area is intensively farmed and agriculture is the major economic base, but major areas of cropland are subject to annual flooding by the Red River and a tributary—the Park River. In this context, an important environmental question arose: should the Park River be dammed to protect farmland and the hub manufacturing and supply center near the juncture of the two rivers from flooding? Some communication data collected on the issue will be discussed later in the chapter.

First, let us consider the functions communication might be expected to perform. A regional supervisor for the Army Corps of Engineers may be interested in developing support for a project which agency studies show to be beneficial in terms of their criteria. This is the patronistic view common to federal agencies. Effective communication is whatever brings about support of the agency's proposed project. But in addition, federal agencies must often be given credit for recognizing the prerogative of local decision, and for trying to inform the public about possible alternatives. Effective communication in this view should increase citizens' knowledge of the pros and cons of available alternatives.

Let's look at the role of communication as implied in two additional viewpoints on the flood control issue: (1) the viewpoint of environmentalists who become antagonists of the agency; and (2) the viewpoint of local people who will most directly experience the effects of the project.

The "environmentalists" could see many roles for communication, from informing the public about the damaging environmental effects of past flood control projects and of the harm likely to result from this one, to gaining acceptance of a broader set of values for assessing the merits of the project. Thus, for environmentalists effective communication may be information gain and it may be value (or attitude) change.

Local citizens anticipate communication from themselves to the agency, as well as from agency to them. They are concerned that the agency become informed about their individual criteria for an acceptable project. These may include such considerations as changes in land value and local tax structure or the relocation and maintenance of local roads. Effective communication in their view would result in recognition of local problems and interests, in addition to the general criteria of project evaluation that are employed either by the agency or by special interest groups.

Communication theory can be helpful here in determining whether the questions being asked are answerable, and whether other reasonable questions have yet to be raised. As we shall see, much past research has been directed at relatively unproductive questions, while more promising questions have gone unstudied.

COMMUNICATION AS A MEANS OF COGNITIVE CHANGE

The Corps of Engineers wants to build favorable opinion toward a proposed project and to increase public knowledge of alternatives. Environmental groups want to increase understanding of ecological effects or perhaps to change environmental values. The desired result of "effective communication" in each case is a form of cognitive change. Each of these ends involves how the individual thinks about the project and about concepts related to its evaluation.

Generally, there are three reasons for the interest in individuals' cognitions concerning an environmental issue:

(1) as an indication of how the individual orients himself to the issue;
(2) as a means of assessing what specific cognitive change might be attempted via communication;
(3) as a means of obtaining desired behaviors.

Each of these reasons contains an assumption about a relationship between cognition, communication and behavior that is vital to our understanding of the role of communication in resolving environmental issues. The next three sections will deal with each of these assumptions in detail.

Do Cognitive Concepts Describe Environmental Orientation?

An important assumption related to the cognitive change view is that concepts such as "knowledge," "opinion," "attitude" are valid descriptors of any cognitive picture that an individual has of environmental phenomena. But do these traditional social science concepts necessarily capture what is significant and revolutionary about ecology, that it is a different way of "picturing" the phenomena of our environment? The answer, that they probably do not, can be explained by comparing the definitions of these concepts with the essence of "an ecological picture of environment."

Ecological Orientation

The "ecological picture" is generally understood to involve the interrelatedness of all life processes. As ecologist Paul Shepard (1969) has put it, understanding of ecology—the subversive science—requires . . . "a wider perception of landscape as a creative, harmonious being where relationships of things are as real as the things." The picture is of relationships. A pond, for example, is defined as a system of interrelated processes, not as a collection of certain kinds of objects.

The importance of the ecological view is that there is much that goes on in, say, a pond that is not likely to be observed or comprehended if we think only in terms of the objects that move about in the pond. We must also think in terms of attributes which vary throughout the pond and explain the presence and behavior of its objects—plants and animals. Variation in the attribute "water depth," for example, explains why floating plants grow in one part of the pond and emergents grow in another part. Processes such as oxidation and respiration help to explain the cycle of life in a pond and how all its organisms are linked together in the constant recycling of energy and nutrients.

Knowledge

The knowledge concept, as used in mass communication literature, refers to the individual's recall of facts about particular events. A recent study (Bailey, 1971), for example, measured whether people knew what the "E" in E-day stood for, and whether they could name the specific calendar date for E-day. In another study (Stamm and Ross, 1966), respondents were asked for such facts as the average life expectancy of small game animals. Neither sort of knowledge test gets at whether the individual perceives interrelationships which comprise an environmental system. The concept of knowledge could presumably encompass much more, but in current mass communication research it unfortunately does not.

Opinion

Opinion, defined as an intellectual (rather than emotional) belief one holds about an issue, could potentially encompass an ecological perspective. This depends, however, on whether the definition of the concept is limited to an individual's orientation to one object at a time (e.g., whether he is for or against flood control dams), or encompasses his orientation to several objects at a time. The latter definition would include the relationships which the individual sees *between the objects.* The essence of ecology is that there are no single object systems; interrelationship is not possible without considering at least two objects at a time. Thus, one might view the timber wolf (as a predator) and a moose (as its prey) as a two-object ecological system. But asking the individual how he views his relationship to each one separately would not tell us whether his view is ecological. In fact the very nature of the question would prevent him from doing so.

In current usage, opinion generally is defined as a verbal, evaluative response directed at a single object. The researcher determines, for example, whether people are for or against building a certain type of flood control project on the Park River, or whether they have a favorable evaluation of the Army Corps of Engineers. Whether there is in fact any intellectual basis for such opinions, such as an understanding of siltation as an attribute that affects a reservoir's ability to support many forms of aquatic plants and insects which is in turn related . . . is not determined. We do not even know whether responses are based on judgments (which would mean the individual's cognitive picture did include a second object) or whether they are largely emotional responses to that object.

The upshot is that current usage of "opinion" tells us whether people are for or against doing certain things to the environment and whether they favor certain remedial policies. But democratic theory also calls for an informed public capable of supporting and promoting a rational environmental policy. The only way to determine whether a public is so informed is some measure of "ecological enlightenment." To date, no such measure exists.

Attitude

The concept of "attitude" has enjoyed much popularity in theorizing about the role of communication and in research on environmental communication (Stamm, 1970; Erickson, 1971). However, the conceptual definition, a stable response to a single object, greatly limits its usefulness for defining differences in individuals' ecological orientations.

The attitude-object need not be a physical object, such as a timber wolf. It may also be an "object" in the sense of an abstract concept or idea. What this means is that attitude scales can be developed to measure the direction of verbal response to ecological concepts. The individual who consistently opposes human exploitation of the natural environment might, for example be characterized as holding a "protectionist" attitude (Erickson, 1971a). The protectionist could not necessarily be said to have an ecological understanding of those objects he wishes to preserve, however.

Attitude scales able to assess the direction of verbal response to ecological concepts would serve as locators of an important aspect of environmental philosophy. However, a person who has learned a certain environmental philosophy or ethic cannot be assumed to also be in command of an ecological understanding. The philosophy embodies a rationale for placing higher value upon certain states of natural systems—e.g., "balanced." Ecological understanding entails a knowledge of how such systems function.

Another limitation of the attitude measures currently used is that they require that the individual have a particular kind of cognition (or "picture") of the environmental situation used as the attitude object. The individual is asked for a picture that includes himself. He has to see himself in the picture in order to report what the observer wants—his position relative to an attitude object.

This rather simple conceptual point has some important implications. First, it raises the question of whether other kinds of cognitions, in which the individual does not include himself, may be just as important as attitude. Is this the only way for the individual to understand ecology—i.e., in terms of cognitions in which he sees himself in relation to environmental objects? It would seem, for example, that a person may well view predator-prey relations without including himself. It may be just as important to picture the dynamics of such relationships as to construct a picture in which you see your position relative to some element of these dynamics.

Second, we might ask whether in our fervor to measure and contrast different attitudinal positions we have not overlooked a far more important distinction—the distinction between having a picture in which you include yourself (attitude) and a picture in which you do not (no attitude). In recent attitude research by Stamm (1968), a large proportion of respondents answered scale items with "don't know," which may well have been their way of telling the observer they had no attitude. Interestingly, the largest statistical differences that emerged in this study were between those who registered no attitude and those holding any attitude at all, not between those of opposing attitudinal positions.

The third major implication bears on desired communication effects. We often say we are utilizing communication strategies to obtain attitude change—i.e., we want the individual to shift his position in the picture. But we can hardly change an attitude unless one already exists, and a necessary condition to having an attitude is that the individual have a cognition about the (observer's) object that includes himself. How often do we end up arguing the reasons for assuming particular attitudes with people who see no reason to be in the picture in the first place? In this sense, the aphorism "nature takes care of herself" may not express an attitude, rather the absence of one.

Environmentalists want other people to see themselves in the context of the workings of an environmental system, to put themselves in the picture, so to speak. This is quite a different thing from changing attitudes, and we may as well begin to keep the two separate.

Research on Environmental Attitude.

Systematic research to describe environmental attitudes has just begun. In a study employing Q-methodology to identify wildlife attitude types, Erickson (1971b) identified two attitude types from the Q-sorts of 49 persons on eighty statements of opinion about wildlife. Erickson labeled the two basic types "protectionist" and "reductionist." The protectionist favors saving vanishing species of wildlife such as the bald eagle, polar bear and whooping crane by protecting them from hunting, preserving their habitat and by feeding starving wildlife. Reductionists, on the other hand, view many types of wildlife as primarily destructive to crops or livestock, and tend to favor the hunting and control of these species.

Erickson argues that identification of these attitude types enables a communicator to predict the kind of message content that will strongly appeal to a given audience. In our example, the Corps of Engineers might seek the support of protectionists by stressing the value of a multiple-use reservoir and greenbelt for preserving the habitat of scarce wildlife species. Undoubtedly a credibility problem would arise, however, if they at the same time advertised as a benefit of the project reductions in the numbers of "pest" species.

In a study by Stamm (1970a), two dimensions of attitude toward the problem of scarce environmental resources were identified in a statewide random sample of 607 Wisconsin adults. A Guttman analysis of responses to the seven items used in the survey indicated that two dimensions of attitude toward scarcity can be distinguished: (1) reversal of trends—i.e., finding some way to reverse the trend toward scarcity; and (2) functional substitutes—i.e., finding equivalents for scarce resources.

One surprising result of the author's study is that ostensibly incompatible environmental attitudes received support from the same individuals. For example, respondents advocated the use of both chemical sprays (a functional substitute) and natural enemies (reversal of a trend) to control an outbreak of a forest insect pest. Supposedly, those who would advocate the chemical spray should be at odds with those who prefer natural means of restoring the forest to its original state, but this can hardly be the case if either remedy seems acceptable. The environmentalist can neither rejoice nor grumble too much over this finding. It provides evidence of both technological pragmatism and conservation ethics in people's attitude toward scarcity.

A modification of the attitude scale described above was used in a "social impact" study of the Corps of Engineers Park River flood control project (our example) as a predictor of support for the Army Corps of Engineers (Ludtke et al., 1971). In this study, 175 randomly selected respondents from the area affected by the project completed the attitude scales and answered a question on their degree of support for the Army Corps.[1] The policy of constructing dams to control and impound water is the epitome of a functional substitutes view, so it was expected that respondents with a functional substitutes attitude would be strong supporters of the Corps. This hypothesis was strongly confirmed by the results. However, the complementary hypothesis, that the stronger one's reversal of trends attitude the less his support for the Corps, was not confirmed. Thus, the attitude scales were useful in locating the "friends" of the Corps, but not in locating its antagonists.

The Park River study further demonstrated the difficulty of obtaining empirically independent dimensions of attitude. In this study, the two conceptually distinguished attitudes—reversal of trends and functional substitutes—were measured by two separate sets of attitude items. However, the intercorrelation between the two scales turned out to be positive and fairly strong.[2] In order to gain some insight into what might account for this degree of intercorrelation, a factor analysis was performed on each set of scale items.

Without going into a technical explanation of the factor analysis results, what it showed was that not all of the items in each scale were highly intercorrelated with one another. This was taken as a warning that the scale might not be "pure," i.e., that the items may not all be measuring the same thing. In the case of the functional substitution scale, the clusters of intercorrelated items could all be interpreted as lower order dimensions of the same attitude concept. However, the item clusters factored out of the reversal of trends scale were not internally consistent, and one of the clusters clearly was not measuring a reversal of trends attitude.

The greater internal consistency of the functional substitution scale was also borne out by the empirical findings of the study. This scale was consistently successful in predicting hypothesized results: support for the Corps of Engineers, knowledge of project benefits, and perceived agreement with the Corps on both benefits and disadvantages of the project. The reversal of trends scale yielded mixed results with the same set of dependent variables.

To conclude, current measures of environmental attitudes serve to describe rather simple, one-object-at-a-time pictures of the environment. An ecological perspective, however, stems from a cognizance of complex systems which are understood in terms of specific relations that can be defined and observed. The (attitudinal) notion of fixed orientations to what should be seen as a constantly changing, evolving environment contradicts the ecological view. This can be illustrated by a chapter from the public experience of the U.S. Forest Service, which has schooled people for decades in the unqualified dictate that forest fires are evil (now enter our hero, that fearless crusader—Smoky the Bear). Many wildlife ecologists in the upper Midwest would occasionally turn the rule around and use fire as a tool in wildlife management, but official and public opposition is too great.

That people do not appear to perceive the relational nature of environmental problems is indicated by a recent survey of 170 Illinois residents (Simon, 1971). The sample was randomly drawn from telephone directories and interviews were conducted by phone. This poll showed a high level of public concern (more than 90 percent) about the specific problems of air and water pollution. But when asked about the reasons for air and water pollution, only 5 percent made any connection between air pollution and population, and even fewer—2 percent—connected water pollution with population. As one might expect, very few people in this survey recommended any form of population control as a means of reducing the pollution problem.

The value of environmental attitude research could be greatly increased not only by distinguishing among the various dimensions of attitude, but also by implementing long-term studies of attitude development. By attitude development, we mean something quite different from the usual study of attitude change. Attitude change research requires that an attitude is already formed—it can only become more or less extreme. Research on attitude development would observe how the structure of an attitude develops, in terms of the identification of relevant objects of orientation and the learning of additional relations among objects.

An an example, consider the problem of obtaining longitudinal measures of individuals' attitudes toward flood control. Following an attitude change approach, we would observe whether attitudes toward the concept flood control become more positive or more negative over time. Of greater significance, however, may be how the individual's concept of flood control changes over time, subject to the influence of communication variables. Changes in attitude complexity might be observed in terms of the number of objects and attributes that are included in the individual's flood control concept. Also, what about the number of relations that the individual sees among the objects in this system? Does his concept of flood control include the relation between prairie pothole drainage and water runoff rates? Or the relation between farm tillage practices and dam siltation rates?

The complexity and relational structure of environmental attitudes may be much more important than their valence. Take the recent problem with "snakenaping" in California (Milwaukee Journal, June 26, 1971). It seems that attitudes toward snakes have become more positive of late among the California pet set. The ecological consequences of this "improved" attitude toward snakes have, however, horrified local ecologists. It seems that so many snakes have been snatched at night from warm blacktop roads that rodent populations have exploded. Unhappily, a fondness for snakes does not necessarily go hand in hand with a knowledge of their relation to populations of other animals in the desert biome. Rangers are reported as trying to "educate" the snatchers they find near area parks, since there is no law against snakenaping except within park boundaries. Unless people are aware of the numerous relations among snakes and other elements of the biome, a positive attitude toward snakes may be detrimental rather than beneficial.

COGNITIVE CHANGE AND COMMUNICATION

"Effective" environmental communication is usually defined as a message that produces change in knowledge, opinions or attitudes relative to environmental objects. Should the environmentalists and the Corps of Engineers necessarily consider attitude change the basis for inferring that their communication efforts regarding the Park River project have been successful? The key issue here revolves around whether mass communication efforts are likely to produce any measurable attitude change. Fortunately, sufficient research evidence is available to allow careful review of such questions.

It is important to consider different sorts of cognitive change separately. For example, the research evidence indicates that changes in knowledge or level of information are much more likely to be produced via mass communication than, say, changes in attitude.

Knowledge Change.

A variety of mass communication research generally shows a positive relationship between mass media exposure and level of knowledge. Tichenor et al. (1970) present data from news diffusion studies, time trends, a newspaper strike and a field experiment which demonstrate that increasing the flow of news on a topic leads to a relatively greater acquisition of knowledge by more highly educated persons. Even the less educated acquire more knowledge as news flow increases, however.

The classic World War II studies of Army training film effects by Hovland et al. (1949), also show gain in knowledge about Allied war strategy from exposure, but indicate little change in attitudes or motivation. More recent research on political socialization shows substantial increase in political knowledge among American teenagers following exposure to mass media public affairs information (Chaffee et al., 1970). Self-report evidence is also available from the study of the Park River flood control project (Stamm and Bowes, 1971), where 25 percent of community members reported gaining knowledge of the project from local mass media sources.

There can be little doubt that mass communication produces increases in public knowledge, although, as Hyman and Sheatsley (1947) pointed out long ago, these increases will not be equal for all segments of society. The impact of differential knowledge on environmental decisions has yet to be studied, but it certainly bears investigation. It would be important to know, for example, to what extent local environmental issues are decided by ecologically uninformed individuals.

Opinion and Attitude Change.

Environmental educators and others interested in the public's orientation to environmental problems often seek more than an increase in the individual's level of knowledge. Gilbert (1964), in a book on natural resources public relations, says that natural resources messages must be presented to the public in such a way that they will be understood *and accepted.* Ross (1970) identifies at least three kinds of communication programs by means of which resource managers seek to obtain opinion and attitudinal change: (1) community relations programs to win public consent for specific projects or policies; (2) public relations programs to build broad support for general agency needs and goals; (3) environmental information programs to engender an ecological conscience on the part of the public at large.

The theoretical point to recognize here is that not all opinions and attitudes are the same. They can be conceptualized as being made up of components which are differentially susceptible to change via communication. This was first pointed out by Hovland (1959) in his attempt to reconcile the conflicting results of experimental and field studies of attitude change. He had noted that attitude change frequently occurred in experimental studies, while in field studies, little or no change was observed. A major reason, he learned, was that the field studies dealt with socially significant attitudes and opinions, deeply rooted in prior experience, while the experimental studies usually did not.

Reconceptualizations of the attitude concept subsequent to the Hovland article have been supported by empirical studies. Fishbein (1962) has separated attitude into two independent components, a belief component—the individual's perception of a relationship between an attitude object and some concept, and his affective evaluation of the concept. Fishbein (1962a) argues that "two individuals may differ in belief but have similar attitudes, or vice versa." The importance of Fishbein's argument is that an individual may be observed to have the same overall attitude before and after a message exchange, when in fact there has been internal change in one or both components that is not reflected in the summary measurement.

The utility of a multicomponent view of attitude has been demonstrated in a recent study by Guerrero and Hughes (1970) in which change in belief and evaluative components were measured separately in addition to a summary measurement of both components. The measures were made before and after a message exchange simulating the decisions of purchasing a car. Individuals participating in the experiment evaluated car features such as performance, comfort, safety, and social acceptability—the evaluative components; and also rated their first and second choice cars on each of these attributes—the belief component. The results of the study strongly support the authors' hypothesis that changes in both belief and evaluative components would be unrelated to the summary measure. In other words, change in either or both belief and evaluative components was not reflected in the summary measurement which lumped both components.

Carter (1965) has also distinguished two attitudinal components—salience and pertinence. Salience, defined as the *psychological closeness* of the object, is a function of the individual's *reinforcement history* with the object. Positive reinforcement, for example, would be expected to increase one's evaluation of the object. Pertinence, the relative value ascribed to an object in comparison with a second object, is a function of the amounts of attributes ascribed to the two objects discriminated. For example, the amount of height ascribed to two individuals allows one to discriminate which is taller.

According to Carter, the salience component would be expected to change only incrementally in much the same way as responses are conditioned in a learning experiment. The pertinence component, however, may change abruptly simply as a result of changing one of the objects or introducing a new attribute as the basis of comparison. That salience and pertinence are separate sources of object value has been demonstrated by Chaffee (1967) and Chaffee and Lindner (1969). In order to begin his experiments with a salience of zero, Chaffee used nonsense words that the subjects would have had no experience with. He manipulated salience then by varying the number of times that each nonsense word was used in completing a puzzle (i.e., by varying the opportunity for positive reinforcement). Pertinence was manipulated by assigning different point values for successfully using a nonsense word in the puzzle. The subjects were instructed to complete the puzzle and get as many points as possible. In the subjects' subsequent ratings of the words, the ratings became more positive the more often a word was used *and* the higher its point value.

The only published study in which mass media exposure has been specifically related to measures of environmental attitude is a statewide study of environmental attitudes by the author (1970b). In this study, an attitude construct, "orientation to scarcity," was identified and measured as two separate dimensions of attitude—a reversal of trends dimension and a functional substitutes dimension (see previous discussion). The hypothesis tested was that those most exposed to conservation media—i.e., newspaper outdoor and conservation columns and outdoor and conservation magazines—would score highest on the reversal of trends scale, since these media generally espouse the predominant conservation philosophy. However, this hypothesis was not supported. Media exposure instead was strongly related to higher scores on both attitude scales, while the nonexposed were unlikely to have any attitudes toward scarcity.

The results of the study suggest that environmental education via the mass media will not be the only (or even the main) influence in shaping individuals' environmental attitudes. The relative lack of orientation shown by the non-exposed as compared to the users of conservation media suggests the media play a role in creating awareness of scarcity problems. But it is just as likely that having an environmental orientation causes greater exposure to conservation media. In fact, there is no reason why both interpretations could not be correct.

The trouble with the above study from the standpoint of trying to locate communication effects is that attitude was measured as a global concept rather than in terms of the structural components we have discussed. Such a study gives only a gross indication of media effects at best. Future research on environmental attitudes would do well to distinguish structural components, or perhaps even study the "attribute structure"[3] of environmental attitudes as Edelstein

(1970) has done with attitudes toward the Vietnam conflict. Edelstein found that attribute structure is strongly related to the individual's level of information seeking about the war; higher information seeking is associated with a more complex attribute structure.

The strategy suggested by Erickson (1971d) of designing environmental persuasion efforts to appeal to existing attitudes does not receive support from a recent study (Donohue et al., 1970) dealing with public understanding of news articles on DDT and nuclear power plants. In an area probability sample of 435 residences drawn from three contiguous areas northwest of Minneapolis, the authors tested the proposition that persons with more extreme attitudes on a controversial public issue will show lower understanding of messages about that issue than persons with neutral positions. Thus, the study represents a direct test of the extent to which attitudes are a barrier to an understanding of environmental issues.

Attitudinal position on DDT and nuclear power plants in each case was measured by summing responses to seven agree-disagree items selected from statements attributed to various interest groups, public officials, and spokesmen. The newspaper articles were taken from actual newspaper coverage over the two months preceding the survey. Each person read and responded to an article on each issue; after the respondent finished reading the article, the interviewer took the article back and asked, "What, as you recall, does this article say?" Understanding was defined as the number of accurate statements offered by a respondent immediately after reading the article.

Results of the study showed that understanding of DDT articles was unrelated to attitudinal position, while understanding of nuclear power plant articles was higher (not lower) for persons with extreme attitudes. The authors concluded that for issues such as pesticides and nuclear waste discharge, ideologically based attitudes may occur so infrequently and the media content may show so little apparent bias (when compared with, say, the propaganda of chemical or electric power companies) that attitudinal selectivity fails to operate among persons confronted with that content. This would seem to suggest that attitudinal selectivity is a significant concern only for the communicator with deliberate and obvious persuasive intentions. The information programs of government agencies such as the Army

Corps of Engineers and the "educational" literature of environmentalist groups would probably be subject to attitudinal selectivity.

The upshot of such theory and research on attitude structure is that it is impossible to make any simple statement about the potency of mass communication to change environmental attitudes. One variable is the salience of the objects involved. It is extremely unlikely that attitudes toward high salience objects could be changed without multiple exposure to messages over a substantial period of time. As an example, we might consider the difficulty of changing a pheasant hunter's attitude toward predators such as foxes. Despite many years of persuasive and educational effort, the call for renewed bounties on foxes is heard wherever pheasant populations show a decline.

This is not to say that environmental education efforts produce no cognitive change where high salience objects are involved, although it does suggest that we should revise our thinking about what we can expect to accomplish. The Guerrero and Hughes experiment, for example, showed that separate attitude components were susceptible to change via communication, but that these changes did not show up in a summary measure lumping both components. Changes in attitudinal structure no doubt will occur as a result of environmental communication efforts, but we are only beginning to develop the concepts and the measuring instruments that will allow us to detect these changes. Prediction of what particular structural changes will occur is yet to be studied.

ENVIRONMENTAL ATTITUDES AND BEHAVIOR

The interest in manipulating environmental attitudes stems mostly from the belief that behavior toward the environment is controlled by the individual's basic attitudes toward the environment. As early as 1949, Aldo Leopold observed modern man's need for an "ecological conscience," pointing out that: "By and large, our present problem is one of attitudes and implements." There are some good reasons, however, for arguing that a concept of environmental attitude never will provide an adequate basis for explaining the individual's environmental behavior: (1) the potency of situational variables such as a vested interest in the resource in question; and (2) the inability of the concept to fully describe environmental orientations.

Environmental educators in general believe that environmental attitudes are the key to changing exploitive and other kinds of behavior they see as undesirable. Southern (1969), for example, proposes that if the individual acquires a broad environmental understanding he will develop social attitudes that will affect his behavior toward the total environment. Covert (1969), too, has offered an environmental education program to "promote an environmental awareness and a sound sociological attitude toward the total environment."

We have already noted that the prospects for using mass communication to generate attitude change are not too bright. But for purposes of discussion let's assume that some change in attitudes can be wrought, and raise the question of what corresponding behavioral change can be anticipated. Research relevant to this topic has been reviewed by Festinger (1964), who points out the absence of research evidence that there are corresponding changes in both attitudes and directed behavior following persuasive messages, and by Mischel (1968) who concludes that changes in attitude are not necessarily accompanied by changes in behavior.

The literature on persuasion affords many examples of lack of behavioral change in conjunction with documented attitude change. A recent review by Leventhal (1970) of the use of fear appeals in persuasion provides many instances of changes in attitudes toward cigarette smoking prompted by fear-arousing messages, but no change in subsequent behavior. In a recent study by Chaffee and Lindner (1969), changes in attitude were demonstrated as a function of salience, pertinence and reduction of cognitive dissonance, but the effects did not carry over to directed behavior toward the objects.

There is scant literature bearing on the relationship between environmental attitudes and behavior, but the few studies available are consistent in demonstrating the lack of any relationship. Medalia and Finkner (1965) surveyed residents of Clarkston, Washington, who were subject to reduced visibility, tarnishing house paint, malodors and suspected effects upon health from a pulp mill. While 85 percent of the sample agreed that air pollution was a problem in Clarkston, only 10 percent said they had considered asking some agency to take action on the problem, and two percent said thay had ever made a complaint.

In a study of environmental opinion in Minnesota, Tichenor et al. (1971) have questioned the notion that increased environmental concern has produced a readiness on the part of the public to act swiftly and boldly to correct environmental problems. They point to a CBS news poll based on a national sample which showed a majority supporting conservation rather than progress, but at the same time largely unwilling to eliminate tax deductions as a population control measure. Similarly, in a 1969 survey of northeastern Minnesota adults (Tichenor et al., 1971a), two-thirds believed DDT constituted a hazard as a pollutant, but still had second thoughts about banning the insecticide. A later survey in the spring of 1970 in four northeastern communities (Tichenor et al., 1971b) found about one in ten willing to accept the rationing of electricity as a course of action, but less than a fourth agreeing with the idea of rationing automobiles. [4]

The authors (1971c) summarize their findings as indicating the degree to which attitudes about control measures are governed by people's own self-interest. Their survey data show very striking differences in attitudes toward control measures among members of separate communities. For example, three-fourths of those surveyed in the taconite mining community of Silver Bay, Minn. disagreed with the idea of preventing discharge of taconite tailings into Lake Superior. Of these same Silver Bay people, two-thirds said they were very concerned about whether mining was to be allowed in the Boundary Waters Canoe Area 140 miles to the north, and were less likely to agree that industry should be allowed to drill and remove minerals, even if it would add to employment and to the economy in that area.

You would think that the individual's personal self-interest in environmental problems would include concern for local environmental quality, as well as concern for the effects of control measures. A recent poll, however, shows that environmental pollution is often perceived as a remote problem not affecting one's own community. These results are reported in a March 1970, survey of a random sample of 300 Durham, North Carolina, residents (Murch 1971). The survey dealt with the issue of environmental damage and attempted to determine how aware people were of the problem, who or what they felt was responsible for it, and how it might be solved.

The surprising finding of this poll was that while nearly three-fourths (74 percent) reported that pollution is a serious problem nationally, only 13 percent felt that pollution was serious in Durham. Yet physical data indicated that air pollution in Durham exceeds the national average, and that the community experiences littering, traffic congestion and aircraft noise.

A similar finding has been reported by Williams and Bunyard (1966), who studied awareness and concern about air pollution in St. Louis, Missouri. In this study, a much greater proportion of people were bothered by air pollution than acknowledged its existence in the neighborhood where they lived.

Murch suggests that the mass media may have helped to produce the tendency to view pollution as a rather general problem external to one's own community. The poll found that mass media—especially television—were most often cited as sources of information about environmental pollution. Network television and national magazines would be expected to focus on broader aspects of the problem. But the same was true of local newspapers, which devoted half their copy on pollution to national and global problems, and less than ten percent to problems within the community.

KNOWLEDGE AND ATTITUDES

Allied with the notion that desirable behavior will follow from proper environmental attitudes is the further notion that proper attitudes result from greater knowledge and information. However, research has not always supported the hypothesis that information gain is positively correlated with attitude change (e.g., Miller and Campbell, 1959). In the environmental area, this finding emerged in the Stamm and Ross study (1966a) of a Wisconsin community's decision to build an artificial lake on a local trout stream. Environmental knowledge bore no relation to community members' attitudes toward the project.

A similar relation was found in the study of public opinion in Minnesota (Tichenor et al., 1971d). Total knowledge of the three issues—taconite tailings, air pollution from a Duluth steel mill, and mining in the Boundary Waters Canoe Area (BWCA)—was markedly higher in the three communities where one of the issues was immediately relevant and was lowest in Grand Rapids, Minn. where the issues were more remote. Yet it was citizens in Grand Rapids who showed highest support for restrictive measures.

The results of the Tichenor et al. study corroborate those of an earlier study by Swan (1970). The Swan study was based on a sample of 173 seniors from a downtown Detroit high school. The school was located in an area subject to severe air pollution, and was heterogeneous with respect to race and socioeconomic level. In this case, a 20-point scale measuring support for actions to solve air pollution problems showed no correlation with knowledge of air pollution.

These findings suggest, contrary to the presently accepted rule, that general public support for environmental measures may in fact fall off as people learn more about the specific nature of the issues involved—particularly as they understand how the restrictions may affect community interests. We should not conclude, however, that a community's appreciation of its own self-interest will lead to decisions that promote further destruction of the local environment. In the Stamm and Bowes (1972a) study of a proposed Army Corps of Engineers flood control project in northeastern North Dakota, those who were personally concerned about the effects of the project were also the most knowledgeable about potential disadvantageous effects. All members of the community were well informed regarding beneficial effects.

COMMUNICATION AS COORIENTATION

The concern of local citizens—that government officials and agencies be informed about their criteria for change—was mentioned previously. Their desire is that communication flow from them, not just to them through the government (or environmental interest groups). Yet the vast majority of the environmental communication literature deals with *intra*personal—not *inter*personal—concepts. This same body of literature implicitly assumes that effective means of creating changes in knowledge, opinion or attitude are sought only by some communicator, but not by local citizens. This is a serious oversight of research on environmental communication, and of mass communication research in general.

The result of this approach to research is that we are forever surveying private citizens to evaluate the effectiveness of agency communication programs or the effects of mass media messages, but we never survey the government agencies or the media with a similar purpose in mind.

Environmental communication research has ignored recent model-building and theorizing in communication circles which have for several years emphasized the reciprocal nature of the communication process (e.g., Bauer and Zimmerman, 1956; Westley and MacLean, 1957; Carter, 1965a; Chaffee and McLeod, 1968). In the case of the Park River Dam, for example, an entirely different set of criteria for "effective communication" would be introduced by considering the reciprocal nature of the communication process. Instead of looking only for changes in citizen's information about or opinion toward the flood control project, we would also begin to ask whether representatives of the Corps of Engineers know what objections citizens might have, whether they know what benefits citizens expect to obtain and correctly perceive citizen opinion toward all aspects of the project.

Public's Perceived Agreement with a Resource Agency

The value of viewing the communication process as reciprocal can be illustrated by examining some of the communication data obtained in the social impact study of the Park River Project (Stamm and Bowes, 1972b). This study obtained data on intrapersonal communication variables such as awareness, knowledge, degree of concern and opinion toward the project, as well as data on a coorientational communication variable. This interpersonal variable, which is derived from a recent coorientational model of communication (Chaffee and McLeod, 1968), can be labeled "perceived agreement." The data concerned the extent to which local citizens perceived similarity between their own view and the view of the Corps on specific effects of the Project such as flood control, environmental changes, tax changes, etc.

The interesting point is that the coorientational data and the intrapersonal data lead to different interpretations of the effectiveness of the information program of the Corps of Engineers. In terms of intrapersonal criteria, the agency program appeared fairly successful. A high degree of awareness of the project had been achieved—

about 65 percent. About 50 percent indicated personal concern regarding whether the project was completed or not. Knowledge of anticipated project benefits was also quite high with 46 percent mentioning flood control, 20 percent improved water supply and 7 percent recreation. Only 18 percent failed to name any benefit of the project.

On the other hand, the comparison between own-views of community members and their perception of the Corps' position on anticipated changes often showed large differences. Community members were considerably less likely to perceive the Corps as sharing their view where they viewed the effect as a disadvantage. This result, it turned out, was largely due to a tendency for community members to be undecided about the Corps position on disadvantageous effects of the project.

The implication of this peculiar "one-sided understanding" between community members and the Corps is that the agency had effectively communicated its viewpoint on beneficial aspects of the project in those cases where community members also thought the effect was beneficial. At the same time, citizens were often left in doubt as to what the Corps would do about potentially harmful changes resulting from the project.

The "one-sided understanding" indicated by the coorientational data could be traced to a decidedly one-sided information campaign in which the Corps produced "handout" sheets stressing benefits of the project. Rather than making independent probes of the project's advantages or disadvantages, the local mass media simply echoed agency handouts. Only when vocal opposition from rural residents and several interested environmentalists was raised at the final public hearing on the project did the local media give extensive play to opposition arguments.[5] However, this coverage came a long time after the favorable arguments had been made public.

Unfortunately, the Park River study did not undertake a full-scale investigation of coorientational variables, dealing as it did only with agreement as perceived by the public sector. The value of the study would have been greater if representatives from the Corps of Engineers and of concerned state agencies had also been surveyed regarding their views of project effects and their perception of local opinion. In this way, the gap between perceived and actual agreement, a measure of the accuracy of perceptions, could have been assessed.

A study by Borton and Warner (1971) lends itself to a coorientational interpretation, although it is not derived from any of the available models. The researchers surveyed 215 persons in the Susquehanna River Basin who had been identified as water resource opinion leaders, and in addition, surveyed agency representatives and staff members of the Susquehanna Study Coordinating Committee (a policy-making group). Both groups were asked to rank order what they considered to be the most important water resource problems in the study area. Committee members were also asked to provide the rank ordering they thought would be given by local leaders.

Committee members ranked flood control as first priority, water supply second and pollution third. They thought local leaders would reverse the order of the first two. In fact, local leaders ranked pollution first and recreation second. Following a series of planning meetings attended by both groups, the priorities of both groups shifted, but the planning committee became more accurate in predicting the ranking of problems by local leaders.

POLICY MAKER ATTEMPTS AT COORIENTATION

As alluded to earlier in this chapter, sometimes government agencies and private corporations do make attempts to determine the opinions and attitudes of communities as a basis for planning more satisfactory environmental projects. Electric power companies have become sensitive to the increased ecological awareness of the public, and have begun to "sound out" public opinion on projects involving nuclear power and discharge of hot water. Such efforts need not be viewed entirely with a cynical eye, as merely providing a basis for planning more effective persuasive strategies. It is also possible that field surveys will be used more and more as a coorientational basis for planning and policy-making because public dissatisfaction has already resulted in unpopularity and costly delays.

In the conclusion to a survey of the environmental perceptions and attitudes of 70 British Columbia engineers and public health officials, Sewell (1971: 57) noted the predominant skepticism of professionals toward involving the public in policy-making, then stressed the dangers of failing to involve them.

Second, it will be necessary to involve the public much more directly in the planning process. It is already clear that the public feels alienated in this process, and that conventional means of consulting public opinion do not accurately reveal their preferences. Presenting the public with a few discrete alternatives has the advantage of simplifying the choice process, but unless the alternatives reflect the values held by the public rather than those of the planners, they may all be rejected.

The social impact study of the Park River Project (Ludtke et al., 1971a) affords an example of the value of local polls in improving an agency's understanding of community views. Not all of the news was bad for the Corps of Engineers either. Generally, the survey found good will toward the Corps and support for its flood control and water impoundment plans. At the same time, the Corps learned that it had overestimated enthusiasm for a multiple-use recreational proposal, and had been ignorant of public objections to such effects as inundation of farms and timberlands, wildlife habitat destruction and possible tax increases.

The objections revealed in the survey finally surfaced at a volatile public hearing, which was to have been the final hearing before a plan was submitted for federal funding. Instead, based on survey findings and the hearing, the Corps decided to hold additional informal meetings with rural groups who most strongly objected to existing proposals. The delay was made in spite of majority support for one of the proposed alternatives, and in spite of nearly unanimous backing from community leaders for this alternative. The community power structure and the general public were not cooriented either.

Agencies involved in the management of public recreational lands, such as the U.S. Forest Service, have been making attempts to increase coorientation with users as a basis for providing higher quality recreation. The surveys have usually included questions about why people are attracted to an area, what values they perceive in a resource, and what facilities they desire.

Much of the recreational research is stimulated by the implied contradiction in trying to provide the wilderness image that some users desire, while at the same time providing minimal facilities to satisfy demands for convenience. A study of Minnesota vacationers by Bultena and Taves (1961) produced the surprising finding that the majority of vacationers did not perceive this contradiction, while most forest supervisors did. Most users of the Quetico-Superior area saw no apparent conflict between their image of the surroundings as wilderness and their desire for convenience.

In a later study of Quetico-Superior recreators (1963), Lucas concluded that all resources are defined by human perception. The interpretation was drawn from a study which showed that the boundary of "the wilderness" as perceived by recreational users not only varied considerably, but also rarely conformed with the official wilderness boundary maintained by the Forest Service. The varying perception of wilderness by the public is a communication problem for the managing agency, but the differences in perception also hold the key to effective management for high quality recreation.

Even this brief consideration of the coorientational nature of environmental issues such as flood control and wilderness area management discloses a significance in public attitudes and perceptions that is not adequately reflected in research. We have discussed throughout this chapter the relation of cognitions to the individual's behavior and the prospects of thereby influencing behavior via communication. But the critical relation may be the influence of perceived public attitudes on environmental decisions, not their influence on the individual's own behavior. To give an example, the Corps of Engineers policy-makers who perceived that dislocation of farms and roads was viewed unfavorably by the community may well devise a plan of several small dams instead of a large dam and impoundment.

White (1971) has described a number of policy decisions which were influenced by perceived public attitudes. A large city electric utility that installed precipitators because it thought conspicuous smoke plumes would impair its relations with its customers; and the decision of the New York City Board of Water Supply to avoid the Hudson River as a water source because it believed users would object to anything other than pure, upland sources are two examples. The questions for communication scholars include how these perceptions come about and whether they are accurate.

The communication problem on environmental issues, as in any other area of social action, involves many sets of opinions and attitudes. White (1971a) suggested a paradigm including the opinions each person holds, the opinions he thinks others hold, and the opinions that he thinks they should hold, and noted that many public administrators confuse these different sets of opinions. Perhaps the greatest contribution that communication researchers can make at this time is to promote appreciation among public officials of the coorientational nature of environmental management decisions, and to provide the methodology for evaluating the state of coorientation between policy-makers and the public on particular issues. The fruits of such research would be much greater than a further search for more effective persuasive strategies. The arsenal of persuasive strategies developed to date has done little to improve the performance of environmental agencies.

NOTES

1. A total of 262 local citizens were interviewed in the survey, of which 175 were asked to complete the attitude items.

2. Gamma = .560.

3. Edelstein (1970) defined attribute structures as unidimensional, mixed-dimensional and multidimensional. For example, a person with a unidimensional attribute structure had only positive or negative attributes for an object. Multidimensional persons had both positive and negative attributes for at least two objects (and no more than one object for which there were only negative or positive attributes).

4. For many readers, the failure to find predictable empirical relationships between attitudes and behavior will come as no surprise. The research of LaPiere (1934) and Minard (1952), to give two examples, is widely known in this regard. The question is still worth raising in this context; first, because of wide acceptance of the proposition that changes in environmental attitudes will bring about behavior changes and, second, because it leads to a consideration of other variables, such as norms, roles and power, that account in large part for our behavior.

5. This finding is consistent with the generally documented function of mass media in local controversies and action campaigns. See, for example, Paletz et al. (1971).

REFERENCES

BAILEY, G. A. (1971) "The public, the media, and the knowledge gap." J. of Environmental Education 2 (Summer): 3-9.

BAUER, R. and C. ZIMMERMAN (1956) "The effect of an audience upon what is remembered." Public Opinion Q. 20 (Spring): 238-248.

BULTENA, G. L., and M. J. TAVES (1961) "Changing wilderness images and forestry policy." J. of Forestry 59: 167-171.

CARTER, R. F. (1965, 1965a) "Communication and affective relations." Journalism Q. 42 (Spring): 203-212.

CHAFFEE, S. H. (1967) "Salience and pertinence as sources of value change." J. of Communication 17: 25-38.

——— and J. W. LINDNER (1968, 1968a) "Three processes of value change without behavioral change." J. of Communication 19: 30-40.

CHAFFEE, S. H. and J. McLEOD (1968, 1968a) "Sensitization in panel design: a coorientational experiment." Journalism Q. 45: 661-669.

CHAFFEE, S. H., S. WARD, and L. TIPTON (1970) "Mass communication and political socialization." Journalism Q. 47 (Winter): 647-660.

COVERT, D. C. (1969) "Toward a curriculum in environmental education." Environmental Education 1 (Fall): 11-13.

DONOHUE, G. A., P. J. TICHENOR and C. N. OLIEN (1970) "Attitudes and mass media learning about two environmental issues." Paper presented at symposium on Mass Communication Research and Environmental Decision-Making, Madison, Wis.

EDELSTEIN, A. (1970) "Attribute structure, education and communication with respect to Vietnam." Paper presented to the Assocation for Education in Journalism, Washington, D.C.

ERICKSON, D. L. (1971, 1971a, b, c, d) "Attitudes and communications about wildlife." J. of Environmental Education 2 (Summer): 17-21.

FISHBEIN, M. and B. RAVEN (1962, 1962a) "The AB scales: an operational definition of belief and attitude." Human Relations 15: 35-44.

FESTINGER, L. (1964) "Behavioral support for opinion change." Public Opinion Q. 28: 404-417.

GILBERT, D. (1964) Public Relations in Natural Resources Management. Minneapolis: Burgess.

GUERRERO, J. and D. HUGHES (1970) "An empirical test of the Fishbein model: its implications for advertising and marketing research." Paper presented to the Association of Education in Journalism, Washington, D.C.

HOVLAND, C. I. (1959) "Reconciling conflicting results from experimental and survey studies of attitude change." American Psychologist 14 (January): 8-17.

——— , A. A. LUMSDAINE, and F. D. SHEFFIELD (1949) Experiments on Mass Communication. Princeton University Press.

HYMAN, H. H. and P. SHEATSLEY (1947) "Some reasons why information campaigns fail." Public Opinion Q. 11: 413-423.

LaPIERE, R. T. (1934) "Attitudes vs. actions." Social Forces 13: 230-237.

LEOPOLD, A. (1949) A Sand County Almanac. New York: Oxford University Press.

LEVENTHAL, H. (1970) "Findings and theory in the study of fear communications," pp. 120-181 in L. Berkowitz (ed.) Advances in Experimental Social Psychology. New York: Basic Books.

LINGWOOD, D. A. (1971) "Environmental education through information-seeking: the case of an environmental teach-in." Environment and Behavior 3: 231-261.

LUCAS, R. C. (1963) "Wilderness perception and use: the example of the boundary waters canoe area." Natural Resources J. 3: 394-411.

LUDTKE, R. L., K. R. STAMM, J. E. BOWES, II, and R. D. KINGSBURY (1971, 1971a) Social and Economic Considerations for Water Resources Planning in the Park River Subbasin, North Dakota. Grand Forks: University of North Dakota.

MEDALIA, N. A. and A. L. FINKNER (1965) "Community perception of air quality: an opinion study in Clarkston, Washington." Cincinnati: U.S. Public Health Service Publication 999-10.

MILLER, N. and D. T. CAMPBELL (1959) "Recency and primacy in persuasion as a function in the timing of speeches and measurements." J. of Abnormal and Social Psychology 59: 1-9.

Milwaukee Journal (1971) "Snakenaping is profitable but ecologically it's slimy." (Saturday, June 26).

MINARD, R. D. (1952) "Race relations in the Pocahontas coal field." J. of Social Issues 8: 29-44.

MISCHEL, W. (1968) Personality Assessment. New York: John Wiley.

MURCH, A. W. (1971) "Public concern for environmental pollution." Public Opinion Q. 35: 102-109.

PALETZ, D. L., P. REICHERT, and B. McINTYRE (1971) "How the media support local governmental authority." Public Opinion Q. 35 (Spring): 80-95.

ROSS, J. E. (1970) "Azimuths in conservation communications research." Environmental Education 1 (Spring): 88-93.

SEWELL, W. R. (1971) "Environmental perceptions and attitudes of engineers and public health officers." Environment and Behavior 3 (March): 23-59.

SHEPARD, P. (1969) "Ecology and man—a viewpoint," pp. 1-13 in P. Shepard and D. McKinley (eds.) The Subversive Science: Essays Toward an Ecology of Man. Boston: Houghton Mifflin.

SIMON, R. J. (1971) "Public attitudes toward population and pollution," Public Opinion Q. 35 (Spring): 95-102.

SOUTHERN, B. H. (1969) "Vitalizing natural resources education." Environmental Education 1 (Fall): 29-30.

STAMM, K. R. (1970, 1970a, b) "Two orientations to the conservation concept of scarcity." Environmental Education 1 (Summer): 134-140.

——— and J. E. BOWES II (1972, 1972a, b) "Communication during an environmental decision." J. of Environmental Education 3 (Spring): in press.

STAMM, K. R. and J. E. ROSS (1966, 1966a) "Rationality of opinion on a controversy in conservation." Journalism Q. 43 (Winter): 762-765.

SWAN, J. A. (1970) "Response to air pollution: a study of attitudes and coping strategies of high school youths." Environment and Behavior (September): 127-152.

TICHENOR, P. J., G. A. DONOHUE, and C. N. OLIEN (1970) "Mass media flow and differential growth in knowledge." Public Opinion Q. 34 (Summer): 159-171.

——— , and J. K. BOWERS (1971, 1971a, b, c, d) "Environment and public opinion." J. of Environmental Education 2 (Summer): 38-43.

WESTLEY, B. and M. McLEAN (1957) "A conceptual model for communication research." Journalism Q. 34: 31-38.

WHITE, G. F. (1971, 1971a) "Formation and role of public attitudes," pp. 105-128 in H. Jarret (ed.) Environmental Quality in a Growing Economy. Baltimore: Johns Hopkins Press.

WILLIAMS, J. D. and F. L. BUNYARD (1966) Opinion Surveys and Air Quality Statistical Relationships. Interstate Air Pollution Study Phase II Project Report. Cincinnati: U.S. Public Health Service.

SELECTED BIBLIOGRAPHY

SELECTED BIBLIOGRAPHY

ARORA, S. K. and H. D. LASSWELL (1969) Political Communication. Holt, Rinehart, and Winston.

ATKIN, C. K. (1971) "How imbalanced campaign coverage affects audience exposure patterns." J. Q. 48 (Summer): 235-244.

——— (1969) "The impact of political poll results on candidate and issue preferences." J. Q. (Autumn): 515-521.

BAGDIKIAN, B. H. (1971) The Information Machines, Their Impact on Man and the Media. New York: Harper & Row.

BAKER, R. and S. BALL (1969) Mass Media and Violence: A Staff Report to the National Commission on the Causes and Prevention of Violence. Washington, D.C.: Government Printing Office.

BAUER, R. (1964) "The obstinate audience: the influence process from the point of view of social communication." American Psychologist 19 (May): 319-328.

——— and A. BAUER (1960) "American mass society and mass media." J. of Social Ideas, 16: 3-66.

BAUER, R. and C. ZIMMERMAN (1956) "The effect of an audience upon what is remembered." Public Opinion Q. 20 (Spring): 238-248.

BERELSON, B. R. (1952) Content Analysis in Communication Research. New York: Free Press.

——— and G. STEINER (1964) Human Behavior: An Inventory of Scientific Findings. New York: Harcourt, Brace, and World.

BERELSON, B. R., P. F. LAZARSFELD, and W. N. McPHEE (1954) Voting: A Study of Opinion Formation in a Presidential Campaign. Chicago: Univ. of Chicago Press.

BERNSTEIN, B. (1964) "Elaborated and restricted codes: their social origins and some consequences." American Anthropologist 66 (2): 55-69.

BREED, W. (1958) "Mass communication and social integration." Social Forces 37: 109-116.
——— (1955) "Social control in the newsroom." Social Forces 33: 323-335.

BOGART, L. (1968-1969) "Changing news interests and the mass media." Public Opinion Q. 32 (Winter): 560-574.

CAMPBELL, A., P. E. CONVERSE, W. E. MILLER, and D. E. STOKES (1960) The American Voter. New York: John Wiley.

CANTRIL, H., H. GAUDET, and H. HERZOG (1940) The Invasion From Mars. Princeton: Princeton Univ. Press.

CARLSSEN, G. (1965) "Time and continuity in mass attitude change: the case of voting." Public Opinion Q. 29: 133-144.

CARTER, R. F. (1965, 1965a) "Communication and affective relations." J. Q. 42 (Spring): 203-212.

CATER, D. (1964) The Fourth Branch of Government. New York: Random House.

CHAFFEE, S. H. (1967a) "Salience and pertinence as sources of value change." J. of Communication 17: 25-38.

——— (1967b) "Salience and homeostasis in communication processes." J. Q. 44: 439-444.

——— and J. M. McLEOD (1968) "Sensitization in panel design: a coorientation experiment." J. Q. 45: 661-669.

——— and D. B. WACKMAN (1972) "Family communication patterns and adolescent political participation." In J. Dennis (ed.) Explorations of Political Socialization. New York: John Wiley.

CHAFFEE, S. H., J. M. McLEOD, and C. K. ATKIN (1971) "Parental influences on adolescent media use." American Behavioral Scientist 14 (3): 323-340.

CHAFFEE, S. H., L. S. WARD, and L. P. TIPTON (1970) "Mass communication and political socialization." J. Q. 47 (Winter): 647-659.

CHESTER, E. W. (1969) Radio, Television and American Politics. New York: Sheed and Ward.

CLARKE, P. (1965) "Parental socialization values and children's newspaper reading." J. Q. 42 (Autumn): 539-546.

CLARKE, P. and L. RUGGELS (1970) "Preferences among news media for coverage of public affairs." J. Q. 47 (Autumn): 464-471.

——— (1971) "Children's response to entertainment." American Behavioral Scientist 14 (3): 353-370.

COLEMAN, J. S. (1957) Community Conflict. New York: Free Press.

COHEN, B. C. (1963) The Press, the Public and Foreign Policy. Princeton, N.J.: Princeton Univ. Press.

COSER, L. S. (1956) The Functions of Social Conflict. New York: Free Press.

CONVERSE, P. (1962) "Information flow and the stability of partisan attitudes." Public Opinion Q. 26 (Winter): 578-599.

DE FLEUR, M. L. (1966) Theories of Mass Communication. New York: McKay.

——— and L. DE FLEUR (1967) "The relative contribution of television as a learning source for children's occupational knowledge." American Sociological Rev. 32: 777-789.

DEUTSCHMANN, P. J. and W. A. DANIELSON (1960) "Diffusion of knowledge of the major news story." J. Q. 37 (Summer): 345-355.

DEXTER, L. A. and D. M. WHITE (n.d.) People, Society, and Mass Communication. New York: Free Press.

DONAHEW, L. (1967) "Newspaper gatekeeper and forces in the news channel." Public Opinion Q. 31: 61-68.

——— (1962) "Communication and readiness for change in Appalachia." J. Q. 44: 679-687.

EDELSTEIN, A. S. (1966) Perspectives in Mass Communications. Copenhagen: Einar Harcks Forlag.

EFRON, E. (1971) The News Twisters. Los Angeles: Nast Publishing.

EISENSTADT, S. N. (1955) "Communication systems and social structure: an exploratory comparative study." Public Opinion Q. 19 (Summer): 153-167.

FESHBACH, S. and B. SINGER (1971) Television and Aggression. San Francisco: Jossey-Bass.

FESTINGER, L. (1964) "Behavioral support for opinion change." Public Opinion Q. 28: 404-417.

——— (1957) A Theory of Cognitive Dissonance. Stanford: Stanford Univ. Press.

FLETCHER, A. D. (1969) "Negro and white children's television program preferences." J. of Broadcasting 13: 359-366.

FRIEDSON, E. (1954) "Communications research and the concept of mass." American Sociological Rev. 18: 313-317.

FRIENDLY, F. W. (1967) Due to Circumstances Beyond Our Control . . . New York: Random House.

FUCHS, D. A. (1965) "Election newscasts and their effects on Western voter turnout." J. Q. 42 (Winter): 22-28.

GALBRAITH, J. K. (1967) The New Industrial State. New York: Houghton Mifflin.

GANS, H. J. (1962) The Urban Villagers: Group and Class in the Life of Italian Americans. New York: Free Press.

GERALD, J. E. (1963) The Social Responsibility of the Press. Minneapolis: Univ. of Minnesota Press.

GERBNER, G. (1958) "The social role of the confession magazine." Social Problems 6: 29-41.

GERSON, W. (1966) "Mass media socialization behavior: Negro-white differences." Social Forces 45: 40-50.

GIEBER, W. (1964) "News is what newspapermen make it," pp. 173-182 in L. A. Dexter and D. M. White, People, Society and Mass Communications. New York: Free Press.

——— and W. JOHNSON (1961) "The city hall 'beat': a study of reporter and source roles." J. Q. 38 (Summer): 289-302.

GLASER, W. A. (1965) "Television and voting turnout." Public Opinion Q. 29: 71-86.

GLESSING, R. J. (1970) The Underground Press in America. Bloomington, Indiana: Indiana Univ. Press.

GREENBERG, B. S. and P. H. TANNENBAUM (1962) "Communicator performance under cognitive stress." J. Q. 39 (Spring): 169-178.

——— and B. DERVIN, with J. BOWES, and J. DOMINICK (1970) Use of the Mass Media by the Urban Poor. New York: Praeger.

HALLORAN, J. D. (1964) The Effects of Mass Communication: With Special Reference to Television. Leicester: Leicester Univ. Press.

HEIDER, F. (1958) The Psychology of Interpersonal Relations. New York: John Wiley.

——— (1946) "Attitudes and cognitive organization." J. of Psychology 21: 107-112.

HERZOG, H. (1944) "What do we really know about daytime serial listeners?" pp. 3-33 in P. Lazarsfeld and F. Stanton (eds.) Radio Research 1943-44. New York: Duell, Sloan, and Pearce.

HESS, R. D. and J. V. TORNEY (1967) The Development of Political Attitudes in Children. Chicago: Aldine.

HIMMELWEIT, H. T., A. N. OPPENHEIM, and P. VINCE (1958) Television and the Child. London: Oxford Univ. Press.

HIRSCH, P. M. (1971) "Sociological approaches to the pop music phenom-enon." American Behavioral Scientist 14 (3): 371-388.

HOCKING, W. (1947) Freedom of the Press. Chicago: Univ. of Chicago Press.

HOVLAND, C. I. (1959) "Reconciling conflicting results from experimental and survey studies of attitude change." American Psychologist 14 (January): 8-17.

——— A. A. LUMSDAINE, and F. D. SHEFFIELD (1949) Experiments on Mass Communication. Princeton Univ. Press.

HOVLAND, C. I. and J. J. FELDMAN (1962) "The Kennedy-Nixon debates: a survey of surveys," in S. Kraus (ed.) The Great Debates. Bloomington: Indiana Univ. Press.

HYMAN, H. H. and P. SHEATSLEY (1947) "Some reasons why information campaigns fail." Public Opinion Q. 11: 413-423.

JANOWITZ, M. (1952) The Community Press in an Urban Setting. New York: Free Press.

JENNINGS, M. K. and R. NIEMI (1968) "The transmissions of political values from parent to child." American Political Science Rev. 62 (March): 169-184.

JONSTONE, J. and E. KATZ (1959) "Youth and popular music: a study in the sociology of taste." American J. of Sociology 62: 563-568.

KATZ, D. (1960) "The functional approach to the study of attitudes." Public Opinion Q. 24: 163-204.

KATZ, E. and P. F. LAZARSFELD (1959) "Communication research and the image of society: convergence of two traditions." American J. of Sociology 65: 435-440.

——— (1957) "The two-step flow of communication: an up-to-date report on an hypothesis." Public Opinion Q. 21 (Spring): 61-78.

——— (1955) Personal Influence. New York: Free Press.

KELLEY, S. (1956) Professional Public Relations and Political Power. Balti-more: John Hopkins Press.

KLAPPER, J. (1963) "Mass communication research: an old road surveyed." Public Opinion Q. 27: 515-527.

——— (1960) The Effects of Mass Communication. New York: Free Press.

KLINE, F. G. (1971) "Media time budgeting as a function of demographics and life style." J. Q. 48 (Summer): 211-221.

KORNHAUSER, W. (1959) The Politics of Mass Society. New York: Free Press.

KRUGMAN, H. E. (1965) "The impact of television advertising: learning without involvement." Public Opinion Q. 29 (Fall): 349-356.

LAING, R., H. PHILLIPSON, and A. R. LEE (1966) Interpersonal Perception: A Theory and a Method of Research. New York: Springer.

LANE, R. E. and D. O. SEARS (1964) Public Opinion. Englewood Cliffs, N.J.: Prentice-Hall.

LANG, K. and G. E. LANG (1959) The Mass Media and Voting. New York: Free Press.

——— (1968a) Politics and Television. Chicago: Quadrangle Books.

——— (1968b) Voting and Nonvoting. Waltham, Mass.: Blaisdell.

LAPIERE, R. T. (1934) "Attitudes vs. actions." Social Forces 13: 230-237.

LASSWELL, H. D. (1949) "The structure and function of communication in society," pp. 102-115 in W. Schramm, Mass Communications. Urbana: Univ. of Illinois Press.

——— (1927) Propaganda Technique in the World War. New York: Knopf.

——— D. LERNER and I. POOL (1952) The Comparative Study of Symbols. Stanford, Calif.: Stanford Univ. Press.

LASSWELL, H. D., L. S. WARD, and K. TANCILL (1965-1966) "Alienation and uses of mass media." Public Opinion Q. 29 (Winter): 583-594.

LAZARSFELD, P. F. and R. K. MERTON (1948) "Mass communication, popular taste and organized social action," in L. Bryson (ed.) The

Communication of Ideas. New York: Institute for Religious and Social Studies.

——— B. BERELSON and H. GAUDET (1948) The People's Choice. New York: Columbia Univ. Press.

LEAVITT, H. J. (1951) "Some effects of certain communication patterns on group performance." J. of Abnormal and Social Psychology 46: 38-50.

LERNER, D. (1958) The Passing of Traditional Society. New York: Free Press.

LEWIN, K. (1951) Field Theory in Social Science. Dorwin Cartwright (ed.) New York: Harper.

LEWIS, O. (1966) "The culture of poverty." Scientific American 215: 19-25.

LIPPMANN, W. (1922) Public Opinion. New York: Macmillan.

LYND, R. S. (1939) Knowledge for What? Princeton, N.J.: Princeton Univ. Press.

MACCOBY, E. E. (1951) "Why children watch TV." Public Opinion Q. 15: 421-444.

MACCOBY, N. and E. E. MACCOBY (1961) "Homeostatic theory in attitude change." Public Opinion Q. 25 (Winter): 538-545.

McCOMBS, M. E. (1968) "Negro use of television and newspapers for political information, 1952-1964." J. of Broadcasting 13 (Summer): 261-266.

MACDONALD, D. (1953) "A theory of mass culture." Diogenes 3 (Summer): 1-17.

MACHLUP, F. (1962) The Production and Distribution of Knowledge in the United States. Princeton, N.J.: Princeton Univ. Press.

McLEOD, J. M. and S. H. CHAFFEE (1971) "The construction of social of social reality," in J. Tedeschi (ed.) The Social Influence Processes. Chicago: Aldine-Atherton.

——— and S. E. HAWLEY, Jr. (1964) "Professionalization among newsmen." J. Q. 41 (Autumn): 529-538.

McLEOD, J. M., R. R. RUSH, and K. FRIEDERICH (1968-1969) "The mass media and political information in Quito, Ecuador." Public Opinion Q. 32 (Winter): 575-587.

McGUIRE, W. J. (1960) "Cognitive consistency and attitude change." J. of Abnormal and Social Psychology 60: 345-353.

McLUHAN, M. (1964) Understanding Media: The Extension of Man. New York: McGraw-Hill.

McQUAIL, D. (1969) Towards a Sociology of Mass Communication. London: Collier Macmillan.

MEAD, G. H. (1934) Mind, Self, and Society. Chicago: Univ. of Chicago Press.

MENDELSOHN, H. and I. CRESPI (1970) Polls, Television and the New Politics. Scranton: Chandler.

MENZEL, H. and E. KATZ (1955) "Social relations and innovation in the medical profession." Public Opinion Q. 19 (Winter): 337-353.

MERTON, R. (1957a) "Patterns of influence: local and cosmopolitan influentials," in Robert Merton, Social Theory and Social Structure. New York: Free Press.

––– (1957b) Social Theory and Social Structure. New York: Free Press.

MYERSOHN, R. (1968) "Television and the rest of leisure." Public Opinion Q. 32 (Spring): 102-112.

NEWCOMB, T. M. (1953) "An approach to the study of communicative acts." Psych. Rev. 60: 393-404.

NIMMO, D. (1970) The Political Persuaders. Englewood Cliffs, N.J.: Prentice-Hall.

NIXON, R. B. and J. WARD (1961) "Trends in newspaper ownership and inter-media competition." J. Q. 38 (Winter): 3-14.

OLIEN, C. N., G. A. DONOHUE, and P. J. TICHENOR (1968) "The community editor's power and the reporting of conflict." J. Q. 45: 243-252.

PALETZ, D. L., P. REICHERT, and B. McINTYRE (1971) "How the media support local governmental authority." Public Opinion Q. 35 (Spring): 80-95.

PARK, R. E. (1940) "News as a form of knowledge." American J. of Sociology 45 (March): 669-686.

PEARLIN, L. I. (1959) "Social and personal stress and escape television viewing." Public Opinion Q. 23 (Summer): 255-259.

POOL, I. and I. SHULMAN (1959) "Newsmen's fantasies, audiences, and newswriting." Public Opinion Q. 23 (Summer): 145-158.

PYE, L. W. (1963) Communications and Political Development. Princeton, N.J.: Princeton Univ. Press.

RILEY, J. W., Jr. and M. W. RILEY (1965) "Mass communication and the social system," ch. 24 in R. K. Merton (ed.) Sociology Today.

ROGERS, E. M. (1969) Modernization Among Peasants: The Impact of Communication. New York: Holt, Rinehart & Winston.

——— (1962) Diffusion of Innovations. New York: Free Press.

——— and D. K. BHOWMIK (1970-1971) "Homophily-heterophily: relational concepts for communication research." Public Opinion Q. 34 (Winter): 523-538.

ROSENBERG, M. J. et al. (1960) Attitude Organization and Change. New Haven: Yale Univ. Press.

RUBIN, B. (1967) Political Television. Belmont, Calif.: Wadsworth.

RUBINSTEIN, E., G. COMSTOCK, and J. MURRAY [eds.] (1972) Television and Social Behavior. Vol. 1-7. Rockville, Md.: National Institute of Mental Health.

RUCKER, B. (1968) The First Freedom. Carbondale, Ill.: Southern Illinois Univ. Press.

SAMUELSON, M., R. F. CARTER, and W. L. RUGGELS (1963) "Education, available time and use of the mass media." J. Q. 40 (Autumn): 491-496.

SCHEFF, T. J. (1967) "Toward a sociological model of consensus." American Sociological Rev. 32: 32-46.

SCHRAMM, W. (1957) Responsibility in Mass Communications. New York: Harper.

——— J. LYLE, and E. PARKER (1961) Television in the Lives of Our Children. Stanford: Stanford Univ. Press.

SCHRAMM, W. and D. P. ROBERTS (1971) The Process and Effects of Mass Communication. Urbana: Univ. of Illinois Press.

SEARS, D. O. and J. L. FREEDMAN (1967) "Selective exposure to information: a critical review." Public Opinion Q. 31: 194-213.

STAR, S. A. and H. M. HUGHES (1950) "Report on an educational campaign: the Cincinnati plan for the United Nations." American J. of Sociology 55: 389-400.

STEWER, G. A. (1963) The People Look At Television. New York: Knopf.

STEPHENSON, W. (1967) The Play Theory of Mass Communication. Chicago: Univ. of Chicago Press.

TANNENBAUM, P. H. (1963) "Communication of scientific information." Science 140 (May) 3507: 579-583.

——— and B. GREENBERG (1961) " 'JQ' references: a study of professional change." J. Q. 38: 203-207.

——— (1968) "Mass communication," in Annual Rev. of Psychology 19: 351-385.

TICHENOR, P. J., C. N. OLIEN, A. HARRISON, and G. A. DONOHUE (1970) "Mass communications systems and communication accuracy in science news reporting." J. Q. 47 (Winter): 673-683.

——— , G. A. DONOHUE, and C. N. OLIEN (1970) "Mass Media flow and differential growth in knowledge." Public Opinion Q. 34: 159-170.

THOMAS, W. I. (1927) The Behavior Pattern and the Situation. Publications of the American Sociological Association 22: 1-13.

TRENEMAN, J. and D. McQUAIL (1961) Television and the Political Image. London: Menthan.

TUCHMAN, S. and T. E. COFFIN (1971) "The influence of election night television broadcasting in a close election." Public Opinion Q. 35 (Fall): 315-326.

TUNSTALL, J. (1969) Media Sociology: A Reader. Urbana, Ill.: Univ. of Illinois Press.

U.S. Government Kerner Commission (1968) Report of the National Advisory Commission on Civil Disorders. New York: Bantam.

WADE, S. and W. SCHRAMM (1969) "The mass media as sources of public affairs, science, and health knowledge." Public Opinion Q. 33 (Summer): 197-209.

WEISS, W. (1969) "Effects of the mass media of communication," in G. Lindzey and E. Aronson (eds.) Handbook of Social Psychology. Reading, Mass.: Addison-Wesley.

WEISS, W. (1971) "Mass communications." Annual Rev. of Psychology 22: 309-336.

WERTHAM, F. (1954) Seduction of the Innocent. New York: Rinehart.

WESTLEY, B. and M. MacLEAN (1957) "A conceptual model for communication research." J. Q. 34: 31-38.

WHITE, D. M. (1950) "The gatekeeper, a case study in the selection of news." J. Q. 27 (Fall): 383-390.

WHORF, B. L. (1956) Language, Thought, and Reality. New York: John Wiley.

WILENSKY, H. L. (1964) "Mass society and mass culture." American Sociological Rev. 29 (April): 173-197.

WRIGHT, C. (1960) "Functional analysis and mass communication." Public Opinion Q. 24: 605-620.

WYCKOFF, G. (1968) The Image Candidates: American Politics in the Age of Television. New York: Macmillan.

INDEX